THE HUMAN RIGHTS MOVEMENT

Western Values and Theological Perspectives

WARREN LEE HOLLEMAN

PRAEGER

New York
Westport, Connecticut
London

Every reasonable effort has been made to trace the owners of copyright materials in this book, but in some instances this has proven impossible. The publishers will be glad to receive information leading to more complete acknowledgments in subsequent printings of the book, and in the meantime extend their apologies for any omissions.

Library of Congress Cataloging-in-Publication Data

Holleman, Warren Lee.
   The human rights movement.

   Bibliography: p.
   Includes index.
   1. Human rights. 2. International relations—Moral and ethical aspects. I. Title.
JC585.H755 1987   172'.4   87-14587
ISBN 0-275-92789-X (alk. paper)

Library of Congress Catalog Card Number: 87-14587
ISBN: 0-275-92789-X

First published in 1987

Praeger Publishers, One Madison Avenue, New York, NY 10010
A division of Greenwood Press, Inc.

Printed in the United States of America

The paper used in this book complies with the Permanent Paper Standard issued by the National Information Standards Organization (Z39.48-1984).

10 9 8 7 6 5 4 3 2 1

CONTENTS

Preface vii

Chapter 1   Universal Human Rights 1

Chapter 2   Western Individualism in the Human
             Rights Movement 13

Chapter 3   Beyond the Individualist-Collectivist Impasse 45

Chapter 4   Western Pneumaticism in the Human
             Rights Movement 73

Chapter 5   Beyond the Pneumatic-Materialist Impasse 97

Chapter 6   Western Political Hegemony 131

Chapter 7   From Global Hegemony to National Sovereignty ... 155

Chapter 8   Western Cultural Hegemony 185

Chapter 9   From Cultural Hegemony to Cultural Integrity 209

Conclusion 225

Bibliography 227

Index 241

PREFACE

My interest in international human rights goes back to the presidential campaign of Jimmy Carter, whose vow to include moral considerations in his foreign policy strategy seemed to me like a breath of fresh air after the cynicism of the Kissinger era. A few years later I was asked to teach a course on the subject at Rice University. Through this experience I was introduced to a wide range of literature, not all of which was complimentary of the policies I had once so vigorously supported. I eventually became convinced that, while moral considerations were important in all realms of life, including foreign policy and international relations, the manner in which they were to be applied was a delicate and complex one.

This complexity could be seen not only by looking at the problems encountered by the Carter administration but also by looking back to earlier attempts to infuse moral concerns into international politics. Even when the motives were good and moral idealism ran high, results seldom lived up to expectations. Sometimes the moral idealism even got in the way of positive results. Time after time the matter proved to be a delicate and complex one, beyond the scope of an ideologically oriented morality that is capable only of simple rights and wrongs.

When dealing with problems of this moral and political magnitude, what is needed is wisdom, and lots of it: wisdom to identify underlying sources of the conflict, and wisdom to suggest avenues by which the conflict might be resolved. Wisdom can come from many sources. Experienced diplomats and bureaucrats can tell us, from firsthand experience, how and why nations act and react as they do. Historians can detect patterns from the history of international relations and can help us avoid repeating past mistakes. Futurologists can prepare us for the many changes that are about to come. Social scientists can provide empirical data and can use the data to test theories of how nations are likely to behave in certain situations. Philosophers can help us think through the issues and conflicts in a logical, objective manner.

One other, less obvious, source of wisdom in dealing with problems related to international human rights is the theologian. The theologian, regardless of his or her religious tradition, comes to the situation equipped with certain insights regarding human nature and human destiny. These insights can inform us about the underlying sources of international conflicts and the prospects for their resolution. Theologians can bring both realism and idealism to the discussion. They can remind us of sin and the limitations to human progress and of the spirit and its capacity to transcend these limitations. They can talk about the meanings and values at stake in any human action and can identify goals toward which we should strive.

Since the Carter era, the human rights movement has lost much of its momentum. I hope it can be revitalized, but I do not believe that this will happen until certain problems are identified and new ways of meeting them are developed. This book is my contribution toward that effort. I have identified four of the most troublesome problems in international human rights diplomacy. I have pointed toward solutions that, I believe, should be acceptable to both Western and non-Western points of view.

I am indebted to a number of people for helping me create this book. James Sellers helped me formulate and structure my argument. Niels C. Nielsen, Jr., William Martin, and James Sellers read early versions of the manuscript and pointed out numerous ways of improving it. Werner H. Kelber introduced me to the world of publishing. Marsha Cline Holleman, Loren Israel and Hannah Koopman helped in the editing and final preparation of the manuscript. I am deeply grateful to each of you, and to all others who offered advice and encouragement along the way.

Finally, I express appreciation to my parents, Carl Partin Holleman and Ruth Warren Holleman, for teaching me to love justice and to pursue excellence. It is to them, with fond love, that this book is dedicated.

1

UNIVERSAL HUMAN RIGHTS

Throughout history there have been numerous social and political movements that could be termed "human rights movements." The democratic urge in ancient Greece; the democratic revolutions in England, America,[1] France, and Russia; the Third World[2] revolts against colonialism in the nineteenth and twentieth centuries; the abolitionist movement; the women's rights movement; the civil rights movement; the gay rights movement: each broadened the scope of justice, and each promoted and protected what we today call human rights. In the past forty years, however, a distinctively new type of human rights movement has emerged: a movement for universal human rights. For the first time, human rights concerns have been addressed not simply at the local or national level and not simply in terms of one minority group or one human rights principle. The movement for universal human rights has addressed human rights concerns in the international forum. It has tried to develop a concept of human rights that transcends particular political or cultural settings, and it has tried to bring all minority groups and all principles of justice within its scope.

The idea of universal human rights was the silver lining that emerged from the dark cloud of the Second World War. In January 1942, the Allied powers declared the ultimate purpose of resisting the Axis nations as humanitarian rather than military. "Complete victory," they declared, "is essential to defend life, liberty, independence, and religious freedom, and to preserve human rights and justice" throughout the world. In October of the same year, Prime Minister Winston Churchill looked forward to the day "when this world's struggle ends with the enthronement of human rights."[3] As the war drew to a close, two bold steps were taken to prevent future human rights abuses and to promote and protect human rights in the postwar world.

The Nuremberg Trials exposed the human rights abuses of the Nazis, punished those responsible, and defined in precise terms what rights they had violated. The Nuremberg Code explicated the rights of all persons, regardless of race or nationality. For the first time "crimes against humanity" were formally recognized. Nazi leaders were punished not simply for "war crimes"; they were punished for crimes against their own people and regardless of whether such crimes violated their own laws. Genocide was formally recognized as a crime during peace and war.

The other major achievement was the formation of the United Nations, not simply as a wartime military alliance but as a postwar humanitarian organization. In the midst of the war, Great Britain, the United States, the Soviet Union, and China met at Dumbarton Oaks (1944) and San Francisco (1945) to establish an international organization that would promote order and justice in the postwar world and thus help prevent future wars. A charter was drawn up, stating that the United Nations should "achieve international cooperation in solving international problems of an economic, social, cultural, or humanitarian character, and in promoting and encouraging respect for human rights and for fundamental freedoms for all without distinction as to race, sex, language, or religion" (Article 1). A Commission on Human Rights was established to write an international bill of rights. On December 10, 1948, the General Assembly adopted the Universal Declaration of Human Rights, proclaiming it as "a common standard of achievement for all peoples and all nations" (Preamble). The commission, under the leadership of Eleanor Roosevelt, also began work on a number of more specific and legally binding documents, most notably the International Covenant on Civil and Political Rights and the International Covenant on Economic, Social and Cultural Rights. The United Nations declared December 10 as Human Rights Day, and it appeared that the dream of universal human rights was well on its way to becoming a reality.[4]

Four decades later, however, the dream seems no closer to realization than in 1948. Anyone who knows a refugee from one of any number of repressive regimes, who has seen photographs of starving children, visited an urban ghetto, or simply keeps up with the news from around the world will wonder whether the dream has not turned into a nightmare. In 1948 it seemed like an idea whose time had come. Today, human rights abuses are as numerous as ever, and there are no real grounds for hope that overall conditions will improve.

Why are universal human rights still a dream and not a reality? Why has the human rights movement failed to achieve its goal of maintaining a universal standard of human rights achievement? Answering these questions will require insights and expertise from a wide range of academic disciplines and practical experience. Social scientists, diplomats, and lawyers certainly have a contribution to make. Less obvious, perhaps, is the way that the theologian can help understand and resolve the problems of universal human rights. I have come to this conclusion after reading through the literature of the human rights movement and realizing that at the heart of the problem is a dispute between Western and non-Western nations[5] over the question of what constitutes a human right. This stems from an even more basic disagreement over what constitutes a human being. The question of human nature and purpose is a fundamental one. It is a question that theological anthropology is prepared to address, and one that theological ethics is prepared to relate to the problems and possibilities of the movement for universal human rights.

My thesis, then, is that theological ethics can help diagnose and solve the problem of universal human rights; this seemingly political problem has a theological solution. More specifically, I argue that, at the basis of the major controversies surrounding the human rights movement, there is a conflict between contrasting visions of humanity: individual versus communal, pneumatic versus material, benevolent versus sinful, and abstract versus cultural. I exploit the resources of Christian theology to develop a via media between each of the conflicting notions, thus offering the movement an alternative vision of humanity. Such an alternative vision will, I hope, do justice to the positive insights of both Western proponents and non-Western opponents of the movement and will provide the basis for reform and peace within the movement and for renewed activity toward the goal of achieving universal human rights.

THREE PRELIMINARY QUESTIONS

Dialogue across national and cultural boundaries is impossible unless we share a common understanding of the terminology we use. So, before we can go very far in developing this new approach to human rights, we must establish a working definition of three fundamental ingredients of univeral human rights. The first concerns the concept of human rights, the second concerns the historical movement for universal human rights, and the third concerns the ultimate basis for human rights.

What Is A Human Right?

Even within the United States, there is a wide range of understanding as to what a human right actually is. To make matters worse, the term "human rights" has become virtually sacrosanct, so that, even though persons disagree as to its meaning, all use it with a high degree of fervor. If a high degree of conviction is combined with a low degree of understanding, the result is likely to be fanaticism and conflict. Such has been the case with the human rights issue.

Oftentimes, persons on opposite sides of an argument will defend their position by invoking the sacrosanct name of human rights. Abortion is condemned in the name of the fetus' human right to life. The outlawing of abortion is condemned in the name of the mother's human right to freedom of choice. The owning of handguns is defended on the basis of the human right to self-protection. Gun control legislation is advocated on the basis of the human right to live in a safe world. Corporeal punishment of children is defended on the basis of the family's human right to privacy. Corporeal punishment is opposed on the basis of the child's human right not to be tortured. Minimum wage legislation is defended on the basis of the worker's right to a decent standard of living. Minimum wage legislation is opposed on the basis of the unemployed person's right to work, or the employer's right to manage. Wiretapping of a political dissident or potential criminal is considered by some to be an infringement of the human right to privacy. Failing to wiretap such a person is considered by others to be an infringement of the public's human right to safety and security. The sacrosanct name of human rights, whatever that name might mean, can be invoked both to oppose and defend just about anything.

We generally think of human rights as a tool for defending the poor and powerless. But it may also be a tool for defending the rich and famous. For example, the state of California recently passed a "celebrity rights" law, which defended the human rights of celebrities not to be oppressed by paparazzi journalists who invade their privacy by taking pictures of them, and by advertisers who exploit their celebrity status by hiring less expensive look–alikes to sell products.[6] Another example: my local public radio station, which markets its product largely to an intelligent, middle class audience, invoked the name of human rights in support of their rather privileged cause. "Art is a human right!"[7] was the slogan they chose to rally aficionados to their cause. One more example: a college professor, overwhelmed by all the bureaucratic regulations with which universities and other institutions are laden by a federal government that insists upon equal opportunities and affirmative action, pondered whether the government had ignored the most fundamental human right of all—the right to be unfair. "The freedom to be unfair," mused Jack Rawlins of California State University, "may be an inalienable right, of man as well as nature."[8]

Statements such as these make one wonder whether human rights is something we might do better without. The privileged claim to be oppressed and accuse the oppressed of being privileged. The privileged demand their human rights: the right of movie stars not to be celebrities when they don't want to; the right of aficionados to their favorite type of music, free of charge and without commercial interruptions; and the right of the powerful to practice Social Darwinism. It seems that human rights have come to mean everything, and nothing.

When a Fiji Island gold miners' union sought to have thirty minutes added to their lunch period, on grounds that they were too tired to enjoy sex at the end of the day, they did so in the name of human rights: their "right to a sex break."[9] When the University of Massachusetts closed the lid on coed toilets, students protested that their human rights had been violated: the right to a coed toilet.[10] When he found out that someone wanted to build a skyscraper in his neighborhood, an eighty-year old Japanese sandlemaker sued for, and was granted, his "right to sunshine."[11] When ophthalmologist and tennis buff Dr. Richard Raskind underwent a sex change operation and became Dr. Renee Richards, she asserted what she perceived as her human right: the right of men who undergo sex change operations to compete in women's athletic competitions. Female tennis pros responded by asserting what they perceived as their human right: their right to compete only against those who could pass a sex chromosome test. When a severely retarded twenty-five year old became self-abusive and gouged out one of his eyes, psychologists developed a behavior modification program involving, as a last resort, the use of an electric prod. When the institution's Human Rights Committee vetoed the program as an "excessive and inhumane form of correction," the inevitable happened. "He is now blind, of course, but he has his rights and presumably his dignity," quipped one of the psychologists. Her conclusion: "Clearly, our society has become almost hysterical about the issue of human rights."[12]

In an apparent effort to bring this human rights epidemic under control, a conference was held in October 1983, at the University of North Carolina. The Frank P. Graham Conference on Human Rights invited a distinguished panel from a range of backgrounds to discuss the issue. The impression given was that there is little agreement as to what human rights really means. South African Dennis Brutus equated human rights with political rights for the twenty-two million blacks in his country. Historian Otis Graham equated human rights with economic rights: the right to a decent level of material well-being which many "underclass" Americans, particularly women and children, do not have. Political scientist Lars Schoultz described the Reagan administration's belief that human rights is a propaganda tool of Communists to undermine "friendly, stable anti-Communist regimes," and that for the United States to promote human rights would lead "to a threat to our national security." (During the Carter years, Communist governments accused the United States of using human rights as a propaganda tool.) Ethicist and Reagan supporter Ernest Lefever argued that

the Sandinistas were greater violators of human rights than their pre-
decessors, the Somozans, because even though the Sandinistas do not torture political prisoners, they had "insulted the pope." In reflecting upon
the conference, journalist Tom Wicker concluded that even though "the
idea of 'human rights' seems simple enough" it "in fact, means different
things—not all of them obvious—to different people." "What does human
rights really mean?", the title Wicker gave to his commentary, turned out
to be a complex question indeed.[13]

What does human rights really mean? In attempting to answer this question, some will err by defining human rights too narrowly, others by defining rights too broadly. Westerners define rights too narrowly when they
focus on the rights of the individual and ignore the rights of the community and the responsibilities of the individual to the community. Westerners also define rights too narrowly when they focus on human
freedoms, such as freedom of speech and freedom of religion, and ignore
basic human needs, such as food, shelter, and medical care. I will argue in
chapters 2 through 5 that a truly universal concept of human rights is possible only if Westerners broaden their view to include communal and
material, as well as individual and pneumatic, notions of human beings
and human rights. Westerners define human rights too broadly when they
ascribe rights to human beings only as abstract entities, forgetting that persons are historical beings: citizens of sovereign nations and members of
particular cultures and subcultures. Persons are granted or denied rights by
and within those nations and cultures. I will argue in chapters 6 through 9
that an effective international human rights movement is possible only if
Westerners narrow the locus of human rights policy to particular nations
and cultures, even though continuing to press for human rights dialogue
between nations and cultures.

The first misconception, then, is that human rights is a Western in-
vention and that promoting human rights and promoting Western values
are the same thing. Rather, human rights is a multifaceted concept. The
West has a solid appreciation of some of those facets: the rights of individuals vis-à-vis their governments, the rights of persons to follow the
dictates of their conscience, a belief in the ability of the human spirit to
transcend nations and cultures and to speak prophetically to a particular
historical condition. The West must, however, develop a greater appreciation for other facets of human rights: communal rights, rights to material
necessities, and rights that accrue to persons as members of particular
nations and cultures.

What Is the Human Rights Movement?

The human rights movement can be just as difficult to define as the concept. One way to come to terms with a complex historical movement is to

reduce the conflict to the simplist of terms. We find a hero, a villain, and a damsel in distress; or, a beginning, a climax, and a denouement; and so on. With some ethical movements, the drama can be fairly straightforward. One thinks, for example, of the American civil rights movement. In this historical drama, Martin Luther King, Jr. was the protagonist, George Wallace the antagonist, and black Americans, particularly Southern Blacks, were the victims awaiting rescue. The movement began with Rosa Parks and the Montgomery bus boycott, reached its zenith with the March on Washington and the Civil Rights Act of 1964, and faded into denouement with both the assassinations and attempted assassinations (the theatrical term is the "killing off") of leading members of the cast. The assassination of John Kennedy may have been a foreboding, but then there was Malcolm X, Robert Kennedy, George Wallace, and Martin Luther King, Jr. There was a degeneration from the confronting of mortal sins, such as racism, segregation, discrimination, to quibbling over venial ones such as busing and affirmative action.

With the human rights movement, the plot thickens, to say the least. Black and white fade into grey. It becomes difficult to agree who are the protagonists, the antagonists, or even the victims. Movie stars, music lovers, and university professors vie with Southern Blacks for minority status. Oftentimes leaders of opposite sides of a human rights conflict both claim to be protagonists of human rights.

Alexander Solzhenitsyn has captured the hearts and minds of many in the West as the leader of an oppressed minority, the Soviet dissidents. But, from a Marxist viewpoint, Solzhenitsyn represents an intellectual and religious elite. The Russian peasant and factory worker are probably better off today than they would be if it had not been for the Russian revolution. This points us to a central question. Whose interests should the human rights movement represent—peasants or professors? One group of human rights advocates claim slain Salvadorean Archbishop Oscar Romero along with the Sandinistas of Nicaragua as the heroes of human rights reform in the region. Another group of human rights advocates, including many of those who embrace Solzhenitsyn's bold resistance to Soviet totalitarianism, condemn the Romeros and the Sandinistas as communists and enemies of human rights and support the more authoritarian but anticommunist regimes in the region. Once again, one faction chooses to promote the rights of the poor, while another chooses to protect the rights of the middle class. Who is the true guardian of human rights?

The human rights drama is indeed a complex one, and attempts to identify heroes and villains will create more heat than light. If we set moral judgments aside, however, we can begin to understand the historical process we call the human rights movement.

The human rights movement, as I have come to see it, is a dynamic historical process consisting of (mostly) Western action to promote human

rights, (mostly) non-Western reaction to Western initiatives, and ethical
reflection to bring about rapprochement between the parties in conflict. At
first glance, it appears that Western nations are "for" universal human
rights and non-Western nations are "against." This misconception is prevalent among many of those active in the human rights movement. Actually, the non-Western opposition reflects objections to certain aspects of
the Western concept of human rights and to the way that the human rights
movement attempts to promote that concept. It does not indicate an objection to human rights per se.

The second misconception, then, is that the human rights movement
consists solely of Western action to promote human rights, and that the
non-Western reaction is opposition to the human rights movement rather
than being what it actually is: the second phase of the movement itself. Just
as the concept of human rights is multifaceted, so the movement for
human rights is multiphased. Western action to promote human rights is
but one phase of that movement. The thesis must be followed by an antithesis and, if universal rights are to be achieved, some sort of synthesis.

The most deliberate Western initiatives to promote universal human
rights have been the efforts of the United Nations beginning in the forties,
of nongovernmental organizations such as Amnesty International beginning in the sixties, and of President Carter in the seventies. Each of these
actions produced a negative reaction which, unfortunately, was often mis-
interpreted as opposition to human rights rather than opposition to Western nations foisting their own truncated concept of human rights upon
the rest of the world. The Western response to this negative reaction was
either to despair and turn isolationist or to be righteously indignant and
turn imperialist. Rather than turning from action to reflection and
dialogue, the Western initiators of the human rights movement grew more
intransigent, took more extreme actions, and precluded the possibility of a
truly international solution.

What is needed at this point is not more action, but more reflection.
We have heard from the activists—those on the front lines of the conflict,
in the heat of the battle. Now we need to hear from those who have distanced themselves from the debate and have weighed the strengths and
weaknesses of both sides. The activist acts and reacts; the ethicist reflects.
The activist is concerned with defending a position or winning an argument; the ethicist with determining what is true and what is good. The activist argues passionately and oftentimes eloquently; the ethicist assumes
a more distanced, dispassionate stance. The activist convinces and mo-
tivates; the ethicist asks questions and decries simple answers. The activist
uses broad strokes to separate black from white; the ethicist uses subtle
strokes to distinguish shades of grey. One seeks to promote an ideology and
a social program; the other seeks to promote no a priori agenda except clear,

consistent reflection upon the moral aspects of human action. Activists carry on the discussion at the polemical level; ethicists carry on the discussion from a more detached stance. Each has an important contribution to make to the human rights movement. Without the activist no one would do the good; without the ethicist no one would know the good that must be done.

Much energy has been expended by Western activists, and yet universal human rights still appear only as a very distant dream. What is needed is to concentrate greater efforts on the third phase—reflecting upon where our actions have taken us and where, in the future, we should take them. This book is one contribution in that direction. I believe that once we begin to understand the differences between Western and non-Western notions of human rights, further action to promote truly universal human rights can be successful. Just as action and reaction create the need for reflection, so reflection can reconcile opposing parties and pave the way for further action. It is for this reason that chapters 2, 4, 6, and 8 begin by "hearing out" non-Western objections to Western initiatives, and chapters 3, 5, 7, and 9 conclude by suggesting new pathways for action to promote universal human rights.

What Is the Basis for Human Rights?

A third area of misunderstanding has to do with the assumption that human rights are rooted in human dignity. One hears this claim being made at every level of the human rights movement, yet there is a wide divergence of interpretation as to what that dignity entails.

The preamble to the Universal Declaration of Human Rights begins with these words: "*Whereas* recognition of the inherent dignity and of the equal and inalienable rights of all members of the human family is the foundation of freedom, justice and peace in the world. . . . " The first article of the declaration also affirms the dignity of the human being and goes on to define that dignity in terms of intellectual freedom. "All human beings," it claims, "are born free and equal in dignity and rights. They are endowed with reason and conscience and should act towards one another in a spirit of brotherhood."[14] Several of the United Nations human rights covenants reiterate this concern by beginning their preambles with the following affirmation of human dignity:

> The States Parties to the present Covenant,
> *Considering* that, in accordance with the principles proclaimed in the Charter of the United Nations, recognition of the inherent dignity and of the equal and inalienable rights of all members of the human family is the foundation of freedom, justice and peace in the world,
> *Recognizing* that these rights derive from the inherent dignity of the human person, . . . [15]

In the same vein, Principle VII, the so-called "human rights clause" of the 1975 Helsinki Agreement, bases its concern for the rights of the person on the dignity of the person. In its second paragraph the document states that "civil, political, economic, social, cultural and other rights and freedoms . . . derive from the inherent dignity of the human person and are essential for his free and full development."[16]

When Presidential candidate Jimmy Carter addressed the Democratic Party Platform Committee in June of 1976, he urged that U.S. foreign policy be based on "certain moral principles," one of which was to "treat the people of other nations as individuals with the same dignity and respect we demand for ourselves."[17] One year later President Carter, delivering his major foreign policy address, told a Notre Dame audience that "our policy must reflect . . . our belief that dignity and freedom are fundamental spiritual requirements."[18]

Throughout the literature of the human rights movement, one theme dominates all others as the basic justification for promoting universal human rights. That theme is the dignity of the human being. It is invoked frequently and with conviction, yet there is little explanation of what is meant by it. It is viewed as a "self evident truth" that one either believes or doesn't believe, and knowing what it means is not so important as simply believing in it.

As a result, those who oppose Western human rights initiatives are often falsely accused of not respecting human dignity. Oftentimes the difference is not between one party that respects human dignity and another that does not, but between one party that defines dignity in Western, liberal terms and another that defines dignity in other ways. From certain non-Western perspectives, it is the West that fails to appreciate the dignity of the human being, for the West fails to respect those aspects of humanity that non-Westerners deem important.

What is needed, obviously, is global dialogue over basic questions of human identity and human worth. A movement that wishes to be truly universal must establish a broad and firm foundation. One inchoate postulate concerning the dignity of the human being is not sufficient. Parties to the dialogue must become aware of what other parties mean when they say that the human being has dignity. In so doing parties will become better aware of their own, oftentimes parochial, assumptions. Western liberals will realize that when they proclaim the dignity of the human being, what they are really proclaiming is the dignity of the human being as an individual being, as a pneumatic being, and as a being abstracted from a particular political and cultural milieu. Perhaps they will learn to appreciate other ways of defining human being and respecting human dignity. In the next eight chapters, I hope to show why the communal, material, political, and cultural dimensions, often overlooked in Western human rights initiatives, are so important.

NOTES

1. Despite the obvious problems with the terms, the English language gives me no other option than to use "American" and "North American" synonymously with the United States.
2. The terms "First World," "Second World," and "Third World" can be interpreted as pejorative toward non-Western nations, since they connote a favored status to the West as the "First World." The terms "Western" and "non-Western" can have the same effect, since the rest of the world is defined in terms of its relation to the West. As Erik Erikson would say, it suggests a positive identity for some and a negative identity for others [*Identity, Youth and Crisis* (W.W. Norton and Co., 1968)]. (This is analogous to the custom of calling blacks and hispanics "nonwhites." Webster's dictionary defines "nonwhite" as "a person whose features and esp. whose skin color are distinctively different than those of Caucasians of northwestern Europe." It does not list "nonblack" or "nonbrown.") Unfortunately, the English language does not give me any other options. "Unaligned nations" and "less developed countries" also suggest a negative or inferior identity of the Third World (though not the Second), and can be misleading as well. Grudgingly, I will use the First/Second/Third World and Western/non-Western distinctions until someone, more creative than I, comes up with better terms.
3. Egon Schwelb, *Human Rights and the International Community: The Roots and Growth of the Universal Declaration of Human Rights, 1948-1963* (Chicago: Quadrangle Books, 1964), 25.
4. For a brief history of human rights activity at the close of World War II, see the following: Schwelb, 24-45; "The Campaign for Universal Human Rights," *The Humanist* 26:6 (November/December 1966): 193–96; and Moses Moskowitz, *The Politics and Dynamics of Human Rights* (Dobbs Ferry: Oceana Publications, 1968), 81–100. For a lengthier analysis of early UN activity, see James Frederick Green, *The United Nations and Human Rights* (Washington, D.C.: The Brookings Institution, 1956).
5. I will use the terms "Western" and "Eastern" in the political sense, not in the philosophical, cultural, or geographical sense. "Western" refers to the United States and its European allies, "non-Western" refers to everyone else.

  Throughout the book the terms "Western proponents" and "non-Western opponents" will appear, and I shall use these labels rather loosely. I do not wish to give the impression that all non-Westerners oppose the human rights movement, or that all Westerners unqualifiedly support it. These terms are used for the sake of convenience. It is assumed that the reader will recognize them for what they are: generalizations that are accurate enough to be useful but, like all generalizations, not accurate in terms of rigorous critical analysis. For example, many democratically oriented Third World leaders expressed appreciation for President Carter's efforts to purge the U.S. State Department of a policy that views the Third World as a theater in which the drama of East–West confrontation is staged. While they applauded the movement away from Kissinger-era cynicism, the movement toward an idealism rooted in Western concepts of human rights and carried out in the sometimes boorish Western manner created mixed feelings of a new hope combined with an old anger. In this sense it remains accurate to speak, in a general way, of these leaders as "opponents" of the human rights movement. There were some for whom the influx of Western concepts and Western manners posed no threat at all. They had adapted to Western ways and stood to benefit from Western cultural imperialism. For the most part, these persons were omitted from the discussion, even though they comprise a rather significant voice. The limitations of space require that I focus on the most representative and authentic non-Western views. Those who have been co-opted by Western interests are not the most representative and authentic voices. Furthermore, their interests are subsumed under the category of Western action promoting universal human rights.

6. Daniel B. Moskowitz, "New Calif. Law Increases Celebrities' Ability to Protect What's in a Name," *Washington Post* (31 December 1984), "Washington Business," 10-11.
7. *KPFT Program Guide* (Houston, Texas) October 1984.
8. Jack P. Rawlins, "My Turn: The Fair-Society Fantasy," *Newsweek*, 15 March 1982, 11.
9. *The Hastings Center Report* 6:5 (October 1976):33.
10. "Ban on Coed Bathrooms at Massachusetts Protested," *New York Times*, 28 February 1981, 6; Fred Ferretti, "Students Like Coed Dorms Despite Problems," *New York Times*, 20 March 1981, sec. B, 4; "Student Protest Fails to End a Ban on Sharing Bathrooms," *New York Times*, 22 October 1981, sec. B, 17.
11. *Hastings Report*, 33.
12. Marilyn Whiteside, "My Turn: A Bedeviling New Hysteria," *Newsweek*, 12 September 1983, 13.
13. Tom Wicker, "What Does 'Human Rights' Really Mean?" *The News and Observer* (Raleigh, NC), 12 October 1983, sec. A., 4.
14. United Nations, *The Universal Declaration of Human Rights* (1948) in *The Human Rights Reader*, eds. Walter Laqueur and Barry Rubin (New York: New American Library, Meridian Books, 1979), 197-98.
15. United Nations, *International Covenant on Economic, Social and Cultural Rights* (1966), and *International Covenant on Civil and Political Rights* (1966), ibid, 208-09, 216. Similar wording is also used in the *Declaration on the Elimination of All Forms of Racial Discrimination* (1963) and *International Convention on the Elimination of All Forms of Racial Discrimination* (1969), ibid., 204-05, 228. The *American Declaration of the Rights and Duties of Man* (1948) begins by acknowledging "the dignity of the individual," ibid., 243.
16. *The Helsinki Agreement* (1975), Principle VII, ibid., 282.
17. Jimmy Carter, "Presentation to the Platform Committee," June 12, 1976, in *President Carter*, (Washington, DC: Congressional Quarterly, c. 1977), 80.
18. Jimmy Carter, "Notre Dame Commencement Address," in *James E. Carter: Chronology, Documents, Bibliographical Aids*, ed. George J. Lankevich (Dobbs Ferry: Oceana Publications, 1981), 95.

2
WESTERN INDIVIDUALISM IN THE HUMAN RIGHTS MOVEMENT

A great supporter of United Nations human rights efforts, Jacques Maritain[1] had one serious reservation—that the human rights movement failed to give sufficient attention to the rights of society vis-á-vis the rights of the individual. Drawing from his background in Thomistic philosophy, with its high regard for the common good, Maritain sought to relate the individual to society in a way that more evenly balanced the conflicting demands of each upon the other. He hoped to work out a notion of human rights that would be rooted in the Western intellectual tradition but more sympathetic to concerns voiced outside the West, namely, the need for a more sympathetic understanding of the rights of the community. In chapter 3 we will examine Maritain's solution to the conflict between individual and communal rights. Before doing that, however, we need to examine the problem more closely. Is the Western concept of human rights excessively individualistic?

OBJECTIONS VOICED BY NON-WESTERN NATIONS

Non-Western critics tell us that individual human rights become meaningless when crime rates are high, when the security of the nation is in danger, when the national political and economic infrastrucure is undeveloped, or when jobs or food are scarce. Persons living under such conditions, they say, view the state not just as a potential oppressor, but as a potential savior. For these critics, too much freedom means anarchy, and they fear anarchy (a lack of governmental power) as much or more than governmental domination. In some contexts, they tell us, more government is needed to integrate a society that has suffered from anarchy ruling in the name of freedom.

Recalling that the human rights debate begins at the "polemical" rather than the "ethical" level, we will in this section simply report what the opponents and advocates of human rights have said. Later on we will deal with these issues more critically. For now, let us first note the perception of Communist, Moslem, and Third World critics that the Western concept of human rights has an individualist bias and, second that this perception is based in the actual events of the human rights movement.

Objections from the Soviet Bloc

Appreciation for communal rights in the Soviet and Eastern European nations was a major factor in their refusal to support the Universal Declaration of Human Rights. From their perspective the Universal Declaration bent over backwards in its advocacy of individual rights but failed to recognize the rights of the community with respect to the individual and the duties of the individual to the community. During the drafting of the Universal Declaration the Soviet bloc nations repeatedly raised two issues related to communal rights. One involved the need to limit individual freedoms in cases where individuals were promoting activities clearly harmful to the common good. The other involved the need to explicate the duties of the individual to society.

The concern to limit certain freedoms reflected the recent experience with fascism. Soviet bloc nations expressed regrets that facism was not openly condemned by the declaration and that the declaration did not give states the right to censor fascist and other "war-mongering" and "racist" propaganda. Freedom of speech, they believed, should be restrained when what is being said is deleterious to the common interest, when freedom of expression is being used as a means of overthrowing a democratic government. The USSR argued, for example, that scientific research should be limited when the purpose of the research was to promote immoral activities such as war or fascism. The USSR argued that freedom of expression should be viewed not simply in terms of what types of ideas should or should not be censored, but in terms of what should be promoted. Not only did Article 19, which gave everyone "the right to freedom of opinion and expression . . . without interference," fail to provide for the suppression of dangerous ideas, but it also failed to provide for the promotion of good ones. If freedom of expression is to be more than a lofty ideal, the USSR argued, the means of disseminating ideas must be available not only to the middle class but also to the workers. Governments should guarantee that working class people have access to the media.[2]

In addition to redefining the government's responsibility for regulating freedom of expression, the Soviet bloc nations urged that the Universal Declaration specify the duties of citizens to the community, the state, and to one another. To them, freedom is not simply a "freedom from" oppression, but a "freedom for" democracy. Freedom is not abstract. It is not simply the right to do whatever one wishes. It is concrete and positive. It is the right to contribute to the development of a democratic society. For the Soviet bloc nations such a "right" is more than a right; it is also a duty. Hence, in many Communist nations citizens are not simply given the right to vote or to serve in public office; they are required to do so. For every right, they argue, there corresponds a responsibility. To ignore this correlation of rights with responsibilities is to encourage anarchy, fascism, and war.[3]

It is interesting that the Western and Eastern blocs diagnosed the rise of fascism so differently. Western capitalist nations perceived the problem as a limitation of individual rights and thus urged the passage of a Universal Declaration of Human Rights that would guarantee individual rights and protect citizens from oppressive governments. Eastern socialist nations perceived the problem as a consequence of too much or, more precisely, the wrong kind of freedom. Citizens had been granted the right to promote racist, militant ideas and they used this platform to overthrow a democratic society and build a war machine bent on conquering the world in the name of fascism.

From the Soviet perspective, the oppression of Jews and other enemies of fascism was simply the implementation of a policy that had been advocated years before when the Nazis were seeking to win public opinion to their way of thinking. From the Soviet perspective, waiting until the opinion of the few has become the policy of the many is to wait too long. At that point democracy has been destroyed and war is the only means of restoring it. To them, it seemed absurd for democracy to allow itself to be subverted by fascism. Thus they could not approve a declaration of individual rights which allowed persons to advocate an ideology whose stated purpose is to ride roughshod over the rights of certain races of people.

The issue of individual and communal rights was raised once again in the 1970's over the question of the rights of Soviet dissidents. From the perspective of Soviet leaders, the dissidents sought to overthrow the Soviet government and thus were a threat to order, security, and the achievements being made under the socialist system. From the perspective of the West, the dissidents were simply exercising their right to express themselves. For the West, human rights means the right of the individual to express himself or herself freely, even to advocate things which would be opposed to the interest of the state. For the Soviets, human rights means the right of the individual to express himself or herself responsibly, and for the public to protect itself against irresponsible expressions that attempt to subvert a democratic government or promote racism, sexism, pornography, or anything else harmful to the common good.

In explicating the Soviet position, Leonid Brezhnev criticized the West for failing to appreciate the threat that the dissidents posed to the Soviet Union. Brezhnev argued that criticizing the Soviet Union in a way that encourages reform of the socialist system is a right guaranteed by Soviet constitutions and by the policy of his government. However, "it is another matter," he argued "if a handful of people who have broken away from our society actively come out against the socialist system and embark on anti-Soviet activities, violate laws, and, lacking support inside the country, seek help from abroad, from subversive imperialist propaganda and intelligence centres." "Quite naturally," he continues, "we take and shall continue to take those measures against them which are in keeping with our law."[4] For Brezhnev, dissidents who work outside the political system, advocate the overthrow of that system and enlist aid from foreign countries to do so, should not be protected by some claim to individual human rights. Society should be protected from them. Thus it is important to assert the rights of society as well as those of the individual.

In June 1975, in a speech entitled "The Indissoluble Unity of the Party and People," Yuri Andropov addressed the dissident issue by explaining the Soviet understanding of individuality and social solidarity. He candidly admitted a number of shortcomings in the Soviet system with regard to individual human rights. He acknowledged that some of the Western allegations were true, and that reform was in order. Andropov then took the offensive, arguing that despite Soviet shortcomings the USSR can boast superiority to the United States in the area of human rights. He stated that the goal of the Soviet system is to create a democracy of the working class. Those individuals who do not share the interests of the working class, like some of the middle-class dissidents, cannot be full participants in a working-class democracy. "Here we have to say frankly: priority must be attached to the interests of all society, all working people. We believe this is a fair principle." Turning to criticize the United States, Andropov observed that while the Soviet parliament consists entirely of workers, "there is not a single worker in Congress, and so-called 'average Americans' are represented by just a few members." Andropov believes that a political system in which the working-class majority can participate at the legislative level is more just than a political system in which they cannot, even though the middle class in the "socialist democracy" may be required to give up some of the privileges they would enjoy in a "capitalist democracy." Andropov goes on to argue that rights are meaningless unless they correspond to duties, and that one of the chief duties of the citizen is to participate in government, working to make it a good one. Dissidents refuse to accept this responsibility. Instead of working within the political structures to build a better government, many dissidents work from without in an effort to undermine the government. Because they do not accept the full responsibilities of citizens, they cannot enjoy the full rights of citizens.[5]

In 1977, Andropov stated that complete freedom of speech cannot be extended to those who divorce themselves from Soviet society and "engage in anti-Soviet activity, violate the law, supply the West with slanderous information, circulate false rumours, and attempt to provoke various antisocial incidents." He considered "the ideological and political unity of Soviet society" to be "a major source of its strength." The "enemies of socialism" would, therefore, direct "their most vehement attacks against this unity." In a 1979 speech, Andropov affirmed the right of loyal Soviets to criticize the Soviet political system, but argued against granting such rights to "renegades ... who slander Soviet reality and sometimes directly collaborate with imperialist secret services." The Soviet people could never grant anybody the right to destroy democratic socialism. Too many lives have been sacrificed and too much effort exerted, he says, to allow a small minority to destroy what has been achieved. "To safeguard society against such criminal activities" is, from the socialist democratic perspecive, "both fair and democratic." It protects "the rights and freedoms of Soviet citizens," and "the interests of society and state."[6]

In a 1983 article of the journal *Communist*, entitled "The Teaching of Karl Marx and Some Problems of Socialist Construction in the USSR," Andropov argued the case for socialist democracy once again. His thesis was that, from the socialist point of view, collective rights were more important than individual rights. "The CPSU attaches top priority," he said, "to the interests of the people, society as a whole." Under capitalist systems, a gulf existed between the interests of the state and those of the citizen. In socialist systems, this gulf had been abolished. "Unfortunately, there are still a few individuals who attempt to oppose [*sic*: impose] their selfish interests on society and its other members." These, known in the West as dissidents, seek to destroy socialist democracy and must be prevented from doing so, for the sake of everyone else. These dissidents must, in Andropov's opinion, be "re-educated." Such re-education "is not a violation of 'human rights' as is hypocritically alleged by bourgeois propaganda but real humanism and democracy which means government by the majority in the interests of all working people."[7]

A number of scholars have commented upon the Soviet concern for communal rights. In 1970, Soviet dissident historian Andrei Amalrik described to Western readers the "bewilderment" that Western talk about individual human rights raises among Soviet citizens, and said that the average Soviet citizen is as likely to view freedom pejoratively as positively, associating freedom with "disorder" and anarchy.[8] In 1980, Australian political and legal scholars Eugene Kamenka and A.E.-S. Tay wrote that although the Soviet Union no longer stresses extreme "anti-individualistic" ideology that once prevailed, and although "the society's concern for the individual and his well-being is much more strongly stressed . . . than it was in classical Marxism or under Stalin," that "this is always balanced by the demand that the individual must show a corresponding concern for society—in practice, loyalty to the Soviet system—and display a feeling of personal responsibility for the course of socialist development under socialism."[9] In 1982, American political scientist Arpad Kadarkay affirmed that "Marxism assigns a higher priority to social purpose than to individual rights," and that "social purpose is invariably defined in collective, not individual terms."[10]

The Russian people's concern for communal rights is rooted in a Russian history laden with invasions and occupations by foreign armies, accompanied by staggeringly high death tolls among both the civilian and military population. Out of these experiences national security has become a major concern. A strong government to protect the Russian people has been as high or higher a priority than protecting individual citizens from that government. The state, as they see it, has the responsibility to be strong and, within reason, the right to require of its citizens what is necessary to make it strong. By contrast, we might note that the United States has never experienced an invasion by a foreign military force.

The United States is, in fact, a nation of foreign conquerors. Europeans invaded the territory in the seventeenth century and took the land away from the native population. The type of injustice that was formative in the American experience was not the experience of being invaded, but the experience of having invaded someone else's territory but then being deprived of the right to govern it. In the Russian consciousness looms the fear of the nation's space being invaded by a foreign government. In the American consciousness looms the fear of having one's private space invaded by one's own government. These differing experiences of injustice account in large part for differing concepts of justice, one conceiving of human rights primarily in communal terms and the other in individual terms.

Even the "darling" of Western human rights activists, Soviet dissident Alexander Solzhenitsyn, has expressed scorn and disdain for Western-style liberal democracy, which he views as corrupt, lacking in moral fiber, and weak, lacking in social purpose. It is materialistic, libertine, and hedonistic. Solzhenitsyn wants a government with the strength of the Soviet government, but with a theistic rather than an atheistic orientation—theocracy, not liberal democracy.[11]

Objections from Moslem Nations

From the Islamic perspective, Western human rights initiatives create an imbalance between individual and society. They bend over backwards to protect individual rights while ignoring the needs of society. They allow individuals and parties of individuals to impose their will on society. Comments Rashid Ahmad Jullundhri, Director of the Islamic Research Institute, Islamabad, Pakistan: "It [Islam] seeks harmony between both; individual and society."[12]

From the Islamic perspective, the Universal Declaration and other Western human rights documents have couched human rights in individualistic, rather than communitarian, terms and have been preoccupied with human rights when they should have been more concerned about human duties. They have been anthropocentric when they should have been theocentric. They have been based upon human contract rather than divine law. Subsequent Western human rights initiatives have glossed over these differences and thus have been unacceptable to the Moslem world. Bridging the gaps between Western Enlightenment concepts of human rights and Moslem communitarian, theocentric concepts of human rights is no small task. The first step, of course, is dialogue. At the very least, Westerners should listen to the Moslem notions of human rights. This is what we will do in the following paragraphs.

During the drafting of the Universal Declaration, the representative from Egypt registered complaints regarding Article 16, which granted freedom of marriage, and Article 18, which granted freedom of religion. In the Moslem religion, he explained to the General Assembly, there are restrictions regarding the marriage of women to men of other faiths. The Universal Declaration had no right to interfere in religious laws and customs. From the Islamic perspective, to grant freedom of marriage is to take away freedom of religion. Freedom of religion is viewed not so much in terms of the right of the individual to practice the religion of his or her choice as the right of the religion to carry out its functions. It is primarily a collective rather than an individual right. The other objection of the Egyptian delegate was that the granting of complete religious freedom would allow Christian missionaries to proselytize in Moslem countries, a practice which Moslems felt they had the right to forbid.[13]

In more recent years, during the Carter administration's human rights initiatives, Abdul Aziz Said, Professor of International Relations at The American University, Washington, D.C., argued that many Western notions of human rights were not only foreign to the Moslem way of thinking, but also were considered inferior to Moslem notions of human rights. Moslems would object to being proselytized by these notions because the anthropocentrism, secularism, and possessive individualism would have a corrupting influence on the Moslem way of life.

While "the West emphasizes individual interests," Said points out that "Islam values collective good." The liberal notion of freedom runs counter to Islamic law, the Shariah. According to the Shariah, the individual is not a sovereign entity, as the liberal concept of human rights assumes. Nor is the state sovereign. Only God is sovereign. According to the Shariah, individuals have no rights to private ownership of property. "All is owned by God alone." The Shariah does establish a "right of use." But it sets limits on the accumulation of wealth because wealth fosters sin. Such a notion of property runs directly counter to the liberal understanding of property rights, as stated in Article 17 of the Universal Declaration: "Everyone has the right to own property alone as well as in association with others," and "no one shall be arbitrarily deprived of his property." According to the Shariah, the freedom God grants is the freedom to exist, not the freedom to act. In the West, freedom is defined as the "freedom from restraint" or, stated positively, "the ability to act." Such a notion of freedom is "alien to Islam." For the Moslem, freedom is theological, not political. "Personal freedom lies in surrender to the Divine Will," Said comments, "and this must be sought within oneself. It cannot be realized through liberation from external sources of restraint." Describing a concept of freedom that is light-years away from Kant and the Enlightenment, but very reminiscent of an Augustine or a Luther, Said explains:

> Since absolute freedom belongs to God alone, the individual realizes freedom by seeking God, the author of human freedom. There is no freedom possible through rebellion against this principle which is the source of human existence. To rebel against it in the name of freedom is to become separated from the potency and grace of the Divine and to lose inner freedom, the only real freedom.

Said refers to the Islamic notion of freedom as "totalitarian voluntarism."[14]

From the theocentric, communitarian Islamic perspective, the ideal form of government is not a liberal state, but an Islamic theocracy. The role of the government is not to guard an anarchistic notion of individual freedom, but to enforce and implement the Shariah. By so doing the government will create "an environment . . . that satisfies the socioreligious needs of the people," as defined by the Qur'an, which is to be virtuous, obedient servents of God. The role of the government, then, is to create an environment in which Moslems can exercise the one, fundamental human right, the right to serve God. For, as the Qur'an affirms, "Man has been created only to serve God!"[15]

Said admits that the Moslem preference for collective human rights has certain weaknesses. In attempting to promote virtue, the Shariah has encouraged the development of "coercive system[s]": governments, customs, and traditions that use repressive means to achieve morally commendable ends. By using a unified religio-cultural approach, Said admits that Islam runs the dangers of identifying moral norms with cultural norms. "Cultural systems . . . usually contain much that impedes human development: prejudice, chauvinism, competitiveness, racism, sexism, and so on." So Islam must confront the problems resulting from trying too hard to promote virtue in society. But, for Said, this is no worse, and may be better, than the situation that Western liberal states face: the need to confront the problems resulting from failing to promote virtue in society. In making the elimination of repression the primary objective of laws and governments, Western democracies have ignored the need to promote individual virtue. Consequently, "individual preferences in music, clothing, drugs, and sexuality have become human rights issues." From the Islamic perspective, as seen by Said, such a situation suggests moral and cultural anarchy, and the failure of the governmental, cultural, and religious institutions to promote what is good for society. People are no longer servants of God and citizens of the community but are individuals preoccupied with their own rights, tastes, and interests. And governments are no longer servants of God, assigned the task of promoting goodness in the community, but are conglomerates with power only to repress. Thus their powers must be limited. Said laments this negative view of government in the West. It is based upon "a false dichotomy between the individual and society." It assumes that the interests of the society can never be those of the individual, that the common good will never mesh with the individual's good.[16]

In the West, then, human rights concerns focus upon the role of the individual in society, guaranteeing him or her the freedom to have convictions, tastes, and preferences, and to express them. "In the Islamic world," Said concludes, "human rights concerns focus on the role of the state and on the essentials of life."[17] Individual life-style preferences are not regarded as human rights which should be protected if the cost is cultural disorder and eternal damnation. It is easy to see why many of the Moslem nations have expressed objections to the concept of human rights that has been promulgated by the Universal Declaration and by the Carter administration.

Objections from Latin American and Africa

Gauging the response of non-Moslem Third World countries to the Universal Declaration is tricky, since most of these nations were colonies of Western powers at that time. Their support of the Universal Declaration does not reflect an authentic Third World response. By the time of the Carter administration, the nations of Latin America, Africa, and Asia had become more independent, and their response to Western human rights initiatives had become more distinctive and authentic. One of the areas of conflict that was to emerge between First and Third World concepts of human rights was the dichotomy between individual and communal understandings of human rights. The varying notions of property ownership and family identity dramatize this distance. Article 17 of the Universal Declaration proclaims that "everyone has the right to own property." In many traditional cultures, property ownership is communitarian and no one has the "right" to own property. Article 16 proclaims that "the family is the natural and fundamental group unit of society." Section 1 of Article 16 defines "family" in nuclear rather than extended terms. And yet the fundamental unit of many Third World societies, and even First World subcultures, is not the nuclear family but the extended family. These two examples dramatize not only the gap between First and Third World notions of individual and societal structure and rights but also the remarkable insensitivity of the Universal Declaration to Third World patterns of culture and justice. We will now examine in more detail the way that Third World cultures tend to relate individual and communal rights, using Latin America and Africa as examples.

Many Latin American scholars trace their notions of human rights back to Spanish philosophers such as Alfonso el Sabio and Francisco de Victoria, who antedated the Western Enlightenment and who thought more in communal than individualist modes. Members of the Uruguayan Delegation to the Second General Assembly of the Latin American Council of Protestant Methodist Churches in Rio de Janeiro, in 1973, reported that the individualist concept of human rights, "largely based on the Anglo-Saxon tradition, " was foreign to their cultural heritage. While interaction with this tradition could certainly broaden their notions of human rights, they expressed concern that the validity of the Spanish concept be affirmed. They pointed out that "One of the first clear references to 'human rights,' is found in the writings of Spanish philosopher Alfonso el Sabio, who spoke about the 'right of the peoples' (derecho de gentes)." His emphasis, "strangely enough, . . . was not on individual but collective rights," and he was very influential upon de Victoria and the development of international law.[18]

C. Neale Ronning, a political scientist specializing in Latin American politics and diplomacy, writes that, from the Latin American perspective, individual civil and political rights must be considered secondary to certain, more basic rights. These more basic rights include not only economic rights [which we shall discuss in chapters 4 and 5] but, more fundamentally, a certain way of conceptualizing the relation between individual and society, expressed variously as "the creation of a new kind of citizen" and

THE ANATOMY OF WESTERN INDIVIDUALISM AND ITS INFLUENCE ON THE HUMAN RIGHTS MOVEMENT

Up to now I simply have presented a perception of many Communist, Moslem, and Third World nations. I have not considered whether such a perception is accurate, that is, whether the concept of human rights as promulgated by Western human rights initiatives does indeed lean toward individual rather than communitarian rights. The individualistic orientation of the human rights movement in the West is fairly widely acknowledged and should not require extensive argumentation. My purpose in this section, therefore, is not to prove something that everyone already acknowledges as true but to explicate in greater detail the features that characterize this individualism and to indicate how this individualism has shaped the character of the human rights movement.

The Western, individualistic concept of human rights is characterized by two prominent and complementary features. One is a positive view of the human being as individual. The other is a negative view of the human being as community, particularly in terms of political community. Combine the two views and the stage is set for the human rights drama as seen from the Western perspective: a conflict in which powerful, tyrannical governments violate the inherent dignity of innocent individual human beings; a conflict in which the ends, individual human beings, are oppressed by the means, their governments.

Rooted deep within the American psyche is a strong faith in the capacities of the individual. We grant individuals a plethora of rights and freedoms. We glamorize the lone pioneers who challenge the frontiers of medicine, outer space, and the Wild West. We idolize the rare rugged individualists and Horatio Algers who succeed when the odds are against them. We put "blind faith" in the "invisible hand" of the free enterprise system, believing that as individuals pursue their own profit-maximizing activities the "invisible hand" of the market will work all things together for the good of all persons. We believe that egotistic impulses somehow serve the common good, thus we justify them. By remarkable legerdemain, selfishness becomes altruism, and greed becomes self-sacrifice.

Coupled with this blind faith in the idividual is a distrust of groups, particularly political institutions. This is why the constitutions of liberal democracies place so many limitations upon governmental power. The source of this fear seems to rest mostly in the experience of political oppression of an emerging middle class in England, France, and America. This fear is summed up by a maxim of Whig historian Lord Acton: "Power corrupts, and absolute power corrupts absolutely."

This combination of faith and unfaith has been very influential upon the concept of human rights that has developed in the West, and this influence is prominent in the literature of the movement. The leading document of the movement, The Universal Declaration of Human Rights, is, almost exclusively, a statement of the rights of individuals against the claims of their governments. The first article affirms its faith in the dignity and worth of the individual by asserting, in Enlightenment fashion, that all human beings "are endowed with reason and conscience." The dignity and worth of the human community is not affirmed. In fact, the next twenty-seven articles explicate the rights of the indivdiual against the community, implying that the authors of the document assumed a natural innocence and goodness of the indivdiual while assuming the state's natural propensity to evil. Articles 2 through 27 follow a linguistic pattern that betrays such an assumption. Each article is stated in one of two ways: "Everyone has the right . . . " or "No one shall be subjected to . . . " The second formula is, of course, simply a reverse expression of the first. These formulas project a moral cosmology in which individuals are basically well-meaning while governments, devoid of "reason and conscience," are not. Only in the next to the last article, Article 29 which appears to be a small concession to Second and Third World criticisms, does the document say anything about the rights of the community and the incompleteness of the individual apart from the community. Article 29 affirms that "everyone has duties to the community in which alone the free and full development of his personality is possible," and the need for "morality, public order and the general welfare in a democratic society." This rescues the declaration from an otherwise exclusive preoccupation with the claims of the individual against the community. But such a statement comes "too little and too late" in the document to make a substantial difference in the declaration's otherwise positive judgment of humanity as individual, negative judgment of humanity as social, and disregard for the duties and responsibilities of individuals to society.

The prominent scholarly and polemical literature of the movement also betrays this combination of faith in the individual and lack of faith in governments and other social and political institutions. Hersh Lauterpacht, author of *An International Bill of the Rights of Man*, which antedated the Universal Declaration and greatly influenced it, wrote that an international bill of rights should limit the powers of the state and increase the freedom of the individual. "The problem which it would purport to solve," he wrote in 1945, "is nothing short of the twin tasks of protecting human freedom against the State and of securing international peace by ensuring lawful government within the State."[28]

In a book commemorating the fifteenth anniversary of the Universal Declaration, Egon Schwelb wrote that protection of the individual from his or her government is the essence of the Universal Declaration. "The question of human rights is mostly, though not always, a question of the relationship between the individual and the government of his State; and it is the State against which the human rights of the individual are in need of protection."[29] Note Schwelb's characterization of governments as transgressors and individuals as innocent victims, of individuals with inherent rights to be protected and states with powers to be limited. The assumption seems to be that in a progressive and democratic society individual freedoms should always be in the process of expansion while the state's freedoms should always be in the process of being curtailed. Such an assumption ignores what we might call the law of political entropy: that greater individual freedom tends to lead not to greater goodness in society, but to greater anarchy.

Schwelb's greater concern for restricting the powers of governments rather than individuals is quite understandable. He views the formation of the United Nations and the human rights movement in general as a response to the Nazis' complete disregard for human rights. He views the Jews of the holocaust and the early American colonists as sharing a common experience: the experience of an oppressive government, a government that ignored individual rights. Just as the American colonists saw fit to declare in a bill of rights that "never again" would a government in their land ride roughshod over its own citizens, so the survivors of the holocaust and their sympathizers saw fit to declare the same thing through an international bill of rights. But the holocaust that many poor people face, the holocaust of hunger, is not caused by governments restricting the freedom of individuals but, if anything, governments allowing a certain class of individuals too much freedom. Would a truly international bill of rights include some restrictions on influential individuals vis-à-vis governments as well as some restrictions on powerful governments vis-à-vis individuals? Does our increasing awareness of the problem of hunger, particularly in the emerging Third World, make the issue of human rights more than simply a matter of protecting individuals from their governments? A truly universal declaration of human rights should proclaim the rights of both individuals and states, and do justice to both.

Another expression of an individualist bias in the Western concept of human rights is that of Myres McDougal, Harold Lasswell, and Lung-Chu Chen, writing on human rights and international law in 1969. They describe the human rights drama as a conflict between passive, innocent, rights-holding individuals and antagonistic governments bent on grabbing those rights away from them. "It is convenient," they say, to "categorize" the actors in the human rights drama "in terms of deprivors (those who impose value deprivations) and deprivees (those who sustain value deprivations).[30] The role of the deprivors is played primarily by "officials at all levels of government—national, sub-national, and, to a far lesser extent, international." The role of the deprivees, of course, is played by individual citizens. Note once again the way that government is cast in negative terms. The Western concept of human rights lacks faith in governments as agents of redemption in society. It sees them only as agents of sin, as "deprivors" and never as "providers," as natural enemies of individuals and not as friends. Is this lack of faith in government an actual "crisis of faith," as non-Western critics would allege? Or is it a turning from a false, albeit powerful, god—the state—to the one who truly bears the image of God— the individual human being?

THE THEOLOGICAL DEBATE OVER INDIVIDUALISM

The question that the theologian must ask is whether this faith of the West is misplaced. Is there too much faith in the individual, and too little faith in the political institutions of society? Expressing the problem in moral rather than fiducial terms, is the goodness of the individual exaggerated and the goodness of the state ignored? As a consequence, do the Western liberal democracies allot too much power to individuals and too little to their governments? To answer these questions the theologian must ask whether these views of individuals and governments are consistent with the Christian theology's insights concerning the nature of humanity.

Thielicke's Defense of Western Individualism

The most reputable theologian to defend the individualist bias of the Western concept of human rights has been Helmut Thielicke. A number of theologians and church denominations have given support to the individualist concept of human rights through their uncritical approval of and involvement in the movement. The World Council of Churches, for example, supported the human rights movement for two decades before questioning its individualist orientation. Thielicke is unique and important because he was conscious of the individual-communal issue from the start and deliberately set out to use theological ethics to defend the individualistic, Western concept of human rights. In this section we will use Thielicke's arguments as a springboard for critically analyzing the theological dimensions of individualist concept of human rights.

As a Reformation theologian, Thielicke expresses some skepticism of the attempt of Western human rights advocates to base human rights on natural law and yet believes that "there is here an insight which cannot be surrendered, however dubious the wrapper in which it is contained."[31] While Thielicke can accept human rights in secular wrappings, he cannot accept them in collectivist garb. The very title of the section of *Theological Ethics* that discusses human rights betrays his individualist bias—"Human

Rights and the Limitation of Power." Thielicke equates human rights with protection of the individual from too strong a government. In this section he could have discussed any number of ways that human rights are violated—the tendency of criminals to violate the rights of law-abiding citizens, of the rich to violate the rights of the poor, of whites to violate the rights of blacks, of men to violate the rights of women, and so on. In each of these examples the rights of human beings are violated, and in each case government can and has served as an agent of judgment upon and redemption from the sins committed by one group of human beings toward other human beings. But Thielicke ignores these examples, and instead discusses almost exclusively the case of the violation of individual liberties by the state. He chooses the one example that puts the state in a negative light, as a perpetrator of human rights violations rather than as a liberator from human rights violations. He chooses the example that puts the individual human being in an altogether positive light. The violator is not a wealthy landowner or an entrenched white majority. It is "the state" or "the government," described in the coldest, most abstract and impersonal of terms. The violated is, of course, the innocent individual human being.

Thielicke's discussion of human rights as individual liberties is replete with proindividualist and anticommunitarian assumptions. Thielicke's very positive view of the individual seems to come more from John Locke and the Enlightenment than from Martin Luther and the Reformation. In support of his individualist concept of human rights Thielicke cites Locke, "who sees a close connection between the rights of the individual—deriving from his freedom in the natural state—and the need to divide the power of the state lest it encroach on the individual rights to freedom." Thielicke's negative view of the state, and his belief that "from the dawn of their first realization," human rights have contained "a protest against the trend of the state towards omnipotence" also suggests that his concept of human rights is shaped largely by Locke. For Thielicke, as for Locke, human rights means the expansion of the rights of the individual and the limitation of the rights of the state, "the protection of man as individual against man as controller of the machinery of the state." A state that "accepts human rights as a binding criterion . . . is in effect limiting its own power by guaranteeing the rights of the individual to freedom."[32]

One of the problems with Thielicke's concept of human rights is that he resists viewing the state as a resource for doing good in society. His argument for a "minimal state" is based on the assumption that governments are necessarily oppressive and ineffective. They are oppressive even when attempting to improve the welfare of society, because they interfere in individuals' private lives. Government welfare programs are ineffective because they do what the church can do much better. In "The Problem of Institutionalizing Love," Thielicke states that the movement toward the welfare state "is an alarming phenomenon" because the welfare state "necessarily seeks to penetrate every sphere of life and hence to take over the care of children, the chronically ill, the sick, and the aged" and because it "hopes to validate itself from a humanitarian standpoint as the representative of social concern." The welfare state becomes, in essence, a sort of totalitarian humanitarianism.[33]

Thielicke believes that the welfare state's communitarian concept of human rights perverts several important Christian notions: *diaconia*, the two kingdoms, love, and poverty.

The Christian notion of *diaconia* stresses that "care for the neighbor . . . cannot consist merely in the supply of material needs," but spiritual ones as well. It must include, Thielicke believes, "a message that will give meaning to what is done." Thielicke accuses secular welfare programs of "perverting" and "falsifying" the gospel by doing the work of the gospel without attaching to it the message of the gospel. Thielicke presses the point way too far. It is clear that the gospel is "ignored" if compassionate governmental action is done out of nontheological humanitarian motives. And it is clear that the gospel would be "truncated" if compassionate ecclesiastical action lacked an accompanying theological motive. But to say, with Thielicke, that the gospel is "falsified" and "perverted" by government welfare programs makes no sense at all. There is some theological validity in saying that good deeds not done to the glory of God contain an element of pride. What could be more hypocritically self-righteous, however, than for the church, particularly if it does little to promote social welfare, to criticize those who do because of an insufficiently theological motivation? Secular welfare programs could only pervert the gospel if they claimed to be practicing it.[34]

What really bothers Thielicke, I think, is that Luther's doctrine of the two kingdoms has been superseded in the modern, pluralistic, Western world.

> The state as universal father, the state which intervenes in all things, exploiting even the inner powers of man (his dispositions and convictions) and registering everything and laying claim to everything, transgresses its allotted sphere on the left hand and—whether latently or deliberately—assumes the role of a pseudo church.[35]

Once again Thielicke objects to state activities that reflect too much compassion and concern for their citizens. He should criticize the church for not doing what it is supposed to, not the state for doing more than it is supposed to. Just as he would not want the state to tell the church how to run itself, he should not expect pluralistic democratic governments to conform to Lutheran notions of what a government should and should not do.

A third Christian doctrine that Thielicke believes is perverted by the communitarian concept of human rights is the Christian notion of love. Once love is institutionalized, as by a state welfare program or even by the "good Samaritan's League," it is "robbed of its very point." In true love of neighbor, there has to be improvisation, spontaneity, and unexpected interruptions. Institutions cannot provide for this. They have to plan, do their work between nine and five, and be cost-effective. Thielicke says:

> There is a tension between love and advance planning, between love and purposeful intent. At its core the living claim of the Thou resists institutionalizing. It cuts right across all order. It always arises as an interruption, a summons to forego all planned order. Just as the Spirit moves where he wills (John 3:8), refusing to be bottled up or encapsuled in orders, so the neighbor is an event, something that happens, a challenge, and hence something which cannot be normalized as part of an orderly scheme.[36]

While I agree that one has to allow for spontaneity and interruptions, I hasten to add that there is also, in the Christian tradition, a notion usually referred to as "stewardship," which offers a healthy corrective to the rather footloose notion of love that Thielicke espouses. Stewardship considers planning and effectiveness to be important. Thielicke says that "love by its very nature is linked with improvisation," and that "love is direct and immediate" while order and planning are "indirect." The implication is that there is no such thing as love that lasts over the long term, or as love that does routine deeds of charity. Visiting an invalid on a daily basis would not qualify as love, according to such standards. Any deed of charity requiring planning would not be a true act of love, since this would lack the immediacy that love requires. Voting or contributing to a worthy cause would not be acts of love, because love must be direct. Thielicke accuses the welfare state's "love" of being too impersonal: "No one is ever summoned personally any more. No one need feel any personal responsibility. The apparatus is available to care for everything." Thielicke criticizes the welfare state for getting in the way of the Good Samaritans in society.

> Those who because of their faith, or because of some particular ethics, would champion personal directness in love of neighbor (as do Christians with their *diaconia*) no longer have any opportunity to live out their love and bring it to men, because the planned machinery of the institution is there before their improvisation can even get under way. And because the planning and organization are so complete that there are no holes left for the seed of *diaconia* to slip through.[37]

Even if welfare agencies were as organized and effective as Thielicke thinks, there would still be plenty of opportunity for the personal and spontaneous love that Thielicke cherishes. Furthermore, Thielicke's argument involves a fundamental contradiction. At one point he says that the state could not replace the personal love that the Good Samaritans could give voluntarily, yet here he claims that it has, and that it has done such a good job, there is nothing left for the Good Samaritan to do! If welfare agencies were this effective, it would be a matter for rejoicing, not sorrow. Since they are not always able to provide the personal, immediate, spontaneous, direct dimension of love that the Good Samaritan can give, most would agree that the welfare agencies leave plenty for the Good Samaritans and the church to do.

A fourth problem with the communitarian concept of human rights, in Thielicke's opinion, is that it has redefined the meaning of poverty. According to Thielicke, poverty has evolved from being perceived as an individual phenomenon to being perceived as a structural phenomenon, a deficiency in the social structure. In the individualistic perception, poverty results from personal vices, most notably laziness. This is Thielicke's view. He musters support from the Book of Proverbs, citing numerous references to a correlation between laziness and poverty. This kind of poverty can be eliminated by loving these individuals and trying to motivate them to be more industrious. In the communitarian perception, poverty results from systemic causes, so the solution is to change the social structure through political and judicial action. Thielicke identifies this view as Marxist, and expresses his abhorrence of Marxism.

Apart from his insensitivity to the situations of poverty in the modern world, which reflects, I think, a lack of love for the poor, Thielicke has ignored the many times that scripture identifies systemic causes of poverty: injustice, greed, and so on. Were the Israelite slaves poor because they were lazy, or because they were treated harshly by their Egyptian masters? Certainly there are many cases of poverty being linked to individual vices: laziness, alcoholism, drug addiction, and so on. But certainly there are systemic causes as well, and one does not have to be a Marxist to affirm such an obvious truth. Thielicke wants to believe that "before the modern age, poverty, though interpreted in a variety of ways, was regarded essentially as an individual phenomenon." As the theologians of liberation have shown us, however, the systemic and corporate roots of poverty are nowhere more explicitly identified than in the Bible itself.[38]

A problem that runs through Thielicke's entire discussion of the welfare issue is his tendency to do morality "from the top." Thielicke is preoccupied with problems related to the dispensing of charity—whether its motives are theological, whether it is a church operation, whether it is spontaneous and direct, and whether it properly defines poverty. These are problems that concern a middle-class Christian. For the hungry person, the concern is not whether the bread comes from an individual Good

Samaritan or a collective government agency, or whether it was given for the glory of God or to get rid of a government surplus. For the hungry person, the main issue is whether it nourishes an empty stomach. Beyond that, the person might be concerned about being treated paternalistically by those who give, and whether to trust the givers to help out the next time there is need. Thielicke ignores these concerns. Thielicke's motivation for feeding the hungry has little to do with a sense of solidarity with the poor, or even with a sympathy for their suffering. He hardly mentions these things. His preoccupation is with the act of giving and with the one who gives, and his concern is that the one who gives do so in a proper way, or not at all. This has some value in the discipleship of middle-class Christians, but it has little to do with solving the problems of poverty, which is what the state welfare programs attempt to do. Earlier we noted that Thielicke was willing to accept the individualist concept of human rights, despite his disdain for its secular packaging. It seems that Thielicke should apply the principle here and accept humanitarian efforts that come in secular wrappers. But he most definitely is not willing to do so.

Thielicke's solution to the individualist-communitarian conflict is what he calls a "relative" or "minimal" welfare state. He approves such minimalist measures as "subsidizing . . . imperiled elements of the economy, protecting workers against dismissal without cause, extending credit with a view to the establishment of economic independence, providing job retraining in cases of personal or general economic crisis, etc." "The payment of pensions and benefits" should be a concern of the state, but he would prefer that it be delegated to the private sector. He does not approve of food, housing, or medical subsidies for the poor. At the time of his writing this volume, 1959, Thielicke believes that governments of the West are *too* involved in welfare activities. The moral directive for Christians living in such a time, he says, is to work to curb such activities. Theological ethics "must espouse the theological thesis that the state ought to be minimal, and give the relevant reasons."[39]

It is interesting that Thielicke, a Lutheran, harbors such a negative view of the state. He admits that he has "inverted" Lutheranism's "original approach to an ethics of the state." Thielicke explains this difference between himself and Luther by saying that "Luther's doctrine of the state was elaborated in answer to the threat of chaos. For Luther the state was a divinely instituted force of order set up to counter centrifugal and destructive egoisms." Thielicke believes that the situation today is reversed. The present threat is "an overabundance of state order" which depersonalizes, isolates, and inhibits "direct I–Thou relationships, and turn[s] love of neighbor into a welfare machine."[40] In assuming that a powerful state will be a tyrannical state, has Thielicke abandoned Luther in favor of Locke? To what extent are his arguments theologically grounded, and to what extent are they Enlightenment concepts packaged in theological terminology? Thielicke accuses the modern welfare states of "selling out" to Marx. It may be that he is the one who has sold out to secular ways of viewing and doing things, at least as regards his rather libertarian view of the state.

The Churches' Challenge to Western Individualism

Although a number of theologians and church bodies have, like Thielicke, defended the individualistic bias of the human rights movement, in recent years quite a few have taken a critical stance toward the individualistic orientation of Western human rights initiatives.

After a period of being very supportive of the individualistic orientation of the human rights movement, Protestantism now seems to be going through a period of soul-searching, questioning whether an individualistic bias is consistent with the Protestant experience and the biblical tradition. For example, the Lutheran World Federation, meeting in Geneva in 1980, was unable to reach agreement concerning the relationship between communal and individual human rights. Some continued to maintain, as Thielicke had two decades before, the absolute priority of individual rights. They based this claim upon their interpretation of the doctrine of justification by grace alone, viewing human collectives as potential surrogate gods. Others viewed individual and communal rights as complementary and equal in priority. They found support for their claim in the triune nature of God and in the biblical affirmation of humanity's likeness to that God.[41]

Protestants who now advocate a dialectical balance between individual and communal rights have begged forgiveness for the role Protestantism has played in promoting the overly individualistic Western concept of human rights. As J. Robert Nelson points out, such expressions as "the private interpretation of the Bible, " "a man and his God," and even "the rugged individualist" have become synonymous with Protestantism. The Universal Declaration of Human Rights, he says, is almost "entirely individualistic," and as such "is a very Protestant document." Nelson's attitude toward this individualism is ambivalent. On the one hand, Protestantism asserts the importance of private freedom and responsibility before God in matters of faith, conscience, and morality. On the other hand, Nelson believes that such rights cannot in all cases be treated as absolutes. A Christian notion of community must balance the concern for individuality. The rights of one Christian cannot be exercised in a way that they impinge upon the rights or well-being of another member of the community. For example, the gifts of one member of the community are to be used in a way that they build up the rest of the community. Another example: when one member of the community rejoices or suffers, the rest of the community shares in the rejoicing and the sorrowing. A third example: sometimes individuals must restrain from exercising rights and privileges if doing so creates more harm than good in the community, as in the case of eating meat sacrificed to idols.[42]

As regards church policy, Nelson points out that the division within Protestantism over episcopalian, presbyterian, and congregational forms of church government is evidence of the struggle to bring about a harmonious balance between individual and communal notions of rights. The episcopalian and presbyterian forms favor the rights of the community, defining the church as an organic communion and the members as parts of that communion. The individuality of the members is subordinated to the identity of the communion, but the individuality is not "dissolved" or "lost." Members can participate as "living stones," not inert or identical bricks in the corporate temple structure. In congregational churches, the church is defined not as an organic communion but as a "gathered church" of individual Christians who have freely, voluntarily, and temporarily associated themselves together. "Where such Protestant communities have thrived in Western Europe, Great Britain, and North America," Nelson comments, "the general popular attitude favors emphasis upon the rights of individual persons over against the rights of society." But Nelson questions whether the almost exclusive preoccupation with individual rights in the West accurately reflects the more balanced approach of these churches which continue to affirm corporate rights and responsibilities through creeds, discipline, the corporate exercise of gifts, and so on. In these "gathered churches" the corporateness of the Body of Christ is not lost or dissolved. It is merely subordinated to certain individual rights and responsibilities.[43]

The recent revival of concern for communal rights is viewed by the Eastern Orthodox Church as a vindication of what it had affirmed all along. Orthodox ethicist Stanley S. Harakas notes that individual rights are a product of the Enlightenment and that the early Christian tradition does not share this concern. The early Christian tradition was concerned primarily with the duties and responsibilities of the individual toward the community, not the rights that the individual could claim from the community. "The tradition emphasizes the idea that love more often than not requires sacrifice of one's 'rights' than the insistence upon them, and forgiveness of their violation by others than insistence upon their fulfillment." Talk of rights would be in terms of what rights the community, political or ecclesiastical, could claim upon the individual. Regarding individual self-fulfillment, the early Christian tradition viewed this in terms of "overcoming sin and distortion in life through a synergy of Divine Grace and the exercise of spiritual self-discipline," not in terms of claiming such "a right to be granted by others." In other words, it was viewed as a spiritual rather than a legal problem, and from the individual's perspective it was a matter of disciplining oneself before God rather than claiming rights before others. Harakas points out, in a more general sense, that "the Eastern Orthodox approach to life as a whole tends not to be cast in a legalistic *quid quo pro [sic]* framework." It is cast in terms of love, not justice. Living the Christian life is described not in terms of advocating justice for the oppressed but in terms of "the imitation of God as giving, grace-filled, compassionate, forgiving, looking toward a communion of human beings which reflects the loving communion of Father, Son, and Holy Spirit—the Holy Trinity." One reacts to oppression not with a cry for justice but with forgiveness and compassion.[44]

Harakas goes on to point out that the Eastern Orthodox tradition is not totally insensitive to individual rights. He cites Orthodox ethicists, such as Panagiotes Demetropoulos and Vasileios Antoniades, who have advocated certain individual human rights and who have asserted that certain rights are inherent in the very fact of being human. He could also have cited the Russian Orthodox advocate of individual rights, Alexander Solzhenitsyn, along with other Orthodox advocates of the rights of Soviet dissidents. But even when insisting upon the inalienableness of human rights, it is difficult for Orthodox ethicists to avoid couching such talk in terms of duty. Rights exist only because duties exist, and so rights exist only as the reciprocal of duties. For example, the worker's right to decent pay is based not, primarily, upon the inalienable dignity of the worker, but on the divinely ordained duty of the employer to be a righteous person.[45]

Like the Eastern Orthodox Church, the Roman Catholic Church has, historically, subordinated the category of the individual to the category of the community. Expressions such as "a man and his God" and "the private interpretation of the Bible" would be out of place in the Roman tradition because the relationship between individuals and their God is mediated by the church, and scripture is interpreted through the auspices of the church. Even so, the Roman church has, in recent years, recognized the need to show greater respect for the individual and through the Vatican II process has begun to move in this direction. A balance was being sought between the traditional concern for the rights of the community and the more modern concern for the rights of the individual. This balance is reflected in *Pacem in Terris*, widely recognized as "the central and classical document of the doctrine of human rights in the Roman Catholic tradition."[46] Although a primary concern of the encyclical was to express the church's new stance with regard to religious freedom, it contained clear implications for the whole range of individual rights. Throughout the document the Pope expresses concern for both duties and rights, and for both the common good and the individual good. The document never mentions a right without listing a corresponding duty, nor an individual good without suggesting that individual goods must be set within a larger context of the good of the community.

In order to achieve a balance between individual and community, *Pacem in Terris* utilizes what we shall call in chapter 3 the philosophy of personalism. At the outset, the encyclical states as its guiding principle "that every human being is a person, that is, his nature is endowed with intelligence and free will. Indeed, *precisely because he is a person he has rights and obligations flowing directly and simultaneously from his very nature*" [italics mine]. As indicated, Catholic personalism asserts the dignity of the person. In contrast to Western liberalism, however, it asserts that this dignity involves responsibilities as well as rights. Personalism asserts the social nature of humanity, suggesting that an integral part of the dignity of human beings is their existence not as isolated monads but as social beings.[47]

The encyclical states the rights of the person, beginning with rights to the basic needs, and then social and cultural rights, religious freedoms, rights pertaining to families, rights pertaining to work, and, last of all, civil and political rights. The encyclical then discusses duties of citizens, asserting that "the natural rights with which We have been dealing are . . . inseparably connected . . . with just as many respective duties. . . . [T]o one man's right there corresponds a duty in all other persons: the duty, namely, of acknowledging and respecting the right in question." The encyclical then directs a sharp criticism at Western liberalism: "Those . . . who claim their own rights, yet altogether forget or neglect to carry out their respective duties, are people who build with one hand and destroy with the other." The basis for the correlation of rights and duties is that "*men are social by nature*" [italics mine] and "are meant to live with others and to work for one another's welfare."[48]

In Part Two, which deals with the relations of citizens to their government, the encyclical continues the strive for harmony between the realms of the individual and the community. The document states that God is the ultimate source of authority and that individuals have the right to disobey governmental authority when it conflicts with the command of God. Here the good of the individual is affirmed. Then the document expresses the other side of the dialectic: "Individual citizens and intermediate groups are obliged to make their specific contributions to the common welfare." Citizens should "bring their own interests into harmony with the needs of the community," and should "contribute their goods and services as civil authorities have prescribed, in accord with the norms of justice and within the limits of their competence." In other words, individual good must be sought within the context of the common good.[49]

Pacem in Terris reflects the Roman Catholic Church in transition from the old church, which favored the rights of the community over the rights of the individual—and thus at times served as an ally of repressive regimes—to a new church, which could strive for harmony between individual and community. The new church would recognize the achievements of the human rights movement in affirming th dignity of the individual human being, but it would continue to speak prophetically to the excesses of individualism. The philosophical framework which would make such a balance possible was the philosophy of personalism, whose roots could be traced to Thomas Aquinas but was reformulated in the modern world, in the context of the human rights discussion, by Jacques Maritain.

Maritain offered the Western world a "middle way" between totalitarian interpretations of the Thomistic notion of the common good and individualistic interpretations of liberal concept of human rights. While *Pacem in Terris* reflects the full flowering of personalism in the form of a major church document, it is in the social and political philosophy of Maritain that we find the development of personalism and the attempt to apply it to the crisis of human rights in the modern world. Maritain's personalism urged reform of the Roman Catholic Church's totalitarian tendencies and of the human rights movement's individualist tendencies.

NOTES

1. Maritain, the most prominent Catholic intellectual of the day, served as French delegate to UNESCO. An Italian priest, Angelo Guiseppe Roncalli, who later became better known as Pope John XXIII, helped write the United Nations' Universal Declaration of Human Rights. Reinhold Niebuhr, whose writings we will examine in chapter 7, served as a U.S. delegate to UNESCO. He also was an advisor to Secretary of State General George C. Marshall and helped formulate the Marshall Plan of economic aid to Europe.

2. United Nations, *Yearbook of the United Nations 1948-49* (New York: Columbia University Press in cooperation with the United Nations, 1950), 528-532; Charles Malik, "International Bill of Human Rights," *United Nations Bulletin* 5:1 (1 July 1948), 521.

3. United Nations, *Yearbook*, 528-29, 533; Malik, 521.

4. Leonid I. Brezhnev, *Pages From His Life* (New York: Pergamon Press, 1982), 94.

5. Y.V. Andropov, "The Indissoluble Unity of the Party and People" (June 9, 1975) in Y.V. Andropov, *Speeches and Writings*, ed. Robert Maxwell, M.C. 2d ed. (New York: Pergamon Press, 1983), 125-26.

6. Andropov, "Faith in Communism as a Source of Inspiration for the Builders of a New World" (September 9, 1977) ibid., 171-72; Andropov, "Under the Banner of Lenin, Under Party Leadership," (February 22, 1979), ibid., 206-07.

7. Andropov, "The Teaching of Karl Marx and Some Problems of Socialist Construction in the USSR" (1983), ibid., 292.

8. Andrei Amalrik, *Will the Soviet Union Survive until 1984?* (New York: Harper & Row, 1970), 34.
9. Eugene Kamenka and A.E.-S. Tay, "Human Rights in the Soviet Union," *World Review* 19:2 (1980): 51, 54.
10. Arpad Kadarkay, *Human Rights in American and Russian Political Thought* (Washington, DC: University Press of American, 1982), 169.
11. Alexander Solzhenitsyn, *Letter to the Soviet Leaders*, trans. Hilary Sternberg (New York: Harper & Row, 1974), 8-9.
12. Rashid Ahmad Jullundhri, "Human Rights and Islam" in *Understanding Human Rights: An Interdisciplinary and Interfaith Study*, ed. Alan D. Falconer (Dublin: Irish School of Ecumenics, 1980), 42.
13. United Nations, *Yearbook*, 532; James Frederick Green, *The United Nations and Human Rights* (Washington, D.C.: The Brookings Institution, 1956), 32.
14. Abdul Aziz Said, "Human Rights in Islamic Perspectives," in *Human Rights: Cultural and Ideological Perspectives*, eds. Adamantia Pollis and Peter Schwab (New York: Praeger Publishers, 1979), 87-96.
15. Ibid., 87.
16. Ibid., 93-96.
17. Ibid., 96.
18. Uruguayan Delegation to the 2nd General Assembly of the Latin American Council of Protestant Methodist Churches, Rio de Janeiro, Brazil, July 18-22, 1973, "The Application of Human Rights in Latin America," in Commission of the Churches on International Affairs of The World Council of Churches, *Human Rights and Christian Responsibility*, Dossier 1 (May, 1974), 42.
19. C. Neale Ronning, "National Priorities and Political Rights in Spanish America," in *Human Rights*, eds. Pollis and Schwab, 112.
20. Simon Bolívar, "Letter to General José Antonio Páez," April 12, 1828, and "Letter to General Daniel F. O'Leary," September 13, 1829, *Selected Writings of Bolívar*, vol. 2, compiled by Vicente Lecuna, ed. Harold A. Bierck, Jr., trans. Lewis Bertrand (New York: Colonial Press, 1951), 689, 738, 740.
21. Diego Portales, "Letter of March, 1822," and "Letter of December 6, 1834," cited in Ronning, 103-04.
22. (a) Ronning, 113.
22. (b) Jean Jacques Rousseau, *The Social Contract or Principles of Political Right*, trans. Henry J. Tozer (London: George Allen and Unwin Ltd., 1895/1948); C. B. Macpherson, "Revolution and Ideology in the Late Twentieth Century," *Democratic Theory: Essays in Retrieval* (Oxford: Clarendon Press, 1973), 157-69; Macpherson, *The Real World of Democracy* (Oxford: Clarendon Press, 1966).
23. Dunstan M. Wai, "Human Rights in Sub-Saharan Africa," in *Human Rights*, eds. Pollis and Schwab, 115; Warren Weinstein, "Africa's Approach to Human Rights at the United Nations," *Issue: A Quarterly Journal of Opinion* 6:4 (Winter 1976), 17.
24. Wai, 116-17; Richard F. Weisfelder, "The Decline of Human Rights in Lesotho: An Evaluation of Domestic and External Determinants," *Issue: A Quarterly Journal of Opinion* 6:4 (Winter 1976), 23; Jeanne Hersch, *Birthright of Man* (New York: UNIPUB, 1969), 95, cited in Wai, 116.

25. Wai, 118–19.
26. Ibid., 119–21.
27. Adamantia Pollis and Peter Schwab, "Introduction," in *Human Rights*, eds. Pollis and Schwab, xiii.
28. Lauterpacht, *An International Bill of the Rights of Man* (New York: Columbia University Press, 1945), 82.
29. Egon Schwelb, *Human Rights and the International Community: The Roots and Growth of the Universal Declaration of Human Rights, 1948-1963* (Chicago: Quadrangle Books, 1964), 9–11.
30. Myres S. McDougal, Harold D. Lasswell, and Lung-chu Chen, "Human Rights and World Public Order: A Framework for Policy-Oriented Inquiry," *The American Journal of International Law* 63:2 (April 1969), 240–42.
31. Helmut Thielicke, *Theological Ethics*, ed. William H. Lazareth, vol. 2: *Politics* (Grand Rapids: William B. Eerdmans Publishing Co., 1979/1959), 67–68. Thielicke believes that human rights had their origin in covenantal faith, but in modern times have been "cut off" from this "soil of faith in which they all had their origin." Thielicke worries that these uprooted rights "are in danger of withering away," and as a theologian wishes that the theological roots of these rights could be restored. But even in secularized form Thielicke sees them as having value: "Every level of faith, even where it is ultimately diluted to the point of complete abstraction, has its practical value."
32. Ibid., 230–31.
33. Ibid., 289.
34. Ibid., 290.
35. Ibid., 290.
36. Ibid., 291.
37. Ibid., 292.
38. Ibid., 296.
39. Ibid., 310–313.
40. Ibid., 290–91.
41. Eckehart Lorenz, "Introduction: How Christian are Human Rights?" in *How Christian are Human Rights? An Interconfessional Study on the Theological Bases of Human Rights*, ed. Eckehart Lorenz (Geneva: Lutheran World Federation, 1981), 6.
42. J. Robert Nelson, "Human Rights in Creation and Redemption: A Protestant View," in *Human Rights in Religious Traditions*, ed. Arlene Swidler (New York: The Pilgrim Press, 1982), 2–5.
43. Ibid.
44. Stanley S. Harakas, "Human Rights: An Eastern Orthodox Perspective," in *Human Rights in Religious Traditions*, ed. Swidler, 13–15.
45. Ibid.
46. John Langan, "Human Rights in Roman Catholicism," in *Human Rights in Religious Traditions*, ed. Swidler, 25.
47. John XXIII, *Pacem in Terris* in United Nations, *Never Again War!* (New York: Office of Public Information, United Nations, 1965), 87.
48. Ibid., 90–91.

49. Ibid., 97. In Part III the encyclical applies the correlation of rights and duties, and of individual good and the universal good, to the relations between states. In concluding the document, John gives one last exhortation to those in the West for whom human rights has become too much a concern for individual rights, to the detriment of the good of the larger community, both local and global: "Once again We exhort Our children to take an active part in public life, and to contribute towards the attainment of the common good of the entire human family as well as to that of their own country" (see 118).

3

BEYOND THE INDIVIDUALIST-COLLECTIVIST IMPASSE

Maritain began developing the personalist alternative in the thirties as a response to National Socialism, Stalinism, and bourgeois individualism. He considered each ideology unacceptable in terms of the way it related individual and society and the way it defined the human person. In the forties, Maritain would become very active in the human rights initiatives of the United Nations and, through books, articles, and speeches, he would present his personalist alternative to the world forum.

PROBLEMS WITH TOTALITARIAN AND INDIVIDUALIST APPROACHES

Like other human rights activists of his day, Maritain became interested in human rights as a response to fascism. His writings on human rights are replete with references to fascism.[1] He expresses unequivocal disdain for both the fascist movement of his day and the philosophical notions which underpin it. The high degree of passion with which he expresses this disdain is not only due to philosophical and ethical objections but also to love for his native France, perhaps a desire to clear his reputation from any tarnishing that may have resulted from his former association with the Action Française,[2] and his naturally polemical temperament. What was it about fascism that awakened a conservative Roman Catholic like Maritain to the dangers of totalitarianism? What was it about the Nazi movement that made a Thomist like Maritain switch from a theocratic totalitarianism to a more pluralistic democratic political philosophy? The aspects of fascism that bothered Maritain the most were its racism and its pseudorealism.

Maritain defines fascism as "the racist conception" of totalitarianism, as opposed to the communist conception. In fascism, the human person is sacrificed not to the god of the economic community, as in communist totalitarianism, but to "the demon of race and blood, which is the god of the racial community." This pseudoreligious racism makes fascism the "worst" form of totalitarianism. Maritain so closely identifies fascism with racism that he uses the two interchangeably, for example, in speaking of "racialist and fascist perversion," and of "Nazi racism." Maritain locates the foundation of racism in the Nazi concept and practice of *zusammen-marschieren* (marching together). Persons march together, Maritain believes, not to achieve some objective end but simply for "the subjective pleasure of being together." This "passion for communion" is dangerous if not directed toward some determining objective because "political communion will carry its demands to the infinite, will absorb and regiment people, swallow up in itself the religious energies of the human being." A powerful pseudoreligion will develop. An ethic of loyalty to the group that marches together will develop, and, because the group is not defined by an external objective, the only way of defiing itself will be through the degradation of other human groups. Such a self-concept is racist and must lead to war because the group

> will have essential need of an *enemy against whom* it will build itself; it is by recognizing and hating its enemies that the political body will find its own common consciousness. And . . . since it must at all cost do something and tend towards something, this something, which is not a determined object, nor an end in the true sense, will be nothing more than the *trend* of a movement, or the *trend* of a dream, an undefined march towards nobody-knows-what conquests.[3]

Erik Erikson discusses the phenomenon of racism in similar terms. He refers to it as a *"positive identity* . . . defined by *negative* images." The group does not know who it is and what it believes in, it only knows who it is not. The group establishes its identity by degrading another group. This results, of course, in racist, destructive behavior.[4]

Maritain defines the pseudorealism of fascism as a failure to acknowledge sufficiently the category of spirit in its concepts of humanity, technology, and law. In the fascist way of thinking, the human being is little more than "a mere parcel of matter, . . . an individual element in nature, such as an atom, a blade of grass, a fly or an elephant." The spirit as the basis of personhood is ignored. There is nothing particular, unique, or special about being human. Individual humans are mere parts of society, they are not "wholes" unto themselves. Maritain is not opposed to utilitarianism, only to a spiritless application of it. In the fascist way of thinking, technology becomes the master of the spirit rather than the servant of it. Instead of the spirit's inspiring technological progress and instead of technology's serving as an instrument of the spirit, technology is used to subdue the spirit. In the fascist way of thinking, the law is simply the Machiavellian "positive law." Because there is no notion of a spirit dwelling in all humankind, there is no concept of "natural law" to temper the oppressive tendencies of positive law. A "might makes right" philosophy of law develops. Widely recognized tenets of natural law are ignored or even subverted. "We are scandalized," Maritain notes, "by the fact that cruelty, denunciation of parents, the lie for the service of the party, the murder of old or sick people should be considered virtuous actions by young people educated according to Nazi methods." Like racism, pseudorealism encourages violence within and among nations. Stripped of their spirit, humans provide the raw material, technology provides the means, and law provides the justification. The "pessimistic pseudorealism that extends from Machiavelli to Hitler," Maritain concludes, "bends man under violence, retaining only the animality which enslaves him."[5]

Most Westerners in the early human rights movement would have agreed with Maritain's critique of fascism. Most would have disagreed with Maritain's solution to the problem. His solution was not to advocate a bourgeois individualist concept of human rights, but to develop a new, personalist concept of human rights. What was wrong with the individualist concept?

First of all, it was irreligious. Maritain once commented that of the three dominant political philosophies at the time of World War II—communism, fascism, and capitalism—"the most irreligious is bourgeois liberalism." Bourgeois liberalism, or capitalism, is "Christian in appearance," but "it has been atheistic in fact." Rather than persecute or defy Christianity, as communism and fascism have done, bourgeois liberalism has perverted Christianity and used it to promote its materialistic and individualistic philosophy. Enlightened self-interest has replaced prophetic morality. A measure of Christianity is allowed to remain as an eternal insurance policy to protect people, "while making money here below, against the undiscovered risks of the hereafter—after all, one never knows!" This dissolves fears that sins will be judged and thus lifts the taboo against self-centered behavior. The prevailing ethic of bourgeois individualism, then, is self-centered and materialistic, has little to do with biblical and historic Christianity, and in fact has perverted Christianity and used it to promote a non-Christian morality. In this sense it is "atheistic," "irreligious," and anti-Christian.[6]

Second, bourgeois individualism and the bourgeois individualist concept of human rights treat the individual as a god rather than, with humility and realism, as a human being. "This philosophy of rights," Maritain complained on numerous occasions, ends by "treating the individual as a god and making all the rights ascribed to him the absolute and unlimited rights of a god." It insists upon grounding everything "in the unchecked initiative of the individual," who is "conceived as a little God," with "absolute liberty of property, business and pleasure." Kant said that "a person is subject to no other laws than those which he gives to himself." Rousseau said that a person should "obey only himself" because any external regulations would destroy the autonomy and dignity of the self. Not only is such a view of humanity inconsistent with the testimony of historic Christianity, but it is unrealistic and self-defeating. Based on the "illusion" that humans and human rights are something more than they really are, it claims something that cannot be met, and thus "compromise[s]" and "squander[s]" the very rights it tries to establish.[7]

Third, the bourgeois individualist concept of human rights ignores the fact that at times the liberty of some must be limited to protect the liberty and well-being of others. Sometimes a society must limit the liberty of those who would abuse it, who would use their liberty to destroy the liberty of others. This was the case with the Nazis, who used "the propaganda tools of racialist and fascist perversion . . . to disrupt the democracies from within and to arouse among men the blind desire to deliver themselves from liberty itself."[8] This is precisely the argument made by the Soviet Union during the drafting of the Universal Declaration, and was one of the reasons that the Soviet Union abstained from approving the final draft of the declaration. The Soviets and Maritain agree that governments should not allow freedom of speech to be used to promote racism or anarchy.

Fourth, the bourgeois individualist concept of human rights fails to recognize the need to limit one type of liberty for the sake of another. Maritain ranks the right to exist and freedom of religion as the most basic of all rights. These might be called "absolute" rights. Freedom of expression and freedom of assembly, on the other hand, are more secondary, and thus cannot be exercised in a way that deprives other persons of more fundamental rights.[9] Prior to World War II, the Nazi Party used its rights to speak and assemble to advocate that Jews, gypsies, homosexuals, and their sympathizers be deprived of their rights to exist and worship freely. Free speech became racist propaganda, free assembly became mob rule, and the Nazis rose to power and turned their racist ideals into policy.

"It is only normal," Maritain believes, "that the various acknowledged rights of the individual should be mutually limitative." "The rights of man as a person involved in the life of the community . . . cannot be given room in human history without restricting, to some extent, the freedoms and rights of man as an individual person." The unwillingness of liberal societies to make distinctions between primary and secondary rights—because all are viewed as "absolute and sacrosanct"—usually results in a de facto distinction. In Germany, free speech became the absolute right and the rights to exist and worship became secondary. A de facto priority will almost always emerge. In liberal societies freedom of speech has emerged as the most "absolute and sacrosanct" of rights. This de facto priority should be acknowledged and, in Maritain's view, changed.[10]

Fifth, the bourgeois individualist concept of human rights affirms rights without affirming the logical corollary—duties. Maritain believes that rights and duties mutually imply one another. If persons have the right to exist, for example, then they also have the duty not to deprive others of the right to exist. Common sense is sufficient justification for such a claim, but Maritain also casts it within a larger metaphysical framework. He argues that the natural law, from which the concept of rights is derived, has been separated from its metaphysical origins, and thus has lost its "realistic dynamism" and "the humility of its connection with nature and experience." As a consequence, the notion of duty has been surrendered. "Only" within a metaphysical framework, he argues, "are we able to understand how a certain ideal order, rooted in the nature of man and human society, can impose universal moral demands upon the world of experience, history and fact, and can found for the conscience as for written law, the permanent principle and primary criteria of rights and duties." Since natural law is the source of both rights and duties, and since rights and duties are complementary ideas, the Universal Declaration of Human Rights is a very incomplete document. "A declaration of rights," he believes, "should normally be supplemented by a declaration of the obligations and responsibilities of man toward the communities to which he belongs, and specially toward the family, the civil, and the international community." The Universal Declaration fails to specify the duties that complement the rights it proclaims, and thus it fails to proclaim human rights in a practical and meaningful way.[11]

Sixth, in bourgeois individualist society neither the community nor the individual person are given their due. There is no basis for community in such a society. "The function of the State is only to insure the material convenience of scattered individuals, each absorbed in his own well-being and in enriching himself." There is no "common work," no "communion," Maritain charges. "Each one asks only that the State protect his individual freedom of profit against the possible encroachments of other men's freedoms." Nor is there any basis for the true personhood. "The true dignity of the person" is replaced by "the illusory divinity of an abstract In-dividual, supposedly sufficient unto himself," leaving the individual "alone and unarmed." Maritain adds that in bourgeois individualist society the poor ["those without possessions"] are particularly alone and unarmed as they stand "before the possessors who [have] exploited them."[12]

Seventh, individualism is the antithesis, not the resolution, of the problem of totalitarianism. The nineteenth century "experienced the errors of individualism" which in turn created the conditions that gave birth to the totalitarian excesses (fascism, Stalinism) of the twentieth century.[13] Maritian argues with considerable passion against totalitarianism, because it is the bete noire of his age. As he looks toward the post–World War II period, however, he fears a pendulum swing too far in the other direction, toward individualism, and a recreation of the conditions that gave birth to totalitarianism. In Maritain's opinion, the human rights movement has proposed a return to the anarchistic, secularistic, materialistic, and lonely individualism of the nineteenth century. Maritain sees this as no solution at all, since it will simply spawn future totalitarian impulses to compensate for the distress and emptiness of the liberal society. Maritain's response to the liberals advocating individual human rights, on the one hand, and the totalitarians advocating economic or racial community, on the other, is a decisive "neither/nor." He finds both approaches completely unacceptable. What he offers as an alternative is a "personalist" approach to human rights.

THE PERSONALIST ALTERNATIVE

The personalist concept of human rights affirms both the "communal" and "personal" aspects of being human in the world. It is communal in that it claims that civil society should be "ordered to a common good which is specifically other than the simple arithmetical sum of the particular goods of the citizens taken singly." It is personal in that it affirms what it considers to be the true dignity of the person. The person is neither merely an individual seeking a private good, as in liberalism, nor a mere part of a larger whole, as in totalitarianism. Whereas in liberalism human dignity is based upon "the power of each person to appropriate individually the goods of nature in order to do freely whatever he wants," and whereas in totalitarianism the mark of human dignity is the power of society "to submit these same goods to the collective command of the social body," in personalism human dignity has both individual and communal dimensions. In the personalist conception, the person has both "wholeness" as a self and "openness" to the larger whole, the community of persons. In the personalist conception, "the mark of human dignity" is based upon the power to make the goods of nature serve both "intrinsically human, moral, and spiritual goods" of society and the "freedom of autonomy" of the self.[14]

The personalist resolution of the debate over individual and communal rights points toward new ways of viewing such central themes as personhood, society, the common good, and natural law.

Personhood

Maritain's most characteristically personalist way of describing the person is as an "open whole." In opposition to utilitarians, Maritain insists that persons are "wholes." Persons are not simply parts of a larger whole, but they are wholes that together form a larger whole. Thus, society is "a whole made up of wholes—since the human person as such is a whole." In opposition to individualists, Maritain observes that one aspect of being a whole person is being a responsible person, performing duties as well as proclaiming rights. Liberal, individualist approaches to human rights, dwelling upon rights but not duties, thus fail to describe persons as morally whole. Persons are not merely wholes, complete unto themselves, but are "open" wholes, with a need for communion with other persons.

> The person is a whole, but it is not a closed whole, it is an *open* whole. It is not a little god without doors or windows, like Leibnitz's monad, or an idol which sees not, hears not, speaks not. It tends by its very nature to social life and to communion.
> This is true not only because of the needs and the indigence of human nature, by reason of which each one of us has need of others for his material, intellectual and moral life, but also because of the radical generosity inscribed within the very being of the person, because of that openness to the communications of intelligence and love which is the nature of the spirit, and which demands an entrance into relationship with other persons. To state it rigorously, the person cannot be alone. It wants to tell what it knows, and it wants to tell what it is—to whom, if not to other people?[15]

To be fully human, then, means being a social being. It is impossible to affirm human dignity, our basis for human rights, without affirming both the wholeness and the openness of the person.

Another term that Maritain frequently uses in redefining personhood is one that he borrows from Aristotle and Thomas. He calls humanity the "political animal." In other words, humanity has a natural predisposition to live in society. "The human person craves political life, communal life, not only with regard to the family community, but with regard to the civil community." Once again Maritain affirms the social aspect of human being. This affirmation serves not only to criticize individualism, as is rather obvious, but also to criticize the utilitarian tendency within totalitarian systems. This craving for political life indicates what distinguishes human societies from animal societies—the struggle for freedom. In a jab at Rousseau, Maritain states that "no animal is born more naked and less free than man. The struggle to win freedom in the order of social life aims to make up for this defect." It is only in the context of a just society that human freedom can develop. And it is only with the development and application of reason that a just society can develop. For Maritain, being a political animal is the equivalent of being a reasonable animal, and that is why it is improper to refer to animal communities as "societies" or "cities." Animal "societies" are governed by instinct. Human societies are governed by reason. Thus human societies develop over time, because reason and understanding, unlike instinct, develop over time. Humanity is a political animal for two reasons. The most obvious is the need for cooperation in the struggle for physical survival. This pertains to "material needs, of bread, of clothes and lodging, for all of which man depends upon the aid of his fellows." Maritain's primary meaning in describing humanity as a political animal refers to the need for the help and cooperation of other persons in doing what is distinctively human: "acting according to reason and virtue." In order to do this, education is needed, and education is a social process.

> It is in this sense that one must give a very strict meaning to the words of Aristotle, that man is naturally a political animal. He is a political animal because he is a reasonable animal, because his reason seeks to develop with the help of education, through the teaching and the co-operation of other men, and because society is thus required to accomplish human dignity.[16]

It is impossible to talk about human dignity apart from this communal aspect.

Maritain also defines persons by distinguishing between person and individual, between personality and individuality. Individuality, Maritain tells us, has to do with the material aspects of being. This "does not concern the true person but rather the shadow of personality." Personality, on the other hand, has to do with the spiritual aspects of being. This involves "the deepest and highest dimensions of being," the soul.[17]

The unity of the self as individual is a precarious one. Like all matter, it is inclined toward disintegration "just as space is inclined to division." It is "subject to the determinism of the physical world." And it is not a whole, but is "a part of the universe" and "a fragment of a species." Because of this incompleteness and finitude, the self as individual feels "forever threatened and forever eager *to grasp for itself.*"[18]

The self as person, or soul, on the other hand, is not a Leibnitzian monad preoccupied with its own existence. It is complete and infinite. Unlike the material dimension, which constitutes the order of existence, the spiritual dimension constitutes the order of knowledge and love. The soul does not seek its own existence, but to know and love others, and hence communication and relationship between persons. In seeking physical wholeness, the self as individual must act in a way that, in the moral terminology of the person or soul, would be described as "selfish." Hence, the self as indivdiual is "detestable" but the self as person "signifies what is most perfect of all nature," a being able to transcend nature through knowledge and love. The self as individual is necessarily egocentric; the self as person is freely social, "a social unit."[19]

In describing human beings as "open wholes," "political animals," and "persons," Maritain's main concern is to emphasize, against the current of the human rights movement, that humans are social beings, and that it is impossible to talk about human dignity and human rights in highly individualized terms.

Society

The second term that Maritain redefines in personalist terms is "society." Society has two components, communion and individuation, and thus is a peculiarly human phenomenon. What distinguishes human society from a group or colony of animals is that human society is a community of persons as well as of individuals. What distinguishes human society from divine communion, on the other hand, is that human society is a community of individuals as well as persons. In animal communities, there is no communion of persons. In divine communion, there is pure communion but no individuation. Human society consists of both. It is "a society of persons who are material individuals, hence isolated each within itself but nonetheless requiring communion with one another as far as possible here below in anticipation of that perfect communion with one another and God in life eternal."[20]

Maritain defines society in this way as a critique of both utilitarian and liberal concepts of society. Utilitarians define society as a community of "individuals" or, to borrow another expression from Maritain, as a "whole" made up of "parts." Although Maritain agrees that humans as individuals exist as parts of a larger whole, he insists that humans as persons exist as "wholes" themselves. "Society is a whole whose parts are themselves wholes." Maritain agrees that society is an organism with a life of its own, but "it is an organism composed of liberties, not just of vegetative cells." Maritain agrees that society has "its own good and its own work which are distinct from the good and the work of the individuals which constitute it. But this good and this work," he insists, "are and must be essentially *human*, and consequently become perverted if they do not contribute to the development and improvement of human persons."[21] The common good is not simply the good of the "economy," or the "state," but is the good of persons.

In Maritain's terminology, liberal advocates of human rights define society as a community of "persons" who are not "individuals." It is a spiritual community without being a physical one. Maritain insists that humans seek society not only out of their spiritual abundance—their "inner urge to the communications of knowledge and love which require relationship with other persons"—but also out of their deficiencies, both material and spiritual. Liberals, in their concern to advocate the rights of persons, tend to ignore the need that persons have for society.[22]

Common Good

The third concept that Maritain redefines in personalist terms is the "common good." Against the liberal individualists he insists upon the primacy of the common good over the private good. Against the utilitarians he redefines the term so as to show greater respect for the person.

Maritain makes it clear that he parts company with the human rights movement's individualistic concept of the good. "Let us not say that the aim of society is the indivdiual good or the mere aggregate of the individual goods of each of the persons who constitute it." Such a goal

> would dissolve society as such for the benefit of its parts, and would lead to an 'anarchy of atoms.' It would amount either to a frankly anarchic conception or to the old disguised anarchic conception of bourgeois materialism, according to which the entire duty of society consists in seeing that the freedom of each one be respected, thereby enabling the strong freely to oppress the weak.[23(a)]

Maritain observes that "at every opportunity" Thomas "repeats the maxim of Aristotle that the good of the whole is 'more divine' than the good of the parts." Maritain finds the liberal, privatistic concept of the good to be totally inconsistent with the Thomistic understanding of justice as the common good.[23(b)]

What Maritain means by the common good, however, is "a common good of *human persons*, just as "the social body itself is a whole made up of human persons." Failure to recognize this personalist aspect of the common good would lead to errors in the other direction from anarchism, such as collectivism and state despotism. Just as the common good is not "a mere collection of private goods," neither is it simply the good of a whole that "draws the parts to itself alone, and sacrifices these parts to itself." The common good of society must be the good of the whole and of the parts which are themselves whole.

> The common good of society is their communion in the good life; it is therefore common *to the whole and to the parts*, to the parts, which are in themselves wholes, since the very notion of *person* means totality; it is

> common to the whole and to the parts, over which it flows back and which must all benefit from it. . . . It involves, as its *chief* value, the highest possible attainment (that is, the highest compatible with the good of the whole) of persons to their lives as persons, and to their freedom of expansion or autonomy—and to the gifts of goodness which in their turn flow from it.[24(a)]

Because the common good is the good of society, and because society is a community of persons, the common good must, necessarily, be the good of persons. This is what distinguishes the common good, which applies only to persons, from the "public good," which applies to individuals. The public good is concerned only about the needs of beings as individuals, hence material needs. The beehive is concerned entirely with the public good, as are most totalitarian systems. Liberal society, on the other hand, tends to be unconcerned about the common good or the public good. Personalist society is concerned about both.[24(b)]

Maritain has masterfully reinterpreted the Thomistic doctrine of the common good in such a way that he can use its utilitarian elements to critique the anarchistic and individualist tendencies of the advocates of human rights, while using its notion of personhood to attack the totalitarian tendencies of its opponents.

Natural Law

The fourth concept that Maritain redefines in personalist terms is "natural law." Just as the common good has been the bailiwick of the utilitarian opponents of human rights, so natural law has served its liberal advocates.

As with the common good, Maritain affirms the principle but redefines it. His affirmation of natural law distinguishes him from the utilitarian opponents of the human rights movement for whom the only law is positive law. His redefinition of natural law shows where he parts company from those advocates of the human rights movement who base human rights upon a liberal concept of natural law. Once again, Maritain finds himself in the middle of the two factions. As a Thomist, he is a utilitarian who believes in the common good, but also in a divine law of nature. For Maritain as with Thomas, this natural law is not of the liberal bourgeois variety, but is more conservative and more theocentric.

Against the legal positivists, Maritain insists upon natural law as the ultimate basis for human rights. Here he stands with the liberal tradition: the Enlightenment, the democratic revolutions, and the human rights movement. He stands with John Locke's claim that humankind is born "with a title to perfect freedom, and an uncontrouled enjoyment of all the

rights and privileges of the law of nature," and that a universal law of nature provides the basis for claiming that all *"mankind are one community,*
make up one society, distinct from all other creatures." He stands with the
American Declaration of Independence's insistence upon those rights "to
which the laws of nature and of nature's God entitle them"; the French
Declaration of the Rights of Man and Citizen's proclamation of "the
natural, inalienable, and sacred rights of man"; the Universal Declaration
of Human Rights' declaration of "the inherent dignity and . . . the equal
and inalienable rights of all members of the human family"; and the
American Declaration of the Rights and Duties of Man's recognition "that
the essential rights of man are not derived from the fact that he is a national
of a certain state, but are based upon attributes of his human personality."[25]

Although Maritain's notions of natural law mesh, at some points, with
liberal notions, Maritain's concept of natural law is derived primarily from
the medieval, Christian, and Aristotelian philosophy of Thomas; not from
the modern, rationalistic philosophy of the Enlightenment. Maritain
makes this clear in a number of ways.

One way is that he calls for a rediscovery of the metaphysical roots of
the idea of natural law. Natural law, he says, has been "distorted" and
"defaced" by the rationalism of the eighteenth century. What has been lost
is not simply a theological problem, but an ethical one as well. Once the law
of nature was lifted from its theological setting, Maritain observes, so lifted
from natural law were its "realistic dynamism and the humility of its relation with nature and experience."[26]

In the theocentric version of natural law, humanity had been a creature endowed with certain rights by the God-given law of nature. Creature-
liness, finitude, and sinfulness had been taken into consideration. Humanity not only had rights, but also duties before God, other persons, and
the rest of creation. Certain limitations were taken into account, and persons were encouraged to be humble in regard to these limitations as well as
proud of their dignity. With the rationalist distortion of natural law, the
realism and humility went out the window. Humans became "as Gods."
Sovereignty now resided neither with God, as in theocentric notions of
natural law, nor with the state, as in Machiavellian-type notions of positive
law, but in the individual human being. Natural law, which had been a
servant of the common good in the theocentric system, became a servant of
the private good in the anthropocentric version. In addition to the obvious
moral consequences, there were practical problems as well. Natural law
was supposed to provide the basis for absolutizing a whole host of individual rights which, in practice, could never be truly absolute because
they would conflict with one another. Even the exercise of one particular
right by one person could conflict with the exercise of the same right by
another person. Maritain believed in respecting persons and also nations,

but not to the point of granting them sovereignty. He did not care to sanction, with natural law, their attempt to maximize private good.

Another way that Maritain distinguishes his notions of natural law from Enlightenment notions is by limiting the number of absolute rights. Absolute rights are those rights which accrue to persons solely by way of natural law and thus are inalienable. For Maritain, absolute rights are the rights to exist, to worship, and to pursue moral perfection. All other rights fall under the categories of the law of nations and positive law. Natural law consists of those rights and duties which follow *"from the simple fact that man is man,"* which are necessary to the first principle of natural law, "do good and avoid evil," and which take no other considerations into account. Positive law consists of the statutes in force in a particular community. Positive or statutory laws differ from community to community, depending upon local customs and the historical circumstances which gave birth to them. The rights and duties specified by positive law should follow from the first principle of natural law, even though they must follow in a *"contingent manner"*; that is, through the historical and cultural conditions of the community. Natural law, then, consists of the rights and duties that can be expressed in universal and transcultural ways. Positive law consists of the rights and duties which follow from the presupposition that humanity is to do good and avoid evil, but whose expression must be culturally specific.[27]

As with his reformulations of person, society, and common good, Maritain challenges the individualistic orientation of the human rights movement. He grants the existence of natural law, and even says that it serves as the philosophical basis for positive law. He is not willing, however, to divorce natural law from its theocentric setting. Nor is he willing to give absolute, universal status to the rights to speak freely, to assemble, or to vote. Such rights are culturally and historically conditioned, and can be expressed in a variety of ways. He does not even believe that their absolute status in the West is justified, given the prior importance of the right to exist and the right to worship and the tendency of the civil and political liberties to displace the right to exist and to worship.

Maritain's Vision of a New Society

In redefining person, society, common good, and natural law, Maritain attempts to transcend the individualist-totalitarian dialectic. He envisions a society that incorporates the strength and unity of monarchical government, the refinement ("differentiation of values" and "the production of the noblest and rarest values") of aristocratic society, and the freedom of democratic society. Such a society would be both "personalist" and "com-

munal." "Personalist" refers to the characteristics of the person that give
the person worth apart from and anterior to society. "Communal" refers to
the person's need for and responsibility toward society. In Maritain's
words, a society is personalist if it "considers society to be a whole composed of persons whose dignity is anterior to society and who, however in-
digent they may be, contain within their very being a root of independence
and aspire to ever greater degrees of independence until they achieve that
perfect spiritual liberty which no human society has within its gift." A
society is communal if it "recognizes the fact that the person tends
naturally towards society and communion, in particular towards the political community, and because, in the specifically political sphere and to the
extent that man is a part of political society, it considers the common good
superior to that of individuals."[28]

What Maritain tries to establish is a dialectical relation of person and
society. "There will always exist a certain tension between the person and
society," Maritain says. To resolve this tension in favor of the person, as in
bourgeois individualism, or in favor of society, as in totalitarianism, is to
fail to appreciate the "dynamic" nature of spiritual and political life. "This
paradox, this tension, this conflict are themselves something both natural
and inevitable," Maritain assures us. On the one hand, the human being is
merely a part of society. On the other, the human being transcends society.
"Man is a *part* of the political community and is inferior to" it, Maritain
says, because of the things in him which "depend as to their very essence
on the political community, and which, as a result, can be called upon to
serve as means for the temporal good of this community." And yet "man
transcends the political community." There are things in a person that are
ordered not to the political community but toward the absolute and which
relate not toward temporal fulfillment of the individual (as a member of
society) but toward "supra-temporal fulfillment of the person" (as a
spiritual being).[29]

MARITAIN'S PERSONALISM AND THEOLOGICAL ETHICS

Maritain's integralist, personalist concept of human rights is vulnerable to a number of criticisms. Some involve the particular way that Maritain argues his case and do not suggest any problem with personalism per
se. Others involve the very substance of Maritain's personalism. Even these
do not necessarily imply any problem with personalism per se, only with
Maritain's version of it.

Problems with Maritain's Method

The most serious formal criticisms of Maritain revolve around his
abstract and polemical style, and his lack of attention to concrete historical

detail and to biblical and theological resources. He makes broad, sweeping statements that mean everything and nothing. He tends to caricature the positions he opposes, ignore the weaknesses and logical inconsistencies of his own position, reduce the alternatives to overly simplified general categories (such as "totalitarianism" and "bourgeois individualism"), and beg the conclusions he wants to reach.[30]

An example of the way Maritain caricatures his opponents and reduces the alternatives to overly simplified general categories is found in his claim, made on numerous occasions, that atheism necessarily spawns a crass utilitarian social policy, and that theism is a firm guarantee against such. "If there be no God," Maritain claims, "the only reasonable policy is that the end justifies the means." Under such a policy "it is permissible to violate any right of any man, if that seems a 'necessary' means" to achieve the common good. "Such," Maritain believes, "is the inner logic of the atheistic ideology." Maritain offers the reader a truncated set of alternatives. The "only" options are a crass atheistic utilitarianism or a full-blown theocratic system. He ignores the various versions of humanism which have given up belief in God but not the sanctity of the person. This contradicts a position he takes elsewhere regarding the relation of atheism to utilitarianism. When making his case for a "theistic" society, in order to avoid sounding harsh, he says that atheists can join in the effort to realize a personalist, communal, and theistic society as long as they "believe in the dignity of the human person, in justice, in liberty, in neighborly love."[31] Maritain also ignores the various incidents of crass, fanatical utilitarianism in the history of the church, such as the crusades and the burning of heretics, in which rules and bodies were broken and individual rights ignored for the sake of a greater common good. The fascist appeal, both in Nazi Germany and in the more recent Aryan supremacist revival, has often been couched in theistic appeals to utilitarianism, and seems to be all the more ironfisted and cold-blooded because of this way of relating genocide to transcendent rather than material or corporate ends.

An example of Maritain's lack of logical consistency and abundance of polemical verve is the way he often disassociates the church from the evils that it has engendered, while giving the church credit for the good things it has done. Maritain does this by distinguishing between authentic Christianity and the many dishonorable actions done throughout history in the name of the church. This is a common distinction rooted in Augustine, but it seems that Maritain abuses the distinction somewhat, wanting to give the church credit for everything good while denying responsibility for everything bad. Sidney Hook accuses Maritain of trying to have his cake and eat it, too. "If it is impossible to deduce from authentic and revealed Christianity the particular programs which M. Maritain condemns, it is just as impossible to deduce their contraries of which he approves." Hook concludes: "*If* authentic Christianity comprises a set of general, eternal and immutable truths beyond history and time, they cannot serve as a guide to *specific* problems of history and time." Hook cites a statement from *Integral Humanism* which exemplifies Maritain's tortuous logic: "The Church, as such, was not involved in these excesses but they were produced within the Church." "How," Hook says, "can an organization not be involved in that which is produced within it?" Hook considers such reasoning to be the logical and moral equivalent of excusing the Nazi Party from the excesses of Nazism.[32]

Has Hook been too harsh on Maritain? Has Maritain done anything more than repeat Augustine's famous distinction between the visible and invisible church? I believe Maritain has used the distinction in an inappropriate way. Traditionally the distinction has been useful in two contexts. One is, in dealing with questions of theodicy, to say that actions done in the name of God are not necessarily the works of God. This clarification is not an attempt to clear the historic church in any way from atrocities it has done, only to clear the name of God from atrocities done by the church. Maritain seems more concerned about clearing the name of the church. He tries to claim that there is an abiding "true Church" which does all the good things done in the name of Christianity, while bad things are done by those who have lapsed from the true way.[33]

The second valid use of the distinction is for the purpose of encouraging reform within the church. The "ought" is pressed against the "is" and the historic church is challenged to measure up to the ideal. The problem with Maritain's use of the classic distinction is that he uses it for neither of these purposes. He uses it as an apologetic tool for dialogue with the non-Christian world, as a way of defending the church's sinful acts through history. It comes off sounding like a shirking of responsibility, and this is what angers Hook. In dealing with those outside the church it makes much more sense simply to acknowledge that the church, and not some imposter masquerading as the church, did something wrong. Theological distinctions between the visible church and the true church should be reserved for specifically theological discussions, and should not be used in discussing the relation of church and society.

Maritain's love for ideas and ideals and his lack of attention to concrete, historical facts are well illustrated by his discussion of economics and human rights in *Freedom in the Modern World* and *The Rights of Man and Natural Law*. Critic Frank H. Knight accuses Maritain of discussing economics and human rights "entirely without reference to the most elementary facts of social life." In other words, the goal should not be to reach the ideal in the abstract, but in history. This can never be achieved apart from translating human rights ideals into the mundane, technical language of economics and political science. This is not to say that Maritain should try to be an economist or a political scientist, but that whatever he says as a theological ethicist should have some relation to historical life. His thoughts should not be such abstract ideas or such lofty ideals that the economist or political scientist would not see in them anything that related to the real world.[34]

Sometimes Maritain seems to string ideals together one after the other without regard to their relation to each other. In *The Rights of Man and Natural Law* he asserts at one point that the worker has "the right to a just wage" not subject to the fluctuating law of supply and demand. Only four pages later, he argues that workers should not be paid wages but should be given "'associative' ownership of the means of production" or "joint ownership of the enterprise."[35] Maritain never acknowledges the apparent contradiction, nor does he specify how the system of joint ownership might work. Comments Knight: "Beyond the advocacy of a radical economic reorganization in accord with vague idealistic principles, admirable enough in the abstract, it seems impossible to make out what the author has in mind."[36] The ethicist should be concerned about the intelligibility and feasibility as well as the morality of his or her recommendations.

Biblical and Theological Resources

From a theological perspective, the greatest formal weakness in Maritain's argumentation is his failure to utilize the resources of Christian theology to their fullest potential. This is partially understandable, since Maritain is more a philosopher than a theologian. His attempt to relate individual and communal rights would have been more powerful and effective, however, if he had couched it not only in the terms of the Aristotelean–Thomistic tradition but also in more widely accepted biblical and theological motifs.

The Trinity provides a wonderful image of the relation of the person to the community. Each "person" of the Trinity is complete. In each divinity dwells fully. Yet the love between the "persons" is so pure that this community of three is a unity of one: one God in three "persons." Since humanity is created in the image of God, we would expect humans to be integral yet social beings as well. Each person constitutes a complete human being, and yet the community constitutes one humanity in a multitude of persons. The notion that God is a social, relational being and that persons are social, relational beings provides a healthy corrective to the individualism of Western liberalism.[37]

The Christian tradition affirms humanity's social nature not only in its most positive judgment that humanity is made in the image of God but also in its most negative judgment that humanity is totally depraved. Sin is not something that one person has and another does not. Humanity is such an integrated community that it is impossible for one to sin without all participating in it. "In Adam's fall, we sinned all" signifies humanity's solidarity in both its dignity and its depravity.[38]

Humanity's social, relational nature is also affirmed by the Christian notion of salvation as a corporate experience. The Protestant preoccupation with justification by faith has contributed to the Western tendency to grant greater sovereignty to the individual. What needs to be rediscovered is that justification by faith is but one of many motifs of salvation described in the Bible. The covenantal nomism of the Old Testament, the kingdom of God and the body of Christ in the New Testament, and salvific events such as the Exodus and the Passion of Christ all connote that salvation is corporate as well as individual, and that personal faith is exercised within the community of faith.

From the perspective of theological ethics, Maritain's failure to utilize fully biblical and theological resources is particularly regrettable. It is to be hoped that any future efforts to integrate individual and communal rights would explore the ramifications of humanity being made in the image of a perfectly social being, of human solidarity in sin, and of the corporate experience of salvation. It is also to be hoped that any efforts to integrate individual and communal rights would avoid some of Maritain's substantive weaknesses as well.

The Relation of Church and State

The most obvious substantive weakness is what Hook perceives as totalitarian tendencies in Maritain and in the pre-Vatican II Catholic Church. "Catholicism is the oldest and greatest totalitarian movement in history," Hook states at the outset. Like "Fascism, Nazism, Stalinism," and other totalitarian systems it utilizes "dogmas, sacred and profane, rituals of canonization and excommunication," and "the directing force of a highly organized minority" to "revolutionize 'the soul' of man." Maritain, in responding to Hook's vindictive critique, accuses Hook of being "blinded by many resentments" and thus of exaggerating Maritain's "totalitarian" tendencies.[39]

Certainly a claim as hyperbolic and all-encompassing as the claim that "Catholicism is the oldest and greatest totalitarian movement in history" belongs more to the rhetorical than the ethical plane of discussion. And certainly Hook's anti-Catholic and anti-Communist prejudices inhibit him from giving Maritain a fair reading. But I would agree with the essential point that Maritain, and the Roman Church at this time, had theocratic tendencies that could be described as totalitarian, even though Maritain and the Roman Church were certainly in a period of transition away from the more repressive aspects of a theocratic society.

After arguing in *The Rights of Man and Natural Law* that society should be personalist and communal, Maritain makes the case for society being "pluralist" and "theist" or "Christian" as well. What Maritain says about the need for pluralism is somewhat blunted by the subsequent argument that society must be "Christian." Maritain denies that his vision of a Christian society involves the expectation that every member would believe in God and become a Christian, or the repetition of "any kind of theocracy or clericalism," or any other "sort of pressure in religious matters." Rather, society would be "Christian" in the sense that "the spiritual activity of the Church" and of other "diverse religious families" would be respected and facilitated by the state.[40] What Maritain has said up to this point is somewhat disturbing because it is so vague. Maritain has raised all kinds of questions regarding the relationship between church and state and has not answered them. It is unclear, for example, how the state is to facilitate religion without getting in the way of religious freedom.

In the next section of *The Rights of Man and Natural Law*, Maritain shifts into a more polemical and prophetic gear, abandoning the conciliatory, "pluralist" language in favor of a most definitely "Christian" approach. He begins the section with the following charge:

> The present war gives us notice that the world has done with neutrality. Willingly or unwillingly, States will be obliged to make a choice for or against the Gospel. They will be shaped either by the totalitarian spirit or by the Christian spirit.

Maritain's intent may be to suggest that the Christian spirit, unlike the totalitarian one, is open and respectful of human dignity. But by expressing this intention in such a dualistic and absolutist manner, it has the effect of connoting a lack of openness and respect for non-Christians. In the subsequent discussion, Maritain abandons any hint of openness and respect:

> The Catholic Church insists upon the principle that truth must have precedence over error and that the true religion, when it is known, should be aided in its spiritual mission in preference to religions whose message is more or less faltering and in which error is mingled with truth.

Once again Maritain qualifies himself somewhat, stating that it is "the spiritual mission of the Church that must be helped, not the political power or the temporal advantages," as in the Middle Ages. Even so, Maritain is unclear as to how much freedom the church should be given in carrying out its "spiritual" mission.[41]

Should the state allow the church to burn its heretics? Although it is difficult to imagine Maritain supporting such a thing, he is vague enough regarding such practical matters of the implementation of his theories that one must be disturbed when those theories would seem to suggest such. In *Integral Humanism* Maritain had shown some respect for the medieval system of dealing with heretics. "I have no mind to condemn this regime in principle," he said. "In a sense, an earthly city capable of the death sentence for the crime of heresy showed a greater care for the good of souls and a higher idea of the nobility of the human community, thus centered on truth, than a city which only knows how to mete out punishment for crimes against the body." Maritain goes on to admit that the types of punishment got out of hand, but attributes this to the state taking over the task from the church: "these became more and more intolerable . . . when after the ruin of medieval Christendon the State, ceasing to act as instrument of a legitimate spiritual authority superior to it, arrogated to itself and in its own name the right to act in matters spiritual," a practice which has continued from the time of Henry VIII to the totalitarianisms of the twentieth century.[42]

I do not share Maritain's confidence that, if the church is allowed to punish its own heretics without any interference from the state, its submission to the divine authority would always be sufficient to check its tendency to abuse such a power. Power corrupts, and absolute power corrupts even churches. In a truly pluralist society there should be a system of checks and balances between ecclesiastical and political authorities. Churches should be given a certain degree of freedom to discipline their heretics, but this should be done within certain parameters set by joint agreement of civil and ecclesiastical authorities, with the state having the duty to intervene on behalf of its citizens if those parameters are violated. Likewise, church members should of course be allowed to participate in government so as to check any abuses of power by the government.

To conclude this line of criticism, it seems fair to say that Maritain's attempt to relate individual rights to collective rights is vulnerable to the criticism that it replaces secular forms of totalitarianism with an ecclesiastical version of the same. I do not believe that Hook is correct in claiming that Maritain is advocating a simple return to medieval theocratic totalitarianism. Maritain denies this on numerous occasions. But I do believe that Maritain's vagueness and lack of attention to the concrete implications of his theory, combined with a sometimes zealous Catholic spirit, leaves the reader wondering just how Maritain proposes to give the church this much authority without creating the conditions for the abuse of that authority.

Three Areas Deserving Further Attention

Apart from the relation of church and state, there are three other areas in which the substance of Maritain's argument is vulnerable to criticism. One is its sometimes pneumatic notion of human being. This elevation of spirit over matter is significant because some in the West—not Maritain—have used it to justify a lack of concern for basic human needs, such as food, shelter, and medical care. I shall argue in chapters 4 and 5 that Christian theology advocates that humanity is a physical as well as a spiritual being, and thus the right to food is as much a human right as the right to free speech.

A second criticism to which Maritain is vulnerable is that his notion of humanity is optimistic. Such an attitude has caused many in the human rights movement to be naive concerning the tendency of states and other institutions to be more concerned about self-preservation than about allegiance to international ideals of justice. I shall argue in chapters 6 and 7 that Christian theology not only asserts the dignity of humanity, but also humanity's sinfulness and finitude, and that this sin and finitude extends to states as well as to individuals, thus making the sovereignty of states an important consideration in any attempt to promote international human rights.

A third criticism of Maritain's political philosophy is that his notion of humanity can be overly "Western" and even "Catholic," in the cultural sense of the term. Ethically, this failure to acknowledge sufficiently the multicultural dimensions of humanity is significant because such an attitude can and has fueled the fires of non-Westerners who felt left out of the leadership of the movement, who felt that Western advocates of human rights had sometimes acted chauvinistically, self-righteously, and hypocritically. I shall argue in chapters 8 and 9 that Christian theology affirms the multicultural dimensions of humanity and militates against any attempt to elevate one culture or family of cultures above another.

Despite these criticisms, it seems clear that Maritain has made a most important contribution to the development of a holistic concept of human rights in his development of a concept that is neither individualist nor totalitarian, but rather is personalist, communal, and, at least in intent, pluralist. Maritain relates the individual to society in a way that affirms "the sacredness of the individual"[43] and the transcendent qualities of the human spirit but also acknowledges that humanity is a social, political being. In this way he has contributed both as a theologian, to the development of a balanced doctrine of humanity, and as an ethicist, to the development of a balanced concept of human rights.

CONCLUSIONS TO CHAPTERS 2 AND 3

1. Non-Western nations have condemned the human rights movement's preoccupation with individual rights and lack of concern for communal rights.

2. This individualism is rooted in Enlightenment anthropology and reinforced by Protestant utilization of justification by faith as the central motif of salvation.

3. Other theological doctrines and motifs, such as the Trinity, original sin, the body of Christ, and the kingdom of God, provide a theological basis for affirming the social, political nature of humanity.

4. The integral humanism and personalist political philosophy of Jacques Maritain and the Roman Catholic Church suggest a way of resolving the individual-communal rights dilemma. By affirming both the Thomistic concern for the common good and the liberal concern for individual rights, recent Catholic teaching insists that humanity is both an individual and a social being. Persons are "integral wholes" and "parts" of a larger whole. It is impossible to be fully human without being both.

5. The thesis of the dissertation is held to be valid. At the root of the differences between Western and non-Western concepts of human rights are differing concepts of what it means to be human. Christian theological anthropology offers a via media between individual and communal conceptions of humanity, which in turn makes possible a rapprochement between individual and communal conceptions of human rights.

NOTES

1. For example, see Jacques Maritain, *The Rights of Man and Natural Law*, trans. Doris C. Anson (New York: Charles Scribner's Sons, 1949), 1, 7, 10–11, 15, 30, 39–40, 43, 46, 48, 52–53, 55, 57–58, 63, 76–77, 100–01.

2. Before 1926, Maritain had written exclusively about metaphysics, epistemology, logic, and aesthetics. "He did not write on political or social or economic questions for the simple reason that he was not the least bit interested in them—was only vaguely aware, in fact, that they even existed," comments one biographer. "He lived in the world without paying much attention to it one way or another, and asked only to be let alone in turn." When Pope Pius XI formally condemned the Action Française in 1926, Maritain's "somewhat aloof and academic attitude" received "a severe jolt." Maritain had never been a member of the Action Française—he was not interested in politics—but a number of close friends, including his spiritual director, Father Clerissac, were very active in the movement. Maritain had written articles for their journal and naively assumed their welding of French nationalism and Catholic fervor to be a good thing. The Pope's condemnation jolted Maritain into thinking more seriously about politics, and he began to realize the danger of leaning too far in the direc-

tion of nationalism and political conservatism. He turned from writing about metaphysics, epistemology, logic and aesthetics to writing about political philosophy, still using Thomistic philosophy as his main springboard of reflection. For all practical purposes, he began a new career, one in which he would make his most prolific and influential contributions to the world of thought as well as to the world of action. When the Second Vatican Council honored Maritain as the most outstanding Catholic intellectual of his time, it was thinking primarily of his political philosophy. See Charles A. Fecher, *The Philosophy of Jacques Maritain* (Westminster, MD: Newman, 1953), 36–39; John M. Dunaway, *Jacques Maritain* (Boston: Twayne Publishers, A Division of G.K. Hall, 1978) 64, 23; Bernard E. Doering, *Jacques Maritain and the French Catholic Intellectuals* (Notre Dame: University of Notre Dame Press, 1983), 4.

3. Maritain, *The Rights of Man and Natural Law*, 39–40; "On the Philosophy of Human Rights," in *Human Rights: Comments and Interpretations*, UNESCO (New York: Allan Wingate, 1950), 77.

4. Erik Erikson, *Identity: Youth and Crisis* (New York: W.W. Norton, 1968), 298–99.

5. Maritain, *The Rights of Man and Natural Law*, 43, 55, 2–4, 10–11, 30, 63, 58.

6. Jacques Maritain, *The Person and the Common Good*, trans. John J. Fitzgerald (New York: Charles Scribner's Sons, 1947), 87.

7. Jacques Maritain, "The Meaning of Human Rights" in Brandeis Lawyers Society, *Publications* (Philadelphia, Vol. 2, 1949), 7; Jacques Maritain, "The Rights of Man: A Comment," *United Nations Weekly Bulletin* 3:21 (November 18, 1947), 672; Maritain, *The Person and the Common Good*, 81–82; Jacques Maritain, *Man and the State* (Chicago: University of Chicago Press, 1951), 83–84. In *Man and the State* Maritain says that the modern version of rights "led men to conceive them as rights in themselves divine, hence infinite, escaping every objective measure, denying every limitation imposed upon the claims of the ego, and ultimately expressing the absolute independence of the human subject and a so-called absolute right . . . to unfold one's cherished possibilities at the expense of all other human beings."

8. Maritain, "On the Philosophy of Human Rights," 77.

9. Ibid., 74–75.

10. Ibid., 75; Jacques Maritain, "Introduction" to *Human Rights: Comments and Interpretations*, 15; Maritain, "The Meaning of Human Rights," 21–22.

11. Maritain, "The Meaning of Human Rights," 10; Maritain, "The Rights of Man: A Comment," 674.

12. Maritain, *The Rights of Man and Natural Law*, 39–44.

13. Maritain, *The Person and the Common Good*, 1–3. Regarding the rise of totalitarianism in the twentieth century, Maritain says: "We have witnessed the development of a totalitarian or exclusively communal conception of society which took place by way of reaction."

14. Jacques Maritain, *Freedom in the Modern World*, trans. Richard O'Sullivan (New York: Charles Scribner's Sons, 1936), 46–47; Maritain, *Man and the State*, 107.

15. Maritain, *The Rights of Man and Natural Law*, 5–6; Maritain, *The Person and the Common Good*, 49–50; Jacques Maritain, *Scholasticism and Politics*, 2d ed., trans. by Mortimer J. Adler (London: Geoffrey Bles: The Centenary Press, 1945), 54–55.

16. Maritain, *The Rights of Man and Natural Law*, 6; Jacques Maritain, "The Conquest of Freedom," in *Freedom, Its Meaning*, ed. Ruth Nanda Anshen (New York: Harcourt, Brace and Co., 1940), 637 (cited in Fecher, 200); Maritain, *Scholasticism and Politics*, 54–55; Fecher, 200–01.

17. Maritain, *The Person and the Common Good*, 21–23. How, Maritain asks, is the theologian to reconcile Pascal's negative view of the self with Thomas' very positive view of the self? Pascal had said that "the self is detestable," whereas Thomas had exulted that "person signifies what is most perfect in all nature—that is, a subsistent individual of a rational nature." Existentially, we know that both claims ring true, and yet they appear to contradict one another. Maritain resolves the apparent contradiction by distinguishing between the material and the spiritual self, identifying the material self with individuality and the spiritual self with personality, and claiming that Pascal is speaking of the former while Thomas is speaking of the latter.

18. Ibid., 27–28.

19. Ibid., 31–39. Maritain is concerned that his distinction between individuality and personality not be interpreted as a bifurcation of the self, or that individuality and personality be interpreted as two separated realities. The self is one. Matter and spirit are not two opposing substances, but rather are the form and the innervating principles of the same self. "Our whole being is an individual by reason of that in us which derives from matter, and a person by reason of that in us which derives from spirit." See 33.

20. Ibid., 37, 48–49.

21. Maritain, *The Rights of Man and Natural Law*, 7.

22. Maritain, *Scholasticism and Politics*, 54–55; Maritain, *The Person and the Common Good*, 37–38.

23. (a) Maritain, *The Rights of Man and Natural Law*, 7–8; (b) Maritain, *The Person and the Common Good*, 18–19.

24. (a) Maritain, *The Rights of Man and Natural Law*, 8–9; (b) Maritain, *The Person and the Common Good*, 39–40. Another way that Maritain avoids some of the pitfalls of a materialist utilitarian definition of the common good is by distinguishing between spiritual and material common goods, and by giving primacy to the former. According to Thomistic philosophy, Maritain writes, the "person is ordained directly to God as to its absolute ultimate end." Persons are created, first and foremost, not for some immanent common good but for "an infinitely greater good—the separated common Good, the divine transcendent Whole." For this reason Thomistic philosophy regards the contemplative life as superior to the political life. And for this reason Thomistic philosophy regards the speculative intellect—through which we know that which is uncreated, separated common Good—as superior to the practical intellect—through which we know the created world and the created common good. Even when necessity or compassion calls us to leave our contemplation, we do so not because action is superior to contemplation but because of the love that our

contemplation has given us. And we do not actually "leave" our contemplation, but take our contemplative soul with us. See *The Person and the Common Good*, 5–19.

25. John Locke, *Second Treatise of Government*, ed. C.B. Macpherson (Indianapolis: Hackett, 1980), 46 (no. 87), 67 (no. 128); *The Human Rights Reader*, eds. Walter Laqueur and Barry Rubin (New York: New American Library; Meridian Books, 1979), 106–07, 118, 197, 243.

26. Maritain, "The Rights of Man: A Comment," 673; Maritain, "On the Philosophy of Human Rights," 73.

27. Maritain, *The Rights of Man and Natural Law*, 68–73. The middle category of law, the law of nations, Maritain defines as "the rights and duties which follow from the first principle [of natural law] in a *necessary* manner" but, unlike natural law, certain conditions, such as "the state of civil society or the relationships between peoples," are presupposed. A law of nations is universal to the extent that these conditions are universal. Maritain's qualitative distinction between the law of nations and positive law is not very clear. His use of "necessary" and "contingent" is somewhat misleading. The quantitative distinction is more obvious. Laws of nations have to do with larger communities, particularly communities of nations, while positive laws can only be worked out on a smaller scale. The right to own property, in a general sense, belongs to the law of nations. But "the particular modalities of this right are determined by positive law." The right to basic material needs and the right to be free from the fear of terror and persecution belong to the law of nations, inasmuch as the nations are capable of providing for these rights. The particular way in which the nations may provide for these rights is dependent upon the economic and political organization and thus positive law. Maritain considers the right to free speech and freedom of assembly (which has acquired an absolute, natural law status in the West) to be rooted in the natural law, of course, but sees its particular mode of expression as culturally and historically conditioned, and secondary in importance to the rights to exist and to worship.

28. Ibid., 50–51, 20. Note that these are the three types of regimes enunciated by Aristotle.

29. Ibid., 16–18. For example, a mathematician learns mathematics from "the educational institutions which social life alone has made possible." Because the community provided this individual a service that he or she could never have obtained alone, the individual owes a debt to the community, and the community has a right to expect the individual to repay that debt by teaching mathematics to others in the community. But mathematical truths transcend the political community. There is no such thing as "Aryan mathematics," or "Marxist-Leninist mathematics," or "bourgeois-individualistic mathematics." There are a variety of mathematical systems, but these are ordered toward the absolute, not toward the political community. So while the political community can require the mathematician to serve the community by teaching mathematics, it can never require the mathematician "to hold as true one mathematical system in preference to another, and to teach such mathematics as may be judged more suitable to the law of the social group." From the mathematician's perspective, he or she has a duty to teach mathematics to the

community, but has a right to choose the type of mathematical system he or she will teach.

30. Frank H. Knight accuses Maritain of seeming "ignorant of and indifferent to facts which are essential to an understanding of the problems," of dealing "only with abstract issues and in highly abstract and ambiguous terms," of being "blind to the contradictions which are involved in advocating any simple abstract principles of conduct," of dealing with complex subjects with "sweeping pronouncements," and of prescribing solutions that "are platitudinous in the abstract and ambiguous and contradictory in the concrete." All Maritain really says, according to Knight, is that he "stands for truth and high ideals and wishes other people to do likewise." Frank H. Knight, "Review of Jacques Maritain's *The Rights of Man and Natural Law*," *Ethics* 54 (January 1944), 124, 130–31.

Sidney Hook accuses Maritain of not being a "rigorous thinker." He finds Maritain "persuasive," but this is based not on the truth of his arguments but on the way that he begs conclusions, caricatures opponents, and remains so vague as to be above empirical criticism. Sidney Hook, *Reason, Social Myths, and Democracy* (New York: John Day, 1940), 84.

31. Maritain, "The Meaning of Human Rights," 9; Maritain, "On the Philosophy of Human Rights," 75–76; Maritain, *The Rights of Man and Natural Law*, 22.

32. Hook, 87.

33. A more realistic approach, it seems, is to claim that the historic church, with all its sins and shortcomings, is the abiding church, the only church there really is. When in its better moments, which are few and far between, the church does something truly good, in those moments the church approximates being what it ought to be. Except for these fleeting moments, the church does not actually become this "true church," for the "true church" is but an ideal. The church cannot become something that is not real.

34. Knight, 136–37.

35. Maritain, *The Rights of Man and Natural Law*, 94, 98.

36. Knight, 136–37.

37. On one occasion Maritain does briefly utilize the Trinity in this regard, referring to it as "a whole ... which is the common good of the three subsisting Relations." Maritain, *The Person and the Common Good*, 47.

38. For further insights concerning the implications of the *imago dei* and original sin for humans as social beings, see James Sellers, "The *Polis* in America as *Imago Dei*: Neither Secular nor "Born Again" in *The Bible and American Law, Politics, and Political Rhetoric*, ed. James Turner Johnson (Philadelphia: Fortress, 1984). See also Sellers' "Jonathan Edwards as an American Thinker," unpublished manuscript. On the relational aspect of the *imago dei*, see Karl Barth, *Church Dogmatics*, vol. 3, 2: *The Doctrine of Creation*, eds. G.W. Bromiley and T.F. Torrence, trans. Harold Knight, et al. (Edinburgh: T & T Clark, 1960), especially 220, 223, 231–42, 274, 294–96, 323–24.

39. Hook, 76; Jacques Maritain, "Ten Months Later," *The Commonweal* (June 21, 1940) in "Appendix," Hook, 102.

40. Maritain, *The Rights of Man and Natural Law*, 22.

41. Ibid., 23–26.
42. Jacques Maritian, *Integral Humanism: Temporal and Spiritual Problems of a New Christendom*, trans. Joseph W. Evans (Notre Dame; University of Notre Dame Press, 1973), 150.
43. Daniel F. Polish, "Judaism and Human Rights," in *Human Rights in Religious Traditions*, ed. Arlene Swidler (New York: The Pilgrim Press, 1982), 41.

4

WESTERN PNEUMATICISM IN THE HUMAN RIGHTS MOVEMENT

"Contrary to the Western liberal tradition, the socialist tradition has always tended to define human rights in economic rather than in political terms. The hallmark of socialist regimes, such as those in the Soviet Union and Cuba, is the attempt to establish a minimum 'floor' which will guarantee a basic standard of living for all members of the society."[1] With these words Fouad Ajami of Johns Hopkins University's Department of Middle East Studies delineates a basic difference between Western and non-Western concepts of human rights. These differences are rooted not simply in ideological distinctions between capitalism and socialism but in the economic realities of the Third World. Chapter 4 will consider the differences between the Western concern for civil and political rights and the non-Western concern for social, economic, and cultural rights. Chapter 5 will argue that at the root of these differences is a fundamental disagreement over what it means to be human, with Western nations defining humanity in more pneumatic terms than Second and Third World nations. Christian theological anthropology suggests that it is not a question of either/or, but of both/and. To define humanity in exclusively pneumatic or materialistic terms is to fail to appreciate the integral nature of the human being.

OBJECTIONS VOICED BY NON-WESTERN NATIONS

The concern for social, economic, and cultural rights has moved into the forefront of the human rights discussion only in the last two decades. In the early years of the UN, this concern was covered, in a general way, by attention to communal rights. A number of factors have contributed to the emergence of economic, social, and cultural rights as a new category of rights. Among these are the failure of developmentalism, the so-called Green Revolution, and other Western approaches to the problem of poverty in the southern hemisphere. Other factors include the growing independence and articulateness of Third World nations and the adoption of the United Nations International Covenant on Social, Economic, and Cultural Rights of 1966. In recent years, opponents of Western human rights initiatives have begun citing the lack of concern for economic, social, and cultural rights as a major reason for their dissatisfaction with the movement.[2] This complaint surfaced in response to the efforts of President Jimmy Carter, Amnesty International, and other international monitoring agencies.

Objections to Carter's Human Rights Policies

When Carter attempted to use U.S. "muscle" to promote Western notions of human rights around the world, a substantial number of Third World and Communist leaders objected on grounds that human rights consisted more of economic, social, and cultural guarantees than of civil and political liberties. Fidel Castro informed a Western audience that "the cultural level and the health level of our people are the highest of all Latin America." Under socialism, prostitution, gambling, and racial discrimination have been eliminated, Castro proudly observed. "The United States does not have anything to show us."[3]

Brazilian Minister of State Antonio F. Azereda Da Silveiro stated that the refusal of Western powers "to facilitate the establishment of a more just and more stable international economic order . . . is a factor which cannot be ignored or overshadowed in the interest of respect for human rights." Unless and until basic human needs are met, "the rights of man, in their wider and truer meaning," cannnot be considered universal rights.[4] African leaders argued that "the priority of African states is economic development and elimination of hunger, disease, and illiteracy," and that infringements of civil and political liberties are justified if in order to satisfy these more basic human needs.[5]

Political scientist Mab Huang observed, in 1979, that "for the past two and a half decades political and civil rights have been substantially neglected" in the People's Republic of China. "Yet," he hastened to add, "impressive gains in economic, social, and cultural rights have been made."[6] This observation sums up well the human rights situation not only in China, but also in a number of other Third World socialist nations. Huang does not deny the need for progress in the area of civil and political rights, but he urges the West to recognize the priority of economic, social, and cultural rights in the previously colonized nations and to recognize the substantial achievements made by some of these nations in meeting these more basic human needs. Such a recognition could dispel much socialist and Third World animosity toward Western human rights initiatives.

Leonid Brezhnev argued in October 1977 that capitalist human rights were an insidious commodity, doing nations more harm than good. Civil and political liberty served as a euphemism for "unemployment, racial discrimination, lawlessness and overpriced medical care," he charged.[7] On December 10 (Human Rights Day) of that same year, Soviets arrested twenty protesters in Moscow. The Government newspaper Izvestia criticized the United States' "noisy, slanderous campaign over human rights," accused the West of distorting the concept of human rights, and asked, "Can a member of society be deprived of the opportunity to work, acquire an education and have shelter be said to be enjoying full rights?" "And yet," it charged, "there are tens of million of such people in the capitalist world."[8]

Four years later, Konstantin Chernenko echoed this line of criticism once again. "What real rights and freedoms are guaranteed to the masses in present-day imperialist society?" he asked in his 1981 book, *Human Rights in Soviet Society*.

> The "right"of tens of millions to unemployment? Or the "right" of sick people to do without medical aid, the cost of which is enormous? Or the "right" of ethnic minorities to humiliating discrimination in employment and education, in political and everyday life? Or is it the "right" to live in perpetual fear of the omnipotent underworld or organized crime and to see how the press, cinema, TV and radio services are going out of their way to educate the younger generation in a spirit of selfishness, cruelty and violence?

"In the West,"Chernenko observed, "the concept of human rights is often limited to exclude social and economic rights." "The majority of bourgeois constitutions" do not guarantee such basic rights as "the right to work, to free higher education or to free qualified medical service." To the Soviet way of thinking, this suggests a failure to take human rights seriously, since "it is socioeconomic rights and freedoms that constitute the real foundation for the enjoyment of political and personal rights."[9]

The tone of Chernenko's book is polemical. It can hardly be considered an unbiased document. His purpose is to convince the reader that the Soviets are superior to the West in terms of human rights. He does not intend, as the book's title would suggest, to give an objective description of the status of human rights in Soviet society. He covers every major area of human rights, from political liberties to housing to education to sexual equality, and in each case the Soviets are shown to score high. On each issue he begins by describing how bad things were in Czarist Russia. He relies heavily on anecdotal evidence to make his point. Then Chernenko describes, with great fervor, the noble struggles of revolutionary heroes to overcome this bad situation. He then describes the situation today which, when compared to a century ago, is invariably much improved. By projecting the progress into the future Chernenko can promise that tomorrow things will be even better.

Chernenko then compares the Soviet Union to the United States, the Federal Republic of Germany, and other Western capitalist nations. Invariably, the Soviet Union is shown to be superior. The reason is that Chernenko compares only in areas of Soviet strength. For example, in the discussion of political rights he focuses on the high representation of workers in the Soviet parliament, the high percentage of women in government, and the high percentage of citizens who vote. He avoids discussing how much power the parliament actually has, or whether citizens who vote are given a meaningful choice. Chernenko concludes each chapter by stating the reason for Soviet progress and superiority in that particular area of human rights: the superiority of socialism to other forms of goverment.

As we pointed out in chapter 1, the discussion of moral issues such as human rights must begin at the advocatory, polemical level. Even though we wish to bring the discussion to a more reflective, ethical level, we must begin by listening to what the parties in the conflict have to say.

Chernenko claims that in the Soviet Union, unlike the United States, economic, social, and cultural rights are considered legitimate human rights that should be protected by law. He points out that the Soviet government has eliminated unemployment, whereas in the West five percent or more of the population is always unemployed. In prerevolutionary Russia, peasants and factory workers labored twelve to sixteen hours a day, six days a week. The new Soviet constitution sets the maximum number of hours for wage and salary workers at forty-one hours a week. In prerevolutionary Russia, housing was so limited in urban and suburban areas that it was the norm for two or three families to share a single room, and for two or three single people to rent the same bed, sleeping in shifts. Between that time and today, he claims, housing conditions have improved dramatically, with costs remaining constant since 1928. "On the average, rent plus the utility service charges come to about three percent of the family budget of a wage-earning or salaried worker." This compares to a figure of twenty to thirty percent in the capitalist countries of the West.[10]

In contrast to the high cost of medical care in the United States, the Soviet Union can boast free medical treatment for all citizens, as well as higher numbers of doctors and hospital beds per capita than in the West.

Even though the Soviet Union comprises but six percent of the world's population, it has over one-third of the world's doctors. Chernenko points out that U.S. citizens spend more money on medical assistance than on clothes and footwear. He cites U.S. sources claiming that, because of high costs, half the U.S. population do not go to a doctor when they need to. Infantile mortality is now one-tenth of what it was in prerevolutionary Russia. Life expectancy in the Soviet Union has risen from thirty-two years at the end of the last century to seventy years today.[11]

Just as remarkable, he claims, are the Soviet achievements in education. "Nearly four-fifths of czarist Russia's adult population could neither read nor write." Today, the vast majority of the population is literate, and "the USSR ranks first in the world for the educational level of the population." Education is compulsory and free. While educational standards and opportunities in the Soviet Union are at an all-time high, Chernenko points out that America is experiencing a crisis in education. At the secondary level, funding is "insufficient," the quality of instruction is on the decline, classes are "unruly." There is "despair" among the teachers and "apathy" among students. At the university level, rising tuition costs make college education unaffordable for forty to sixty percent of American young people.[12]

In the Soviet Union, women are guaranteed the same rights as men. In the West, Chernenko observes, women earn less pay than men, have less access to higher education and professions such as law and medicine, and are underrepresented in positions of governmental leadership. In the midseventies, "women constituted 1.1 percent of engineers, seven percent of doctors, and less than one percent of physicists and mathematicians" in the United States. In the Soviet Union, they constituted almost half of the engineers, two-thirds of the physicians, and forty percent of the scientists. Compared to the handful of women in the U.S. Congress, the Soviets boast that women constitute one third the total members of the Supreme Soviet. Chernenko points out that the U.S. Constitution is silent on the rights of working women, but that the Soviet Constitution guarantees "legal protection and material and moral support, including . . . paid maternity leaves . . . and the gradual reduction of the working time of women having small children."[13]

In terms of cultural rights and achievements, the USSR has made dramatic improvements over prerevolutionary Russia. Entrance fees for museums and theaters have been abolished, public libraries have been established, literature has been published at affordable prices, and foreign cultural interchange has been encouraged. Chernenko cites UNESCO figures indicating that Soviet citizens lead the world in the number of visits to museums and theaters and in the amount of literature read. UNESCO figures also indicate that the USSR translates twice as many books as the

United States, Japan, and France. "Films from capitalist countries make up about 10 percent of all films shown in the USSR," Chernenko notes, "while films of all socialist countries account for only five percent of foreign films shown in the West." (And these, he adds, are shown mostly "in small cinemas, without proper publicity and press reviews.")[14]

Objections to Amnesty International and Freedom House

The lack of concern for economic, social, and cultural rights has also been cited as a reason that Amnesty International, Freedom House, the International Commission of Jurists, and other private Western human rights organizations have not been as successful as they might otherwise have been. Richard H. Ullman, editor of *Foreign Policy*, notes that while Amnesty International's focus on civil and political rights enables it to gain broad support in the West and to concentrate its efforts upon one particular type of injustice, such a focus has some detrimental effects as well. "It is precisely their concentration on civil and political liberties," Ullman believes, which makes them "seem to citizens of poor countries like political agents of the industrialized West." If they wish to establish credibility "within the societies whose abuses of civil and political liberties they pinpoint," Ullman says they must "call attention to deprivations of human needs" as well as of civil and political rights. Otherwise, they seem to "feel the pain only of the tortured and not of the starving."[15]

Nigel S. Rodley, legal advisor of Amnesty International and part-time lecturer in law at the London School of Economic and Political Science, admits that Amnesty's "civil rights emphasis (as opposed to economic and social rights) opens them to the charge of Western orientation." Coupled with the fact that its constituency is "predominantly Western," it is difficult for Amnesty to claim to have a truly global understanding and concern for human rights.[16]

Jorge I. Dominguez, Professor of Government at Harvard University, compares Freedom House with the Bariloche Institute in Argentina and concludes that the former could be more effective if it incorporated more of the socio-economic concerns of the latter. Dominguez criticizes Freedom House and similar Western human rights groups for focusing too exclusively upon civil and political rights. Such a focus, Dominguez believes, suggests that social and economic rights are not important. "This tendency is aggravated in the United States," he says, "by identifying the term 'human rights' exclusively with civil and political rights." Such a focus also suggests that "only under nonauthoritarian governments is there freedom of any kind or respect for human rights." It fails to see the good that can come from the more authoritarian-type governments. What all this indicates to Dominguez is that Freedom House, and similar human rights monitoring organizations, are too closely identified with U.S. and First World interests to be an objective assessor of global human rights. A very different sort of human rights monitoring organization is the Bariloche Institute, which lists certain basic needs essential to human development. The four most basic needs, according to the Bariloche Institute, fall within the "socio-economic" category: food, health care, housing, and education. Such a priority, Dominguez believes, is good for the poor. Civil and political liberties are not their most pressing needs. But Dominguez does express a concern that the Bariloche Institute not forget about liberties altogether. Dominguez concludes the comparison of the two organizations by saying that for purposes of comprehensiveness and for gaining international acceptance, the more libertarian human rights organizations would benefit by showing a greater concern for economic and social needs.[17]

THE ANATOMY OF WESTERN PNEUMATICISM AND ITS INFLUENCE ON THE HUMAN RIGHTS MOVEMENT

How legitimate are these objections? Do they reflect genuine concerns or political rhetoric? There is certainly a temptation among Western advocates of human rights to assume the latter. Oftentimes this has been the case. Talk of economic or social or cultural rights has been used as a smoke screen for unconcern for civil and political rights in situations in which the problem was not a conflict between two noble principles—basic human needs versus basic liberties—but a lack of concern for the person as either a physical or pneumatic being. In fairness, however, Westerners have often been guilty of much the same thing. In the name of freedom, corporations have been allowed to treat workers not as human beings but as virtual slaves of corporate greed and economic cycles. As before, the problem is not an ideological conflict between food versus freedom, but is a prostitution of freedom to preserve the status quo.

The job of the ethicist is to sift through the polemics of the human rights discussion to find what might be valid and worthwhile in the claims of both sides. Just as the use of freedom as a smoke screen by some does not diminish the value of freedom, so the abuse of basic human needs language by others should not diminish the value of basic human needs. Regardless of the motivations of Castro, Da Silveiro, Brezhnev, and Chernenko, the substance of their complaints deserves the respectful attention of Westerners concerned about the failure of the human rights movement. It points to a real barrier to international acceptance of universal human rights. The substance of their complaint is that Western human rights initiatives ignore or underestimate the significance of social, economic, and cultural rights. There is quite a bit of evidence to support this contention, both in the UN human rights documents and in more recent efforts by private human rights organizations and by the Carter administration.

The major United Nations human rights documents reflect a bias against social, economic, and cultural rights. The Universal Declaration contains thirty articles. The first twenty-one relate to civil and political liberties. Article 22 guarantees the right to social security and to "economic, social and cultural rights." This sweeping offer is rescinded, however, by the qualification that such an entitlement must be "in accordance with the organization and resources of each State." No such qualification was made with regard to civil and political rights. This disclaimer has the unfortunate effect of nullifying what Articles 23 through 27 say concerning social, economic, and cultural rights.

Article 23 "guarantees"[18] the right to work, to choose one's line of work, to decent working conditions, to protection against unemployment, to equal pay for equal work, to a fair wage, and to form and join trade unions. Article 24 protects "the right to rest and leisure," including limitations on working hours and "periodic holidays with pay." Article 25 lists basic human needs such as food, clothing, housing, medical care, and emergency relief. Article 26 presents the ideal of free, compulsory elementary education. Article 27 discusses cultural rights such as the right "to enjoy the arts and to share in scientific advancement and its benefits."

If the United Nations had been as serious about social, economic, and cultural rights as civil and political rights, the Universal Declaration would have been written differently. First, the declaration would have enumerated as many social, economic, and cultural rights as it did civil and political rights. Only six articles deal with the former, while three times that number concern the latter.

Second, the declaration would not have adopted a double standard for the two types of rights. Article 2 states that "no distinction" be made for any reason in the question of who is entitled to the rights listed in the declaration. Then Article 22 contradicts Article 2 and states that social, economic, and cultural rights be dependent upon "the organization and resources of each State." Such a qualifier is inappropriate both logically and morally. In the next section of this chapter we will consider the claim of Western human rights activists that social, economic, and cultural rights are of a different species than civil and political rights, with only the latter being protectable by law.

Third, the declaration would have attempted a greater balance between the libertarian right to private property and the more materialist right to basic economic necessities. The right to private property is stated in Article 17 and is affirmed as an absolute right. The other economic rights are qualified by the disclaimer in Article 22. The clear implication is that the rights of capitalists to own and manage their assets as they wish takes precedence over the rights of workers to just wages, guaranteed employment, and so on. Rather than maintaining some sort of dialectical tension between these two conflicting human rights, priority is given to the economic rights of the wealthy. The economic rights of workers and the poor, although enumerated in Articles 23 through 27 are, for all practical purposes, nullified.

Despite the small conciliation made to Communist, Moslem, and Third World nations concerned with social, economic, and cultural rights, the Universal Declaration is little more than a reiteration of the bills of rights of the great Western democracies. Adamantia Pollis and Peter Schwab state that the document is much too Western and, more particularly, American, to claim any universal status. It is "abundantly clear," they state, "that the overriding philosophy underlying" the declaration "is the Western concept of political liberty and democracy, inclusive of property rights in contradistinction to economic rights or egalitarianism." More specifically, "the Universal Declaration of Human Rights . . . is based on the Jeffersonian credo." Such a conclusion, by the way, would be agreed to by most everyone familiar with the Universal Declaration, including supporters as well as opponents of the human rights movement.[19]

The other major United Nations human rights documents are the International Covenant on Civil and Political Rights and the International Covenant on Economic, Social and Cultural Rights. These covenants were conceived as sequels to the Universal Declaration of Human Rights. The Universal Declaration was intended as a declaration of some general ideals. It was not to be legally binding, but was to be promoted through educational means. The two "follow-up" covenants were intended to be more specific and more binding. Rather than declaring ideals, they were to establish binding covenants. By 1954, the Commission on Human Rights had completed the drafts of the two covenants and submitted them to the General Assembly for approval. Twelve years later they were finally approved.

The differences between the documents reflect the libertarian bias of the United Nations human rights efforts. The Covenant on Civil and Political Rights defines its rights in very specific terms. It insists upon instant and total compliance of member nations. It proposes that a Human Rights Committee be established which could hear complaints regarding the failure of member nations to comply with the covenant, as well as an International Court of Justice for purposes of appeal. On the other hand, the Covenant on Social, Economic, and Cultural Rights defines rights in a general fashion. Rather than demanding instant and total compliance, it asks for "progressive implementation" (Article 22) of its provisions. The degree of compliance is to be commensurate with the economic and political conditions of the country. Instead of setting up committees and courts to regulate member nations, it simply recommends that nations give periodic reports on progress made in areas of social, economic, and cultural rights. Even if the reports fail to show progress, this may be acceptable if nations "indicate factors and difficulties affecting the degree of fulfillment of obligations under the present Covenant" (Article 17).[20]

It is clear that the United Nations has adopted a double standard with regard to civil and political liberties, on the one hand, and economic, social and cultural rights on the other. One demands instant, total, universal compliance. The other must be implemented gradually because certain nations are not yet capable of compliance. Why, opponents ask, are some governments excused from their responsibility to provide for physical necessities but not from responsibilities to protect civil and political liberties? In the next section, we discuss why Westerners consider libertarian rights more capable of being universalized than socialist types of rights. What must be pointed out here is that non-Western opponents of UN human rights initiatives certainly appear to have just grounds for being angry. It appears that the UN has adopted a double standard for these two types of rights and has reneged on its original intention of adopting two equally binding human rights covenants.

A libertarian bias continued to prevail in Western human rights initiatives up through the initial phase of the Carter era. Writing in 1978, Fouad Ajami cites President Carter's "single-minded focus on political freedoms" as a major factor in the "varied reception" that his human rights policies received around the world. "One-sided efforts," says Ajami, "will merely serve to undermine the political credibility of their proponents and/ or the legitimacy of their particularistic values."[21]

A study commissioned by the Australian government in 1977 and completed in 1979, entitled *Human Rights in the Soviet Union*, exemplifies the continuing libertarian bias in the human rights movement. The study purports to be as accurate and comprehensive as possible. It contains over one thousand pages of transcripts of interviews with Australians who had visited the Soviet Union and Soviets who had emigrated to the West. It deals with nine questions related to human rights. Unfortunately, the document does not raise any questions related to economic rights. Nor does it take up the issue of sexual discrimination.[22] On these two human rights issues the Soviet Union would score high marks, but the Australian government chose to ignore those human rights issues in which the West did poorly and the Soviets did well. Consequently, the document is more likely to be interpreted as a polemical work than as an accurate and comprehensive statement of human rights conditions in the Soviet Union. This is unfortunate since the contents of the document, though accurate, will never be considered credible among those it is intended to impact. Ajami's "law" can be applied: "one-sided efforts will merely serve to undermine the political credibility of their proponents and/or the legitimacy of their particularistic values."

Many of those who acknowledge the legitimacy of social, economic, and cultural rights still can be naive regarding the way that civil and political rights can proscribe social, economic, and cultural rights. Amnesty International's Nigel Rodley wrote in 1979 that he saw no reason "why, in a given situation, particular measures to improve the enjoyment of economic, social, and cultural rights necessarily entail infringements of specific civil and political rights."[23] Rodley fails to appreciate Third World situations in which new national governments need to regain control from colonial influences, and in which the gap between the rich and the poor necessitates that the freedom of the powerful be limited lest they use their freedom to take advantage of the weak.

In this section we have presented the claim of non-Western opponents of the human rights movement that the human rights movement favors civil and political liberties over social, economic, and cultural rights. We have shown that although this claim is often motivated by political expediency and expressed in polemical terms, there is still a legitimate basis for the claim that must not be overlooked if there is to be a truly universal understanding of what constitutes a human right. In the pages that follow we shall examine the arguments most frequently cited in the West for the priority of liberty. Then, in chapter 5, we shall critique these arguments and offer an alternative way of viewing the human being and human rights, based on an integralist understanding of humanity as both a physical and a pneumatic being.

THE CASE FOR THE PNEUMATIC APPROACH TO HUMAN RIGHTS

The argument for the priority of liberty is made by two factions within the human rights movement. One I will call the "liberal idealists," the other the "liberal realists." Because the liberal realists have been the most vocal and effective opponents of the basic human needs movement, most of the discussion will focus on them. However, a few words must be said concerning the liberal idealists.

The Liberal Idealist Argument

The liberal idealists are heirs to the natural rights tradition. They believe that certain rights are inalienable because they are commensurate with the essence of human nature. For them, human nature consists primarily of the capacity to be free and rational. John Locke begins the Second Treatise of Government by stating that all persons are entitled to "all the rights and privileges of the law of nature." Similarly, Jefferson begins the Declaration of Independence by speaking of the entitlements granted by "the laws of nature and nature's God" and by proclaiming that persons "are endowed by their Creator with certain unalienable rights." And the French Declaration of the Rights of Man and Citizen begins by stating its intention "to set forth . . . the natural, inalienable, and sacred rights of man."[24]

In 1955, H.L.A. Hart wrote an essay entitled "Are There Any Natural Rights?" The essay is the most highly regarded attempt to relate the concerns of the Enlightenment natural rights tradition to the human rights movement. Hart's thesis is that "if there are any moral rights at all, it follows that there is at least one natural right, the equal right of all men to be free." The essay attempts to justify the claim of Locke and Jefferson, and later advocates of universal human rights, that civil and political liberties are natural rights.[25]

By the term "natural" right, Hart refers to rights that persons have simply by being human, not because some community conferred it upon them or because they exist in some special relation or agreement that entitles them in some special way. By the term "right" Hart refers to "that branch of morality which is specifically concerned to determine when one person's freedom may be limited by another's." There are many forms that virtue may take, such as charity, loyalty, telling the truth, and so on. The particular form known as "rights" involves the conditions in which one person's freedoms may be limited by another's. Hart argues that such a limitation is justified in the area of civil and political rights, but not in the area of economic rights. He reasons that in the economic sphere competition is acceptable ("competition is at least morally unobjectionable"), whereas in the sphere of personal liberties it is considered objectionable for persons to exercise their natural capacities in ways that inhibit others from doing so. This example illustrates an important principle: that natural rights are those rights for which there are correlative duties. Persons who claim a right to 800 calories a day cannot claim that to be a "natural right" because they cannot point to anyone who has a duty to feed them. They may claim that it is "wrong" for other persons not to feed them but they cannot claim that all persons, or any particular person, have a "duty" to feed them. They cannot claim, in Hart's opinion, that other persons' freedoms should be limited in order to feed them. Hart believes that persons can claim the right to free speech as a natural right because everyone has a duty to respect that right. Therefore, civil and political rights are natural rights. They are natural: being human means being free and rational and able to make choices and act upon them. And they are rights: they make a claim which not only is consistent with human nature and purpose but which all other beings have a duty to respect. Basic economic rights are "natural" in the sense that humans have the capacity to eat, although not "natural" in the sense that eating is not what makes us distinctively human. Regardless, eating is not a right that all other persons have a duty to respect to the point that coercion may be used against one group to make it possible for another group to eat.[26]

The Liberal Realist Argument

The liberal realists usually base their argument on two distinctions. One is a distinction between rights and ideals. The other is a distinction between positive rights and negative rights. They accuse advocates of economic, social, and cultural rights of blurring these important distinctions.

Rights Versus Ideals

The difference between a right and an ideal, they argue, is that a right is something that persons actually have, whereas an ideal refers to something that persons ought to have and may want very badly to have, but do not necessarily have. A person obtains a right by being granted it by government, employer, family, or any other authority qualified to do so. Rights said to be granted by God or the laws of nature or other transcendental sources are not true rights, but are ideals. They become rights only when granted by an authority willing and able to enforce them.[27]

Liberal realists believe that a human right should consist of both elements: the transcendental moral concerns that human ideals have, and the pragmatic concerns that legal rights have. Ideals without actual rights are empty dreams; rights without ideals are morally blind. The highest and loftiest ideals are worthless without laws to guarantee them and governments to enforce them. The best secured legal rights are no true human rights at all unless consistent with high and lofty moral ideals. Antigone's appeal to a higher law, though morally sound, had no power to protect her from being punished as a criminal. Creon backed his rule (that a traitor's corpse not be buried) with positive law and with the strong arm of government authority. But his "right" to do so was strictly a legal right, not a human right, because his positive law defied a higher moral law. Only when human ideals are translated into legal rights do they become human rights.

The concern for human ideals has stemmed from the natural law tradition. The concern for positive rights is rooted in both the social contract tradition and the utilitarian tradition. The genius of the American and French declarations of rights is that both, though heavily influenced by the natural law tradition, recognize the worthlessness of ideals not backed by the authority of the state, that is, a social contract. Thus, immediately after declaring humanity's "unalienable rights" to "life, liberty, and the pursuit of happiness," the Declaration of Independence states that "to secure these rights, governments are instituted among men." Sandwiched between declarations of ideals that "men are born and remain free and equal in rights," and that "the natural and inalienable rights of man ... are liberty, property, security, and resistance to oppression," the French Declaration recognizes the need for coercion: "the aim of every political association is the preservation of the natural and inalienable rights of man."[28] The emphasis on positive law reflects the concerns of the social contract tradition. The writers of these documents were inspired by the ideals of the natural law tradition, but to translate these ideals into realities they sought to express them in terms of positive law. Because they recognize that human rights consist of both human ideals and positive laws, these documents have served as paradigms for the "middle-of-the-road" approach preferred by most leaders of the human rights movement.

At the opposite end of the spectrum from the natural law tradition is the utilitarian tradition. If the peril of the one is utter idealism, the peril of the other is utter cynicism. The motivation for initiating and sustaining the human rights movement has been to protect civilization from inhumane practices carried out under the guise of positive law. Aroused by the cynicism of Nazi Germany, the human rights movement has since challenged similar abuses in the Soviet Union, the Republic of South Africa, and throughout the world. The human rights movement recognizes that a human right consists of more than a "lawful entitlement;" there must also be a "just entitlement."[29]

Even so, in challenging amoral utilitarian governments, the human rights movement has learned a lesson from its enemies. It has learned to counter immoral force with moral force, not moral ideals. Although much moral idealism surrounds the movement, its intellectual leaders have also learned from Machiavelli, Hobbes, and Bentham that universal human rights must be stated in specific and enforceable terms[30] or else they die the death of countless other vague and well-intentioned ideals.

Bentham wisely informed the idealists of his generation that hoping for something is not the equivalent of having it, that declaring an ideal to be a right does not make it a right. It only becomes a right when it becomes an actual law backed by a government intent upon enforcing it. Eloquent declarations of rights, without the backing of government authority are, at best, a waste of time: "*Natural rights* is simple nonsense," he said, "nonsense upon stilts." At worst, they are counterproductive: "want is not supply—hunger is not bread."[31] They give persons the illusion of having something that they do not have. They substitute words and promises for bread. Chapters 6 and 7 will continue this discussion of idealism versus cynicism, not in regard to the food versus freedom debate, but in regard to the debate over national sovereignty versus international government.

Influenced by all three traditions, there has emerged a middle-of-the-road or "realist" approach to human rights that emphasizes both the moral idealism of the natural law tradition and the positive law concerns of the social contract and utilitarian traditions. Like the American and French declarations of rights, it seeks to translate ideals into laws. Unlike these declarations it prefers to use the term "ideals" rather than "natural rights" because it has accepted the utilitarians' judgment that the only true rights are positive rights. In this respect, the middle-of-the-road approach diverges from the more "idealistic" or "natural rights" approach that was influential enough to have the UN's Universal Declaration labeled a declaration of "rights" instead of "ideals" even though no provision was made for enforcing them.

The first assumption of the liberal-realist human rights ideology, then, is that somewhere between the power vacuum of human ideals and the moral vacuum of positive rights is the human right. The reason that basic economic and cultural rights are not human rights is that they belong to the category of ideals. It would be nice, they say, if everyone had food, a home, a job, good health care, and an education. But trying to express these ideals in legal terms would lead to absurd consequences. Positive laws must be specific, so how can laws be specific about material needs when needs differ so much among individuals? Is a fat person entitled to more food than a skinny person? Are sickly persons entitled to more health care than healthy persons, even if their sickliness is due to smoking or overeating? Positive laws must be enforceable, so how can laws be enforced for crimes in which there are victims but no criminals? Those who are hungry or unemployed or homeless or illiterate are victims of circumstance, they say, not of willful criminal action. Western human rights activists have argued, therefore, that concerns regarding basic human needs should be expressed as human ideals, but not as human rights, for they can never be expressed in binding terms of positive law. Concerns for human needs may be expressed in a declaration of ideals, but not in a declaration of rights. To list economic, social, and cultural "rights" side by side with civil and political rights will not raise the status of the former to that of the latter. It will only diminish civil and political rights to the level of economic, social, and cultural rights.

Negative Rights Versus Positive Rights

The second assumption of the human rights movement has been that a clear distinction must be made between "negative rights" and "positive rights." Here the meaning of "positive rights" is completely different from the meaning used in the preceding discussion, where the term "positive rights" was used in contrast to ideals, or "natural rights." They referred to actual rights—rights guaranteed by law or contract or mutual understanding or custom—as opposed to ideals which some might like to become actual rights but are not at the present time. The term "positive" was derived from its use in the expression "positive law;" positive rights referred to those rights guaranteed by positive law.

In the present discussion "positive rights" is used in contrast not to ideals or natural rights, but to "negative rights." In this sense, positive rights refers to rights that must be secured through positive action; negative rights refers to rights that must be secured through negative action. Economic, social, and cultural rights are considered positive rights. Civil and political rights are considered negative rights. It takes positive action, such as benefits and subsidies, to secure basic economic, social, and cultural rights. It takes negative action, such as a limitation of government and other corporate power, to secure civil and political rights. One involves redistribution of resources, the other involves retribution toward those who violate the freedom of others. One guarantees certain standards of living, the other protects against threats to personal freedom. One gives poor persons something they do not have, the other helps all people keep that which they already have—their ideas and beliefs. One gives citizens that which they need to survive, the other insures that they will have what they need to thrive intellectually and spiritually. One provides that which is good, the other protects against that which is evil. One is positive, the other is negative.

The current debate over positive and negative rights is a reenactment of the debate between Luther and Calvin over the functions or "offices" of the law. Luther believed that the law served only negative functions. On an individual level, it showed people how bad they were, relative to the high standards of God, and thus their need for grace. On a societal level, the law served as a "dike" against evil. It did not foster goodness in society, but it did keep things from being as bad as they might otherwise be. It did not make things better, but it did keep them from getting worse. It did not create a utopia, but it did prevent, as it were, "all hell from breaking loose." Calvin agreed that the law showed individuals their sinfulness and restrained evil in society. He also believed, however, that the law served a positive function. It could promote goodness. It could serve, as the psalmist had said, as "a lamp to my feet and a light to my path."[32]

Those who argue today that the only true human rights are negative human rights are saying in regard to human rights what Luther said regarding the second office of the law. Luther believed that the law could help protect the status quo. Human rights activists believe that human rights can help persons keep that which they already have: an ability to think and to express their convictions. Human rights legislation can protect persons from being robbed of that which nature and nature's God have already given them, namely, a free mind. Human rights legislation can serve a negative function, protecting persons from external threats to their freedom. It does not "give" persons anything, it merely protects them from having anything taken away.

Those who argue today that there can be positive as well as negative human rights are saying with regard to human rights what Calvin said regarding the third office of the law. Calvin believed that the law could actually do something positive. It could make society more righteous, more like the kingdom of God. Many Communist, Moslem, and Third World leaders, along with those Westerners who adhere to the basic human needs philosophy, argue that human rights can do more than protect persons from violations of their person or property. They believe that human rights legislation can promote the physical and educational development of persons. It can guarantee persons that their basic human needs will be met. They believe that human rights declarations and covenants should have a positive as well as a negative component. In doing so they need not appeal to Marxist or Third World revolutionary ideology. They can appeal to John Calvin.

The second distinction of the liberal realists, we have seen, is between positive and negative rights. Economic, social, and cultural rights are strictly positive. Civil and political rights are strictly negative. Negative rights are the only rights that can be considered truly human rights. Later on we will question this rigid distinction,[33] but for now let us elaborate the reasons liberal realists give for distinguishing among positive and negative rights and for claiming that negative rights are uniquely capable of being universal human rights.

The Case for Negative Rights

Negative rights are not contingent upon individual life plans and social or economic roles. Each person has a "station" in life: some are farmworkers, others are doctors, others are homemakers, others are engineers. One's economic rights are determined largely by one's particular station. A steelworker may have the right to form a union, whereas a soldier may not. A school teacher may be entitled to a minimum wage and holidays with pay, whereas a self-employed business person may not. A computer operator may be guaranteed a job; a blacksmith may not. A factory worker may be protected against having to work overtime; an obstetrcian or a farmer may not. A person's educational rights are also determined by certain uncontrollable factors. An imbecile does not have the right to a secondary or post-secondary education. A National Merit Scholar does not have the right to participate in special educational programs for the handicapped. Whereas economic and educational rights are commensurate with individual capabilities and life plans, liberal realists believe that civil and political rights are truly universal.[34]

Secondly, civil and political rights are not contingent upon the economic status of the nation. A person's right to a certain level of income or a certain level of education is dependent upon the wealth and stability of his or her nation. If a nation is poor, it cannot be expected to provide what it does not have. Economic and educational rights are limited by the criterion of attainability. Civil and political rights, on the other hand, are attainable regardless of the nation's economic situation. As negative rights they do not require that anything be provided to the individual, only that nothing be taken away. They only ask that the government restrain its "own executive arm" (Maurice Cranston), "leave its citizens unmolested" (Hugo Adam Bedau). This does not require wealth (at least, according to the liberal realists). It requires merely a respect for the inviolability of the human person. And it can be "readily" secured, Cranston maintains, by "fairly simple legislation." Negative rights qualify as universal rights because every nation is capable of implementing all (Cranston) or many (Bedau) of them. Bedau thinks he has discovered a criterion for universality: "the more fundamental a right is the less its provision and protection depend upon a society's resources and wealth."[35]

A third distinctive feature of negative rights is that they deal with matters of "paramount importance." Negative rights address urgent matters that involve threats to life or liberty. Positive rights, Cranston argues, address the quality of life but not human life itself. One cannot be fully human, Cranston and others maintain, in societies that do not regard life and liberty as sacred. The difference between a poor person and a wealthy person is measured in degrees. One has less money than the other, but the poor person is no less a human being than the rich one. The difference between a free person and an oppressed person, on the other hand, is a difference of kind, not degree. The oppressed person is deprived of that which makes one truly human, and lives an animal existence. One can be truly human, in the fullest and highest sense of the term, only if one is free. Cranston argues that there should be a sense of urgency regarding that which makes a person truly human. Matters of such paramount importance should be respected as human rights. On the other hand, one can be fully human regardless of whether one is rich or poor. Rich persons may derive more pleasure from life than poor persons. But they have no more civil, religious, or political freedom than poor persons. Poor persons may be deprived of the things that make human existence enjoyable. But they are not deprived of the things that make their existence authentically human. Bedau writes that "it is an insult to one's dignity to have welfare rights at the same time one is subject to arbitrary detention without charge or trial, but the converse is not true." Thus negative rights, unlike positive rights, guarantee those things liberal realists consider essential to being distinctively human, those things which are of paramount importance.[36]

A fourth feature of negative rights, the liberal realists say, is that they are judicially enforceable. When a person is tortured or not allowed to vote or held without a trail, a crime has been committed and the person or persons responsible can be prosecuted. (Obviously, this is contingent upon the power of the judiciary vis-à-vis military juntas, client elites, and other loci of power, a factor which liberal realists tend to overlook.) Each person has a duty not to restrict the freedom of any other person (except to protect the freedom of oneself or any third party). When one person arbitrarily restricts the freedom of another person, the victim can be defended by the prosecution of the criminal. In the case of "violations" of economic, social, or cultural rights, there is a victim but there is no crime and no criminal. No one has a duty to provide the basic material or social needs of everyone else. There is no guilty party to be held accountable. There is no judicial solution to this problem. No one has committed a crime. The worst thing that has been done is that certain benefits have not been conferred. As John Stuart Mill once said, "A person may possibly not need the benefits of others, but he always needs that they should not do him hurt. Thus the moralities which protect every individual from being harmed by others, either directly or by being hindered in his freedom of pursuing his own good, are at once those which he himself has most at heart, and those which he has the strongest interest in publishing and enforcing by word and deed."[37]

A fifth feature of negative rights is that they are widely recognized and respected in the West. Indeed, this is one of the great achievements of Western culture. Economic, social, and cultural rights have not been as high a priority among Western nations, particularly the United States. Bedau argues that it would be inappropriate for Western nations to launch a global human rights campaign for any rights other than those recognized and respected in the West. "If the United States is going to link human rights with its foreign policy," he says, "the rights in question must be rights that we have already undertaken to recognize in our domestic law." They should not "be rights that our own government has ignored or violated with impunity until recently." Nor should they be "rights about which there is still ideological . . . controversy in our own country." They should be rights that are "rooted in our constitutional history and practiced throughout the land." By this criterion, Bedau rules out economic and social rights. It would be hypocritical as well as ineffective to preach abroad what had not been practiced at home. By this criterion, Bedau also brings into question many civil and political rights, since the American history of racism and sexism indicates a lack of concern for the civil and political rights of a substantial portion of the population. Bedau does feel that America's record on certain civil or personal rights is outstanding. These rights include the right to privacy and the right not to be tortured: what Justice Brandeis called "the right to be let alone," and what Secretary of State Vance called "the right to be free from governmental violation of the integrity of the person." Vance listed as examples: torture, inhuman or degrading treatment or punishment, arbitrary arrest or imprisonment, denial of due process, and invasion of the home. Since these rights are recognized and respected in the West, Bedau would argue that the United States is qualified to advocate them in the world forum.[38]

NOTES

1. Fouad Ajami, *Human Rights and World Order Politics* (New York: Institute for World Order, 1978), 15.
2. Non-Western views on basic economic, social, and cultural rights are discussed at a more theoretical level in a number of sources.

    For the Soviet Marxist view, see Eugene Kamenka and A.E.-S. Tay, "Human Rights in the Soviet Union," *World Review* 19:2 (1980), 51–56; David Hollenbach, S.J., *Claims in Conflict: Retrieving and Renewing the Catholic Human Rights Tradition* (New York: Paulist Press, 1979), 20–27; and Marnia Lazreg, "Human Rights, State and Ideology: An Historical Perspective," in *Human Rights: Cultural and Ideological Perspectives*, eds. Adamantia Pollis and Peter Schwab (New York: Praeger Publishers, 1979), 36.

    Kamenka and Tay argue that concern for basic economic rights has dominated Soviet policy since 1917. Even though Soviet constitutions have affirmed many civil and political rights (the RSFSR Civil Code of 1922 was patterned after the 'bourgeois' civil codes of Western Europe), they interject a caveat that these rights are not to be exercised in a manner inconsistent with the larger purposes of Soviet society. Marxist teaching does not regard political and civil rights as separate from economic rights. In Kamenka and Tay's words: "Such rights and rules ... cannot be treated simply in the abstract. In particular, the political sphere cannot be divorced from the social and economic. Rights must not be seen as freedoms from but as freedoms to, and as such they require constant attention to the economic and social setting in which men live and, in societies of private property and class conflict, total reorganization." Kamenka and Tay do see signs that Soviet-Marxist ideology may be moving toward a more balanced relation between economic rights and civil and political rights. "The society's concern for the individual and his well-being is much more srongly stressed, and presented in more individualist terms, than it was in classical Marxism or under Stalin." "In contrast with the end-directedness and moral relativism of Lenin and Trotsky, there is now some foundation in current Soviet theory, at its more academic levels, for treating human rights as embodying unconditional human values." But, they add, "no orthodox writer, or no writings that survive the censorship, push matters to this point." They also qualify by saying that recent criticism of Soviet human rights policies "has led to a certain hardening—to an insistance that economic rights or welfare are more important than civil liberties or political rights, [and] that the 'bourgeois' elevation of rights is hypocritical and anti-Soviet."

Hollenbach agrees with Kamenka and Tay that "social and economic rights such as the rights to work and material security are preeminent in Marxist theories of rights." As Marx himself said, "Rights can never be higher than the economic structure of society and cultural development conditioned by it" (Critique of the Gotha Program). He also agrees that economic rights and civil rights are inseparable: "Individual and social freedoms can only be realized if they are realized together. Thus political and economic rights are correlative." Civil and political liberties can become inimical to basic economic, social, and cultural rights: "Unrestricted liberty in a society stratified according to classes leads to a denial of social and economic rights."

Lazreg also agrees that economic, social, and cultural rights are at the top of the Soviet agenda. She says that the Soviet constitution (1936) was "unlike the United Nations Declaration" in that it "emphasized the right to work—for which it provided a definition and legal guarantees (Articles 12 and 118) whereby the state pledged to supply jobs." It also guaranteed the right to free education (Article 121). The Soviet constitution also differed from the United Nations Declaration in that it was addressed specifically to workers and peasants. In so doing, Lazreg comments, "the Soviet state expressed the intention, at least theoretically, to uphold the rights of these classes, whereas the United Nations Declaration addressed itself to an abstract supranational individual." The Soviet constitution and its supplements also showed a concern for social rights by listing anti-Semitism and fascism as barriers to equality and by delineating individual duties as well as rights.

The Moslem view of economic, social, and cultural rights is discussed in Rashid Ahman Jullundhri, "Human Rights and Islam," in Understanding Human Rights: An Interdisciplinary and Interfaith Study, ed. Alan D. Falconer (Dublin: Irish School of Ecumenics, 1980), 35–36, 41–42; and Abdul Aziz Said, "Human Rights in Islamic Perspectives," in Human Rights, eds. Pollis and Schwab, 93–94.

In most strains of the Moslem tradition, basic economic and cultural rights are considered as important or more important than civil and political rights. Jullundhri argues that "every citizen of a Muslim state has the right to a decent living and to hold property. In addition, he has freedom of opinion, profession and movement." Every citizen is entitled to basic economic necessities: "The State or society, according to Islamic teachings, is bound to provide man with the basic requirements of life: i.e., food, housing, clothing." The concern for economic justice goes back to the earliest days of Islam: "the Prophet and his early successors introduced land reforms with a view to bringing to an end humiliation, repression and exploitations which prevent man from gaining happiness." Regarding the primacy of cultural rights, Said writes that "in Islam the cultural community must be served by the political, economic, and social systems—rather than the other way around." This is quite different from the way that capitalist societies attempt to separate and communist societies attempt to subordinate traditional culture from the institutions of the state.

3. "News in Brief," *Los Angeles Times,* 13 December 1977, pt. I, 2.

4. Ajami, 1.

5. Dunstan M. Wai, "Human Rights in Sub-Saharan Africa," in *Human Rights,* eds. Pollis and Schwab, 120. See Wai's critique of the basic needs argument, 120–28.

6. Mab Huang, "Human Rights in a Revolutionary Society: The Case of the People's Republic of China," in *Human Rights,* eds. Pollis and Schwab, 79.

7. *New York Times,* 19 October 1977, A5, cited by Arpad Kadarkay, *Human Rights in American and Russian Political Thought* (Washington D.C.: University Press of America, 1982), 167 [Note: the NYT citation is erroneous].

8. *Izvestia,* 10 December 1977 cited by David K. Shipler, "Russians Confine 20 on Rights Day," *New York Times,* 11 December 1977, 12.

9. Konstantin U. Chernenko, *Human Rights in Soviet Society* (New York: International Publishers, 1981), 142, 4.

10. Ibid., 84, 86–89, 105–11.

11. Ibid., 91–98.

12. Ibid., 115–22.

13. Ibid., 51–60.

14. Ibid., 123–130.

15. Richard H. Ullman, "Introduction: Human Rights—Toward International Action," in *Enhancing Global Human Rights,* eds. Jorge I. Dominguez, Nigel S. Rodley, Bryce Wood, and Richard Falk (New York: McGraw-Hill Book Co., 1979), 10.

16. Nigel S. Rodley, "Monitoring Human Rights Violations in the 1980s," in *Enhancing Global Human Rights,* eds. Dominguez *et al,* 146.

17. Jorge I. Dominguez, "Assessing Human Rights Conditions," in *Enhancing Global Human Rights,* eds. Dominguez *et al,* 31–32, 43–46.

18. I use quotation marks because the disclaimer in Article 22 implies that social, economic, and cultural rights are not guaranteed in the same sense that the previous civil and political rights were.

19. Adamantia Pollis and Peter Schwab, "Human Rights: A Western Construct with Limited Applicability," in *Human Rights,* eds. Pollis and Schwab, 3–5. See, for example, the statement of Egon Schwelb, an ardent supporter of the universal human rights movement. Schwelb says that the roots of the Universal Declaration "are in the legal and political thought of the seventeenth to twentieth centuries" in France, England, and the United States. Egon Schwelb, *Human Rights and the International Community* (Chicago: Quadrangle Books, 1964), 12.

20. "The Campaign for Universal Human Rights," *The Humanist* 26:6 (November/December 1966), 193–94.

21. Ajami, 27.

22. report of the Joint Committee on Foreign Affairs and Defense of the Parliament of the Commonwealth of Australia, *Human Rights in the Soviet Union* (Can

berra: Australian Government Publishing Service, 1979), cited in Kamenka and Tay, 58–59.
23. Rodley, 130.
24. *The Human Rights Reader*, eds. Walter Laqueur and Barry Rubin (New York: New American Library, 1979), 62, 106–07, 118.
25. H.L.A. Hart, "Are There Any Natural Rights?" *The Philosophical Review* 64:2 (April 1955): 175.
26. Ibid., 175–81.
27. Maurice Cranston: "What is characteristic of a positive right is that someone actually has it. Positive rights are those rights conferred (or confirmed) and enforced by the system of municipal law that prevails in any country." And: "Positive rights are facts. They are what men actually have. What men *ought* to have is another question." See Cranston, "What Are Human Rights?" in *Human Rights Reader*, eds. Laqueur and Rubin, 17 [hereafter Cranston, 1979].
28. *Human Rights Reader*, eds. Laqueur and Rubin, 107, 118.
29. Cranston, 1979, 19.
30. Maurice Cranston, *What are Human Rights?* (New York: Basic Books, 1964), 8–9 [hereafter Cranston, 1964]; Maurice Cranston, *What are Human Rights?* (New York: Taplinger Publishing Co., 1973), 5–6 [hereafter Cranston, 1973]. [Note from "Acknowledgements" page: "This book is a revised and greatly extended version of an essay originally published in London as *Human Rights Today* (Ampersand Ltd., 1962) and in New York as *What are Human Rights?* (Basic Books, 1964)."]
31. Jeremy Bentham, *Anarchical Fallacies; Being an Examination of the Declarations of Rights Issued during the French Revolution* in *The Works of Jeremy Bentham*, Part VIII, collector John Bowring (Edinburgh: William Tait, 1889), 501.
32. Martin Luther, "The Freedom of a Christian" and "Secular Authority: To What Extent Should It Be Obeyed?" in *Martin Luther: Selections from His Writings*, ed. John Dillenberger (Garden City: Anchor Books, 1961), 57, 370–71; John Calvin, *Institutes of the Christian Religion*, Bk. II, Ch. VII, esp. 12 in *The Library of Christian Classics*, Vol. XX, ed. John T. McNeill, trans. Ford Lewis Battles (London: S.C.M. Press, 1961), 348–66; Psalm 119.105.
33. In addition to Cranston and Bedau, proponents of the positive-negative distinction include: Charles Frankel, *Human Rights and Foreign Policy*, Headline Series No. 241 (New York: Foreign Policy Association, 1978), especially 36–49; and Thomas Nagel, "Equality," in *Mortal Questions* (New York: Cambridge University Press, 1979) 114–15. [Source: Henry Shue, *Basic Rights: Subsistence, Affluence, and U.S. Foreign Policy* (Princeton: Princeton University Press, 1980), 185–86.] Critiques of the positive-negative distinction can be found in Shue, 35–40, and John Langan, S.J., "Defining Human Rights: A Revision of the Liberal Tradition" in *Human Rights in the Americas: The Struggle for Consensus* (Washington, D.C: Georgetown University Press, 1982), 82–90.
34. Cranston, 1973, 70.
35. Ibid., 66; Hugo Adam Bedau, "Human Rights and Foreign Assistance Programs," in *Human Rights and U.S. Foreign Policy*, ed. Peter G. Brown and Douglas MacLean (Lexington, MA: Lexington Books, 1979), 36–37.

36. Cranston, 1964, 38–39; Cranston, 1973, 67; Bedau, 37–38.
37. Cranston, 1964, 36–38; Cranston, 1973, 69, 66; Bedau, 38–39; John Stuart Mill, *Utilitarianism*, in *Utilitarianism, Liberty, & Representative Government*, ed. Ernest Rhys, (New York: E.P. Dutton, 1917).
38. Bedau, 39; Justice Brandeis, *Olmstead v. United States* 277 U.S. 438, 478 (1928) in Bedau, 39; Cyrus Vance, "Law Day Speech on Human Rights and Foreign Policy," April 30, 1977, University of Georgia Law School, in *The Human Rights Reader*, eds. Laqueur and Rubin, 299–300.

5

BEYOND THE PNEUMATIC-MATERIALIST IMPASSE

In 1977 a significant change began to take place within the human rights movement. For the first time, many politicians, social scientists, and theologians began to talk seriously about placing economic, social, and cultural rights on an equal plane with civil and political rights. The catalyst for this new development was the negative, even hostile reaction President Carter's human rights campaign evoked in many parts of the world. The hostility was triggered largely, as shown in the previous chapter, by Carter's "single-minded focus on political freedoms"[1] and lack of concern, in particular, for basic economic rights.

After a few months in office, certain members of the Carter administration began expressing a concern for subsistence-level rights. In his Law Day Speech on Human Rights and Foreign Policy, at the University of Georgia on April 30, Secretary of State Cyrus Vance defined human rights not only as "the right to be free from govermental violation of the integrity of the person" and "the right to enjoy civil and political liberties" but also as "the right to the fulfillment of such vital needs as food, shelter, health care, and education." In this tripartite definition of human rights, Vance seemed to be putting the basic needs of the poor on an equal footing with the more "middle class" types of rights. Vance tried to accommodate Third World and Communist critics. But what he conceded with one hand he may have withdrawn with the other. After asserting the right to food, shelter, health care, and education, Vance interjected a familiar qualification: "the fulfillment of this right will depend, in part, upon the stage of a nation's economic development."[2]

In a major foreign policy address three weeks later at Notre Dame, President Carter reiterated his commitment to human rights, but he hinted at broadening his definition to include rights to basic human needs. "Hunger, disease, illiteracy, and repression": these were the problems Carter considered most prevalent in Latin America, Africa, and Asia, and which the United States should address through its foreign policy. "We know a peaceful world cannot long exist one-third rich and two-thirds hungry." Carter also proclaimed that "the time has come for the principle of majority rule to be the basis for political order" in southern Africa. Years later, Carter admitted that, in the first few months of his administration, he had been "inclined to define human rights too narrowly." He quickly learned, however, that "the right of people to a job, food, shelter, medical care, and education could not be ignored."[3] The theme began to reverberate through the Carter staff.

The week after Carter's foreign policy speech, American Ambassador to the United Nations Andrew Young made the point that "where there is poverty . . . there cannot be full political participation and freedom." Jessica Tuchman of the National Security Council staff told one reporter that "in much of the world the chief human right that people recognize is 800 calories a day," and that "we're beginning to recognize that fact." By June, Angus Deming of *Newsweek* was reporting that "Washington has adopted a broader definition of human rights." He summed up the shift toward economic and cultural rights: "Food, shelter, health care, and education—the rights that the Soviets like to boast they are best at providing—have now been added to Washington's list, along with such traditional U.S. concerns as free speech, the right to travel and freedom from torture and arbitrary arrest."[4]

Deming may have exaggerated the shift toward basic human needs. After all, many prominent elements within the Carter administration, such as the State Department's Bureau of Legal Advisers, never supported Vance's attempt to grant the same status to subsistence rights as had been granted to civil and political rights. Even so, the shift was significant enough to impact key elements within the human rights movement.[5]

It was not long before many Western human rights leaders were recognizing the validity of basic human needs. "To have freedom of speech and assembly while living in squalor," wrote political scientist and Lutheran leader George H. Brand in 1978, "is as inimical to human dignity as is living in relative economic security while being denied fundamental rights of self-expression." Brand reiterated what Communist and Third World leaders had been saying for some time: "Though we readily perceive the political injustices of the Soviet sphere, we show a peculiar blindness to economic injustices of our own system." Historian Norman A. Graebner echoed Tuchman's insight that Western experience and Third World experience can be quite dissimilar. "For the bulk of humanity," Graebner concluded, "economic and personal security are more important than democratic institutions."[6]

This emerging awareness among certain Western supporters-turned-critics of the human rights movement has set the stage for a new debate on Western soil. Prior to this time, the "food versus freedom" debate was primarily an international debate between East and West, and between South and North. It was between Western advocates of international human rights and non-Western opponents. Now, with the increasing support for basic human needs in the West, the debate can be found within the human rights movement, between those who want to continue to focus upon civil and political rights and those who want to broaden the focus to include economic, social, and cultural rights.

THE CASE AGAINST PNEUMATICISM

In the last decade or so, a substantial body of literature[7] has called into question the human rights movement's favoritism toward civil and political rights over economic, social, and cultural rights. This literature has become identified by its concern for the most basic of human needs: clean water, food, housing, jobs, health care, education, and freedom from bodily harm. (Some also include minimal civil and political rights: due process and political participation.)

Basic human needs literature has criticized liberal human rights ideology on three grounds. First, its knowledge of human rights is based upon an all-too-limited experience; the "freedom first" ideology has emerged from the rather narrow experience of Western liberal democracies and lacks understanding of the needs and priorities of other peoples and nations. Second, the liberal ideology is based upon faulty reasoning. Third, it is based upon a concept of humanity that fails to appreciate the physical dimension of existence. The second criticism has been expressed in the literature of political philosophy, political science, international studies, and United Nations reports. The third has been alluded to in some of these studies, but ignored or contradicted in most. It has been the theological literature, particularly the social teachings of the Catholic Church since Vatican II, that has expressed this anthropological concern most cogently and exhaustively. The first criticism has been implicit in both strands (secular and religious) of the literature. It is here that we begin the basic human needs critique of liberalism.

Parochialism

Many of those committed to the basic human needs perspective have come to the human rights movement by way of involvement in issues such as hunger, limits to growth, and immigration, and through missionary and Peace Corps work among the poor, particularly in the Third World.[8] Through this involvement their experience has been expanded beyond the realm of middle class life in the Western world. They have witnessed another way of life in which the primary concerns are not free speech but are food and clean water (among the poor) and local control of political and economic institutions (among previously colonized peoples). This experience has given them the opportunity to view the human rights movement from a non-Western perspective. From this perspective the particular experiences of Western liberal democracies are seen to be just that: particular experiences, and not universal ones.

Western human rights leaders have been slow to recognize the importance of basic economic rights because the Western experience of oppression has been political rather than economic. The great revolutions of the West were precipitated by political exploitation of middle-class persons whose basic economic and cultural needs were being met. In the case of the English and French revolutions, the emerging middle class fought for political rights that the aristocracy sought to keep for themselves. In the case of the American Revolution, the American middle class objected to not being given the same political rights as the English middle class. In all three revolutions, the primary concern was freedom, not food.[9] In all three situations, the aspect of human dignity that was violated was human freedom. Thus Westerners have come to identify human dignity and human rights with human freedom.

The primary oppression in the Third World colonial experience was economic. Civil and political rights were denied as well, but the level of poverty of most of the people was such that meeting basic economic concerns became a necessary preoccupation. Little or no food for the hungry, bacteria-infested drinking water for the thirsty, no medicines for the sick, no shelter for the homeless, no jobs for the unemployed or underemployed: these concerns took precedence over all others. As with the Western experiences of oppression, persons felt their human dignity violated. But here it was a case of being denied the right to function as a healthy physical being, not as a moral and spiritual being. Thus in the Third World, human dignity and human rights have come to be identified with basic human needs.[10]

How have Western human rights advocates justified their relative lack of concern for economic, social, and cultural rights? They argue that economic, social, and cultural rights are not true rights but, at best, are vague ideals or nonlegislative rights. They may justify their claim with appeals to human nature and reason, but what they are actually doing is attempting to translate a particular historical experience into an abstract universal principle. Such an effort is, at worst, chauvinistic polemics or, at best (if done naively) an example par excellence of the limitations revealed by the sociology of knowledge. Certain types of experience give rise to certain types of knowledge. Those whose experience is primarily Western and, moreover, middle class, tend to understand human rights primarily in Western and middle-class terms. Those Westerners who have significant experience in the Third World or among the poor tend to have a different understanding of human rights. As long as the concern is to promote rights at the local level, there is no compelling reason to expand one's experience beyond cultural and national boundaries. But when the concern shifts to universal rights, then global dialogue and experience become essential. The problem with Western human rights advocates prior to 1977 was that they assumed that what had been good for the West would be good for the world. Instead of incorporating the concerns of the Third World poor, they merely reformulated their argument for the priority of civil and political liberties in more elaborate though not necessarily more logical terms. There are two ways they do this, and these comprise the second point of the basic human needs critique of liberal human rights ideology.

Faulty Reasoning

Prioritizing Rights According to Ideological Rather Than Logical Criteria

One way that Hart, Cranston, Bedau and others who argue the priority of liberty use faulty reasoning to buttress their position is by declaring certain rights to be primary (e.g., freedom) and others secondary (e.g., food), even though it may be necessary to possess some of the secondary rights before it becomes possible to enjoy some of the primary rights. It is illogical to make one right absolute without making its prerequisite absolute. If South Korea allowed North Korean sports fans the right to purchase tickets to the 1988 Olympic games, but denied them the right to obtain visas necessary to enter the country, most observers would agree that South Korea had in fact refused to grant North Koreans the right to attend the 1988 Olympics. Similarly, if a university granted students the right to use pocket calculators to take exams, but required that all exams be taken in the library, where calculators were forbidden, then in fact the university has refused the right of students to use calculators to take exams. To guarantee someone the right to speak without guaranteeing them the right to eat is, in conditions of scarcity or gross inequality, to deny them both rights. Those who suffer from malnutrition cannot exercise the right to free speech. Without realizing it, the liberal ideologues have not only denied the right to food, but also the right to free speech.

Henry Shue, of the Center for Philosophy and Public Policy of the University of Maryland, states that his motivation for writing a book on *Basic Rights* was "anger at lofty-sounding, but cheap and empty, promises of liberty in the absence of the essentials for people's actually exercising the promised liberty." Shue identifies a number of "basic rights": rights that must be secured before other rights can be enjoyed, rights that are "inherent necessities" for the enjoyment of any other rights. Among the basic rights is the right to security, that is, protection against hunger, exposure, and disease. These rights are "basic" because they are needed "for the fulfillment of all other rights." Shue proposes that liberals apply the transitivity principle to the prioritizing of rights: "If everyone has a right to y, and the enjoyment of x is necessary for the enjoyment of y, then everyone also has a right to x." Such a "transitivity principle for rights" has two merits. It corrects the faulty logic of those who insist upon the priority of liberty. And it develops a priority appropriate to situations of scarcity. In North Atlantic countries there has been an abundance of subsistence goods and services. Liberal theory has been developed under the assumption that scarcity will not be a factor. Thus liberty can be "first" because subsistence items can be assumed to be already available. While it may be reasonable to postulate their availability in the North Atlantic region, the situation is completely different in the poorer nations of the Third World. A "new" priority must be devised for these situations. What was assumed in the West must be made explicit: that for persons to enjoy their liberty, their need for certain biological necessities must be met.[11]

This idea, and the whole concept of subsistence rights, is not a new one. It is a rediscovery, Shue says, of a very old idea common in "traditional societies that are often treated by modern societies as generally backward or primitive." Shue, who has written extensively on U.S. policy, foreign and domestic, regarding poverty, concludes that many Westerners view subsistence rights as new or "strange" simply because "Western liberalism has had a blind spot for severe economic need."[12] In fairness it should be reiterated that this blindness is due more to a narrowness of experience than to malice or greed. Even so, the narrowness may reflect a certain callousness toward suffering, given the fact that pockets of extreme poverty do exist in the West, and given the fact that exposure to global poverty is readily available through various media of communication and transportation. Regardless of whether the West's failure to take subsistence rights seriously involves a moral error, it certainly involves an error in reasoning. It is illogical to assume that a person has the right to something without also assuming that he or she has the right to whatever else is necessary to enjoy that right.

Part and parcel of this same problem is the way that liberal human rights theory categorizes and prioritizes rights according to ideological rather than personal or psychological categories. There is nothing illogical about "categorizing" rights according to ideologically related groupings such as the right to life, liberty, material wants, and equality. It is illogical to "prioritize" rights according to these groupings. Each grouping contains a wide range of rights, some more essential than others. For example, the right to consume one thousand calories per day and the right to holidays with pay are both considered economic or material rights. Most would consider the former to be among the most essential of all rights, whereas the latter could be guaranteed only in a highly developed economy. Similarly, the right to participate in the political process is a more basic right than the right to bear firearms or the right to publish racist, pornographic, or anarchistic literature. Only the more stable nations could grant complete freedom with regard to the latter.

Ideologically zealous liberals who insist upon making all civil and political liberties prior to all economic and material rights, and ideologically zealous materialists who insist on the opposite priority, make the logical error of ranking secondary and tertiary rights ahead of more basic ones. Cranston points out at every opportunity the ludicrousness of listing "holidays with pay" (Universal Declaration of Human Rights, Article 24) among the universal human rights, as if to imply that the authors considered it as essential as the right not to be tortured or to due process of law. Cranston errs, however, in concluding that since one economic right is frivolous or secondary, all are secondary.[13] He assumes an absolute trade-off between basic economic rights and civil and political liberties, that one category must be entirely prior to the other. Certainly many advocates of basic economic rights may have made the opposite error: assuming that all civil and political liberties are as unessential as, say the right to publish pornographic literature.

Advocates of human rights as basic human needs urge that prioritizing of rights be based upon personal and empirical, rather than ideological, criteria. The most basic rights would be those essential for the enjoyment of all other rights.

Obviously, some material rights are more essential than some libertarian rights, and vice versa. Basic human needs advocates, such as Johan Galtung, suggest that we "cut through [the ideological] rhetoric" and focus upon "what is essential and basic."[14] What is essential and basic is determined by an empirical study of human needs, not by debating the merits of the various ideologies. Basic rights concern themselves with what persons need, not what ideologies advocate. The criteria are "physiobiological"[15] or psychological[16] or simple experiential knowledge.[17] They concern themselves with least common denominators and "the poorest section of the population"[18]—in short, with human essentials—not with human potential.

One problem with some of these versions of basic human needs is that they define human needs entirely in biological terms, forgetting the political frameworks through which these needs must be met. Thus physical necessities are equated with basic needs and civil and political rights are given a back seat. To combat this tendency, Henry Shue has suggested that basic rights be defined as any rights necessary for the enjoyment of all other rights. By this definition not only do food, clean water, shelter, clothing, and health care qualify as basic rights but so do political participation, due process, freedom of physical movement, and freedom from bodily harm. Although Shue does not do so, the right to a basic education could also be added to the list.[19]

Shue's criterion is logical rather than biological. He reasons that it would be difficult for one to enjoy any other rights as rights if one had no power to influence the process by which rights were granted and denied, if one were being imprisoned or tortured, if one had no means for redress of grievances when those rights were being denied, or if one had no way of learning how to acquire and protect these rights. One could still enjoy the "substance" of the rights. For example, a population deprived of the right to political participation can still eat if the dictatorial government is benevolent and provides for all physical necessities. However, they could not enjoy eating as a "right" because the food has been provided as a gift, not as a right. There is no guarantee that the food will be provided tomorrow. The provision of food is contingent upon the daily whims of the ruler, not upon the will of the people.

Conclusion: the absolute prioritizing of rights according to ideological categories is illogical and impossible. It is impossible to enjoy civil and political liberties without a modicum of physical necessities. It is tempting to place biological needs first, but this too does not work, since certain civil and political liberties, and certain educational skills, must be possessed if a person is to enjoy food, clean water, and so on. The logical solution is to form a new category of essential human needs and to call it "basic human rights."

Exaggerating the Distinction between Negative and Positive Rights

The other way that North Atlantic liberals use faulty reasoning to buttress their position is by making an artificial and exaggerated distinction between negative and positive rights. "Negative" rights are more "positive" and "positive" rights are more "negative" than Cranston, the U.S. State Department, and others would care to admit.[20]

Personal security and civil and political liberties are considered "negative" rights because they require simply that citizens not interfere in the lives and thoughts of other citizens. These rights do not give people something they do not have, but help people maintain what they naturally have. It is true, Shue says, that one can *"avoid violating"* a civil, political, or security right by avoiding committing certain acts. But it is impossible to *"protect"* these rights without taking positive actions. Laws, police, courts, prisons, taxes: these institutions must be established and nurtured if the so-called negative rights are to be protected. This involves an extensive outlay of capital and a large labor force. The amount of effort needed to protect "negative" rights certainly calls into question whether they are as negative as liberals say they are.[21]

Economic, social, and cultural rights are considered "positive" rights because, instead of protecting what people naturally have, they give needy people what they do not have. As liberals see it, providing for economic and cultural rights consists of various forms of governmental aid to persons in need. This is "positive" because it requires that a lot of positive action take place—revenues must be raised and spent, bureaucrats and social workers must be hired, and programs must be developed. It is not so much a matter of the government "protecting" a citizen's right as it is "providing for" a citizen's need. Government serves less as a policeman and more as an eleemosynary organization.

Basic human needs thinkers have pointed out several flaws with this assumption. In many cases, they argue, persons are not deprived of basic economic, social, and cultural rights because of natural catastrophes or economic downswings, or because of laziness or lack of resourcefulness of the poor, but because of positive actions whose adverse consequences for the poor are predictable and preventable.

A fundamental problem in many Third World countries is what political scientist Richard Fagen has called "illiberal state capitalism." Illiberal state capitalism works in the following way. A poor country wants to borrow money to promote economic growth, but creditors require a favorable balance of trade. Because it is hard to increase exports significantly in the short run, these countries must cut imports to save hard currency. Rather than directly levying tariffs and quotas, they cut imports by devising policies that decrease the general buying power of the population. Such policies include suppressing trade unions to keep wages low, raising the levels of unemployment, and decreasing government expenditures for welfare and public works. The purchasing power of the nation is thus decreased, imports are decreased, a favorable balance of trade is attained, and the nation is able to continue borrowing money, continue increasing its national debt, and continue keeping the poor, poor. If any economic growth is realized, it does not trickle down to the poor. In fact, the whole sructure is devised so as to place the cost of economic growth on the shoulders of the poor. The ruling elite continues to enjoy its high level of consumption and to reap the benefits of any economic growth. Basic human needs thinkers have observed that this phenomenon, far from being a situation in which natural catastrophe, unforeseen economic cycles, or individual laziness have left some persons poor, is a situation in which a government has caused certain citizens to become poor as a matter of deliberate policy. The issue is not whether the government should "step in" and take "positive" action to help poor persons suffering from natural, economic, or personal problems. It is instead an example par excellence of what the liberals call a negative right. Citizens have had their buying power taken away from them by their government. These citizens are not asking the government to give them a handout, only that the government stop taking away what the citizens already have. In this case the plea for basic economic rights is no more positive than the plea for the right to free speech or the right not to be tortured, because all that is being requested is that the government refrain from oppressing its citizens.[22]

In addition to illiberal state captialism, another major cause of Third World poverty is land redistribution involving a switch from food crops to cash crops and from labor intensive to labor extensive production. The following would be a typical situation. The bean farmers in a given region receive an offer from a flower corporation to lease their land for the next ten years. The farmers are guaranteed an income over that time period equal to or better than their average income as bean farmers in exchange for serving as foremen on the new flower farm. They are encouraged to buy machines that would cut their need for labor by fifty to seventy-five percent. From the perspective of the corporation and the individual farmer, the switch from beans to flowers appears rational and in the best interest of both parties. However, the following adverse consequences begin to unfold after the transition is made. A number of farm laborers are left without employment opportunities. The reason they worked on someone else's farm was that their own land, if they had any, was too poor to produce enough food on which to subsist. Now they and their families must either starve, steal, or try to move where employment opportunities are better. Another consequence is that the price of beans rises sharply. Beans are the basic staple of the diet. Fewer people are now growing them. Demand has remained constant while supply has decreased, thus driving up the cost. The farmers discover that the income paid them by the flower corporation is now insufficient to buy the amount of food needed to feed their families. Malnutrition can be alleviated in the short run by selling the farm to the flower corporation, but since the nation is industrially poor, the possibility of resettling and returning to their original standard of living is slim. What has happened is that the land has been redistributed out of the families of peasant farmers who owned them for generations and into the hands of corporations concerned only about profit maximization.[23]

According to liberal theory, such a phenomenon is unfortunate, but cannot be prevented or resolved since no crime has taken place. Persons and corporations have the right to buy and sell and lease their property. The contract was freely entered into, and so it must be honored. Whether the intent of the parties to the contract was malicious is irrelevant, although in most cases this does not appear to be the case. According to basic human needs philosophy, the issue in not whether the parties to the contract freely entered into the contract, but whether the state has a right to honor contracts which it knows will cause unemployment, homelessness, and malnutrition among a significant portion of its population. The situation is not the same as a sudden natural disaster or an unforeseeable economic trend. The increase in food prices may be beyond the prognosticating abilities of a peasant farmer, but certainly could be predicted by the government's economists. Nor is the situation the same as a nationwide depression in which the deprivation suffered by the poor is unpreventable and cannot be ameliorated until the economy gets back on its feet. The situation can be prevented simply by the government's refusing to honor contracts calculated to bring extreme poverty to innocent persons who otherwise could live above the poverty level. Once again, guaranteeing basic economic rights is not a matter of a government's giving out doles to the poor, but rather is a matter of a government's not allowing transactions that would make certain people become extremely poor. This is analogous to a government not honoring transactions which involve slavery or the suppression of other "inalienable" rights. This is just as "negative" a right as any civil or political or personal right. The government is not asked to give anybody anything, only to protect persons from having what they already possess taken away from them. Ironically, if the government fails to take negative actions to protect this right, it is faced with having to take positive actions to feed its hungry citizens, or else to let them starve.[24]

Even in situations in which the government takes positive actions to help those suffering severe poverty (e.g., Medicare, Medicaid, Aid to Families with Dependent Children, WIC), the action may not be any more expensive and interventionist than other actions generally regarded by liberals as acceptable. (Recall that two of the main criticisms liberals make of "positive" rights are that protecting them is costly and requires government to be too active in the private sector.) For example, if the crime rate in a community causes persons to feel insecure, then they may be very supportive of efforts to lower the crime rate: improvements in the police force, neighborhood watch programs, drug rehabilitation programs, teenage recreational programs, and so on. These programs, designed to protect the right of (usually middle-class) citizens to the security of their persons and their property, may be as expensive and interventionist as food stamp programs and health care programs designed to protect the right of poor persons to basic physical necessities.[25]

Shue concludes that the liberals' distinction between negative rights (rights to forbearance) and positive rights (rights to aid) is "intellectually bankrupt" and "thoroughly misguided." "This misdirected simplification is virtually ubiquitous among contemporary North Atlantic theorists," he says, and is therefore "all the more pernicious for the degree of unquestioning acceptance it has now attained." Shue argues that every right involves both forbearance and aid. Only the societal duties that correlate to the various individual rights can be accurately labeled in terms of "positive" and "negative." For every type of right there are three corresponding duties: (1) "duties to *avoid* depriving," (2) "duties to *protect* from deprivation," and (3) "duties to *aid* the deprived." The first of these is a negative duty; the other two are positive. These duties apply equally to the right to free speech as to the right to food. Liberals would maintain that society should protect persons from being deprived of free speech (thus a legal, peaceful assembly is given police protection to prevent disruption), and that society should aid those so deprived (thus someone who disrupts a legal, peaceful assembly is arrested and removed from the scene). Thus they are being hypocritical if they argue the priority of civil and political liberties on the grounds that these rights are "negative" while other rights are "positive."[26]

Conclusion: positive action is necessary to guarantee every sort of right. This is true regardless of how "negative" that right might seem in the minds of North American liberals.

A Contempt for Human Physicality

From the perspective of theological anthropology, the basic human needs argument as it has been developed thus far fails to address the problem of physical needs in as fundamental and radical a manner as it should. It reaches the proper conclusion: that basic physical needs take priority over some of the less basic "pneumatic" needs. But it reaches this conclusion for the wrong reason. Its reason for the priority of certain physial rights is simply a matter of logic—these rights must be met before certain pneumatic rights can be enjoyed. While such an argument may be logially sound, it is ontologically unsound, for it suggests that the physical dimension of human existence is important only as a means to higher, pneumatic ends. From the perspective of Christian theological anthropology, the physical dimension of human existence has a dignity all its own. It bears or reflects the image of its creator, and thus is important as an end in itself. Thus a strictly pneumatic concept of human nature and purpose is incompatible with Christian anthropology.

What is the basis for theology's claim that conventional formulations of the basic human needs argument fail to address the problem of physical needs in as fundamental and radical manner as is demanded by the situation? There are two bases. One involves the shortcomings of the conventional formulations. The other involves the vast potential of formulations rooted in Christian notions of what it means to be human, particularly as expressed in the integralist notion of humanity developed in the recent social teachings of the Roman Catholic Church.

The shortcoming of these conventional formulations of the basic human needs argument is that they unquestioningly accept the pneumatic anthropology of the liberal opponents. Their only disagreement with the liberals is the faulty logic that liberals employ in trying to preserve and protect the pneumatic dimension of human existence.

With regard to the distinction between positive and negative rights, the proponents of basic human needs rightly point to a logical flaw in the liberal argument. This does not prove, however, that food and housing are to be regarded as primary rights, only that this particular argument for the primacy of pneumatic rights is flawed and that a better argument should be found. If I were to claim that one baseball team is better than another, and base my claim on the argument that one team has better relief pitchers than the other, and if you then proved to me that the relief pitchers were equally good on both teams, you would not have disproved my claim, only the evidence I used to support that claim. I may very well be able to muster other, more reliable evidence to support my claim. If I can do so, then my general conviction remains true. The basic human needs advocates have shown that it is illogical to distinguish among pneumatic and physical rights on the basis of one being more negative than the other. This does not mean that there may not be other, more valid, ways of distinguishing between and prioritizing among the two that might still result in the elevation of pneumatic over physical rights.[27]

With regard to the claim that basic rights are the prerequisite for all other rights, the advocates of basic human needs not only point out a flaw in the liberal argument but also they give a reason for the priority of some physical rights over some pneumatic rights. The reason is not that physical rights are as important as pneumatic rights, or even that physical rights are important, although less important than pneumatic rights. The reason is simply that some physical needs must be met before one can enjoy any other rights. No positive valuation is ascribed to the physical dimension. It has no value in and of itself. Or it may even have a negative value, as a "necessary evil," as it were. The strength of this argument is that, unlike the previous one, it goes beyond mere criticism of the liberal mode of arguing and establishes a positive case for the priority of basic human needs. The weakness of this argument is that the same mode it uses to establish the importance of the physical dimension also denigrates that dimension. It says that we need something, not because that something is important in its own right, but because it is a necessary means to acquire something that is important. It is the same sort of backhanded compliment that educational, civic, and charitable organizations often give the wives of wealthy men. A wife is appointed to the board of trustees, not because they want her advice, but because they want her husband's money. Another analogy would be that of the fundamentalist missionary who feeds hungry natives not because he considers their physical well-being an important end in itself but a means to gain converts. Most would consider such an attitude crass and inhumane. Yet, such an attitude is not far removed from the basic human needs claim that "security and subsistence are basic rights . . . because of the role they play in the enjoyment and the protection of all other rights."[28]

THE CASE FOR THE HUMAN RIGHT TO PHYSICAL WELL-BEING

A more extended discussion is required to indicate the positive potential of rooting an argument for basic human needs in the claims of Christian theological anthropology. Such a discussion must include the following points. First is the claim that the human person possesses a special dignity which serves as the basis for human rights and correlative duties. Second is the claim that the human being is an "integral" being, both in terms of the individual and communal dimensions and in terms of the pneumatic and physical dimensions. The third claim follows logically from the first two. If the human person has a dignity sufficient to serve as the basis for human rights, and if the human person is a physical as well as a pneumatic being, then it follows that the physial dimension has as much dignity as the pneumatic, and that rights to the one are as important as rights to the other. Since the time of John XXIII, the Catholic Church has expressed a strong concern for human rights. Human dignity, human integrity, and the right to basic human needs have been the three distinctive features of this concern.

Human Rights Are Rooted in Human Dignity

The basis for the Church's involvement in human rights is its belief concerning human nature and human dignity. John XXIII's loud praise of Leo XIII for proclaiming "a social message based on the requirements of human nature itself" in *Mater et Magistra* (1961) may have set the tone for Vatican II's insistence that human dignity serve as the basis for claims concerning justice, peace, and human rights. It was Leo XIII who, three-quarters of a century before, had charted a new course for Catholic social teaching when he proclaimed, "No man may with impunity outrage that human dignity which God Himself treats with great reverence."[29]

Many of the Catholic social documents around the time of Vatican II expressed at the outset an affirmation of human dignity, indicating that this belief serves as the basis for concern for human rights. John XXIII opens *Mater et Magistra* by stating that his reason for addressing social concerns is that Catholic Church "has always held in the highest respect and guarded with watchful care" "the lofty dignity of this life." He introduces *Pacem in Terris* by asserting that humanity is made in the "image and likeness" of God. The first chapter of part one of the Second Vatican Council's *Gaudium et Spes* is entitled "The Dignity of the Human Person." This chapter establishes the anthropological assumptions upon which the rest of the document's discussion of social and economic issues is based. The Second Vatican Council's *Dignitatis Humanae*, which addresses the question of religious freedom, begins with this statement: "A sense of the dignity of the human person has been impressing itself more and more deeply on the consciousness of contemporary man." Paul VI's message *To the Peoples of Africa* praises traditional African cultures for their "respect for the dignity of man."[30]

These documents insist that the criterion for judging any action or policy or state of affairs is based on its effect, positive or negative, upon human dignity. Does it affirm and elevate human dignity, or does it negate and demean human dignity? Thus working conditions are to be judged not in terms of whether they enhance productivity, but whether they enhance human dignity—whether they are "truly in accord with human dignity." Thus progress in technology and economic life is not to be judged according to the sophistication of the machines or the amount of wealth engendered, but whether it helps humanity "to realize how great is their dignity; for they have been created by God and are His children." Thus the purpose of work is not activity for activity's sake. "What is the meaning and value of this feverish activity?" asks *Guadium et Spes*. The purpose is for humankind, "created in God's image," to create a world in which God's values, "justice and holiness," are realized. Thus the purpose of the community is to enhance human dignity. Thus the "dignity of the human person . . . lays the foundation for the relationship between the Church and the world, and provides the basis for dialogue [rather than enmity] between them;" all the world are members of God's human "family." Thus, both education and food are essential, because lack of either is "debasing" to human dignity. Thus certain ceremonial rites in traditional cultures must be condemned for being "in violent contrast with the respect due to the human person." Thus "the Second Vatican Council clearly and repeatedly condemned racism in its various forms as being an offence to human dignity," for "the aspirations of all men desiring to enjoy those rights which flow from their dignity as human persons are wholly legitimate." Thus sexual discrimination is condemned. A woman should "never be considered or treated as an instrument," for this violates "her dignity as a woman," which is equal to that of men. Thus situations of dependence (colonization, welfare systems, foreign aid) in which persons are deprived of their political power must be condemned. For example, "when whole populations destitute of necessities live in a state of dependence barring them from all initiative and responsibility, and all opportunity to advance culturally and share in social and political life," such a situation violates "human dignity." It is not sufficient simply to give aid to suffering peoples. The manner in which the aid is given is important: "the dignity of people receiving aid must be respected absolutely." They must be aided in such a way that they are enabled to "become artisans of their own destiny." Advancement is truly human advancement only if it is "carried out in such a manner that we respect his personal dignity and teach him to help himself." *Gaudium et Spes* summarizes the foregoing concerns: "the equal dignity of persons demands that a more humane and just condition of life be brought about."[31]

These documents base their claims concerning human dignity on three theological doctrines: creation, incarnation, and resurrection. The doctrine of creation teaches that humans are created in the "image and likeness of God," which suggests that humans have a certain dignity that identifies them more closely with God and which distinguishes them from the rest of creation. From the doctrine of creation a number of metaphors have developed which point to the dignity and equality of humanity. The Vatican documents refer to humanity as God's children, as God's co-creators, and as managers of God's creation. *Pacem in Terris* suggests that God, who created "the universe and man himself," is the prototypical scientist and technologist. Since humanity is created in God's own "image and likeness," endowed with "intelligence and freedom," and granted lordship over creation, it follows that an important aspect of bearing God's image is having the ability to create. Science and technology must be used to enhance human dignity, not to demean it, as with the technology of warfare and other destructive creations.[32]

The doctrine of the incarnation teaches that "the Word became flesh."[33] Such a claim implies, among other things, a strong affirmation of human dignity. God could not have assumed human nature if its dignity had been annulled by the Fall. God was not ashamed to experience human life and human death and to share that experience with other persons. "For by His incarnation," *Gaudium et Spes* teaches, "the Son of God has united Himself in some fashion with every man." Not only does the incarnation affirm human existence, but it also elevates it. It is through the incarnation that human redemption takes place. In this act the divine likeness (not image) which had been lost in the Fall was restored, and human nature was "raised up to a divine dignity." In this act humanity is recreated after the manner of Christ Jesus: "By faith and baptism he is transformed, filled with the gift of the Spirit, with a new dynamism, not of selfishness, but of love which compels hm to seek out a new, more profound relationship with God, his fellow man, and created things." The incarnation inspires persons to live up to the potential implied by their dignity: "the ferment of the Gospel . . . has aroused and continues to arouse in man's heart the irresistible requirements of his dignity." Concludes *Pacem in Terris*: "If we look upon the dignity of the human person in the light of divinely revealed truth, we cannot help but esteem it far more highly. For men are redeemed by the blood of Jesus Christ. They are by grace the children and friends of God and the heirs of eternal glory."[34]

The doctrine of the resurrection is less prominent in the Vatican documents. *Gaudium et Spes* exhorts its readers not to "despise" the physical body because "God has created it and will raise it up on the last day."[35] In the conclusion of the chapter we shall have more to say regarding the relevance of the doctrine of the bodily resurrection to basic human needs.

Human Beings Are Integral Beings

Christian theological anthropology defines the human being in integral terms. Individual versus communal and pneumatic versus material bifurcations are resisted in favor of a more holistic or integral concept of humanity.

"What must be aimed at," Paul VI writes in *Populorum Progressio*, "is complete humanism," citing Jacques Maritain's *L'humanisme integral.* The Vatican documents develop the notion of integral humanism in the context of discussing poverty in the Third World and the way that capitalist and Communist blocs impose equally unsuitable options upon the nations of the South. These nations fear ideologies that are so individualistic as to impede social progress, but also fear ideologies that, in promoting the good of the community, run roughshod over individual freedom. One produces inequality and poverty, the other terror and torture. They are afraid of ideologies which define the human being solely in pneumatic or materialist terms, once again creating the Scylla and Charybdis of hunger or torture. The Vatican documents offer a third option. Define humanity neither as an individual nor as a community, they say, but as both, and particularly in terms of the relation between the two. And define humanity neither as spirit nor as matter, but as both, never forgetting that both dimensions have dignity and that the two are inextricably related. In presenting the

"Christian vision of development," Paul VI suggests that development must involve more than a simple elevation in the gross national product. It must involve the development of people, not simply capital. And it must include their complete development: as individuals and as communities, as pneumatic and as physical beings. "In order to be authentic, it must be complete: integral, that is, it has to promote the good of every man and of the whole man." The Medellin documents have this same idea in mind when they speak of salvation in holistic or integral terms. The Latin American theologians and clergy insist that salvation is communal as well as individual, material as well as spiritual, present as well as future. "In the economy of salvation the divine work is an action of integral human development and liberation." John XXIII opens *Mater et Magisra* by expressing concern that social progress be integral. It is the Church's responsibility, he says, to guide "the life both of individuals and of peoples," and to offer individuals and peoples "salvation as well as the fullness of a more excellent life." Note that John does not define salvation as broadly as the Latin American bishops (writing seven years later), but he still maintains a broad definition of humanity. Lest there be any doubts concerning his commitment to the present and physical dimensions, he concludes the first paragraph with these words: "The lofty dignity *of this life*, she has always held in the highest respect and guarded with watchful care" [italics mine].[36]

The relationshp of the individual to the community is a subject that we discussed in chapters 2 and 3, and I mention it here to indicate the way that Maritain's pioneering work in the thirties and forties came to fruition in the sixties. *Populorum Progressio*'s discussion of "The Church and Development" shows a heavy indebtedness to Maritain. Integral development must involve both "personal and communal development." It must be personal: "In the design of God, every man is called upon to develop and fulfill himself, for every life is a vocation." It must be communal: "But each man is a member of society. He is part of the whole of mankind." Maritain's concern for the interdependence of person and society and their relation to the common good is a theme that permeates *Gaudium et Spes.* "Man's social nature makes it evident that the progress of the human person and the advance of society itself hinge on each other." The human person must be "the beginning, the subject and the goal of all social institutions," but the human person "by its very nature stands completely in need of social life." It is only through this social life that a person "develops all his gifts and is able to rise to his destiny." Only in the community can persons discover identity, vocation, reason for living. Only through promoting the good of persons can the community promote the common good.[37]

One outgrowth of this emphasis upon the interdependence of individuals and communities is the concept of "solidarity." Thus workers and employers are urged to work together in a spirit of brotherhood. Thus farmers are urged to bind together in farm cooperatives to promote their common (as opposed to their "solitary") interests. Thus nations are exhorted to work together to promote "the universal common good." Rich nations are urged to share in the destiny of the poorer nations. Thus the wealthier portions of the church are reminded of "the inestimable value of the poor," the "obligation of solidarity of those who suffer," and that "solidarity in action at this turning point in human history is a matter of urgency."[38]

In regard to the integral relationship of the pneumatic and physical dimensions of being, the Vatican documents emphasize the dignity of the physical dimension and the unity of the pneumatic and the physical. The dignity of the physical is emphasized to counter the Western tendency to devalue it. The Christian is "not allowed to despise his bodily life," says *Gaudium et Spes*. Because it is a creation of God, the Christian "is obliged to regard his body as good and honorable." Throughout the documents a concern is expressed for the physical needs of persons—food, shelter, and so on. But their readers are also reminded not to become concerned exclusively with the physical, nor to hope that salvation can be found there and there alone. The Church must "anchor the dignity of human nature against all tides of opinion," all ideologies, both "those which undervalue the human body" and those which "idolize it." Hence, both the pneumatic and the physical must be respected. John XXIII reminds readers that "the common good touches the whole man, the needs both of his body and of his soul." The common good "embraces the sum total of those conditions of social living whereby men are enabled to achieve their own integral prefection more fully and more easily." For this reason John urges civil authorities to "promote simultaneously both the material and the spiritual welfare of the citizens."[39]

The pneumatic and physical dimensions each have a dignity that must be respected, but the more fundamental point that the documents make is that the two are inextricably related. "Though made of body and soul, man is one," states *Gaudium et Spes*. "The teaching of Christ *joins*, as it were, earth with heaven" [italics mine], states John XXIII, and the work of the Church must do the same. It must embrace "the whole man, namely, his soul and body, intellect and will." Although the Church has "the special task of sanctifying souls," she must also be concerned about "the requirements of men in their daily lives," for Christ was concerned that persons be nurtured in both the physical and spiritual sense, and Christ seemed unwilling or unable to bifurcate the two.[40]

The Physical Dimension Has as Much Dignity as the Pneumatic

If humans have an inalienable dignity and if humans are integral beings, it follows that this dignity must therefore apply to the whole person and not just to the pneumatic dimension. After discussing the more middle-class concerns of familial and cultural rights, *Gaudium et Spes* turns to "the socio-economic realm" and insists that there, too, "the dignity and total vocation of the human person must be honored and advanced along with the welfare of society as a whole."[41] It is humanity as an integral being—individual and communal, pneumatic and physical—that is endowed with dignity. Therefore, the needs associated with each of the dimensions of life are human needs and deserve to be respected as such. It is inappropriate, therefore, to regard the right to food as an "animal" or "lower" need, just as it is inappropriate to regard the rights of communities as inferior to the rights of individuals. Freedom and individuality may be what distinguishes us from other species, and food and community living may be what we share with them, but this in no way suggests that the right to food or the rights of communities are inferior to the more pneumatic and individualist rights. As the discussion of integral humanism suggested, it is impossible to abstract one and separate it from the rest. All dimensions are essential to being fully human and all have dignity because all are created by God.

Because dignity applies to the socio-economic realm, a complete list of human rights must include rights of a more physical as well as those of a more pneumatic nature. *Pacem in Terris* develops a typology of human rights, and basic human needs head the list. They include "the right to life, to bodily integrity," and to basic physical necessities—"food, clothing, shelter, rest, medical care," and social security in situations of "sickness, inability to work, widowhood, old age, unemployment, or in any other case in which he is deprived of the means of subsistence through no fault of his own." John goes on to list rights pertaining to moral and cultural values, freedom of religion, freedom to choose one's vocation, economic rights (not basic human needs, but rights related to working conditions and property ownership), right of assembly and association, rights to emigrate and immigrate, and political rights. *Gaudium et Spes* makes a similar, although more concise, delineation of rights. Once again basic human rights are not only listed but are placed at the head of the list—"there must be made available to all men everything necessary for leading a life truly human, such as food, clothing, and shelter."[42]

If the pneumatic and the physical dimensions are essential to the integral human being, what should be done in situations of scarcity, in which preservation of one may require the denial of the other? For example, if in an impoverished nation some are starving while others live in luxury, whose right is to be favored—the right of the rich to keep that which they legally gained, or the right of the poor to basic necessities? Choosing in favor of the rich would result in a dehumanization of the poor, as they would be deprived of rights to basic human needs. Choosing in favor of the poor would result in a dehumanization of the rich, as they would be deprived of rights to private ownership of property. Either the rich lose their freedom or the poor lose their lives. In these situations, the Vatican documents consistently rule in favor of the poor. Decisions in this regard are governed by the principle of subsidiarity, which states that initiative and development are most effective if allowed to take place at the grass roots level. However, when efforts at this level fail so miserably that persons lack basic human needs, it is the responsibility of larger governing bodies to intervene. Larger governing bodies should "not only avoid restricting the freedom of private citizens, but also increase it," John XXIII says, "*so long as the basic rights of each individual person are preserved inviolate*" [italics mine]. John suggests that the principle of subsidiarity, developed by Pius XI in 1931 to oppose state socialism, was never meant to be used as a justification for poverty. It was developed to counter a different problem, the denial of individual freedom. In situations in which local bodies fail to provide basic needs, John (and the rest of the Vatican documents as well) assume that intervention is necessary: food takes precedence over freedom. And what if the larger bodies should fail to intervene on behalf of the poor? Then the poor are left with no viable option but to steal from the rich: "If a person is in extreme necessity, he has the right to take from the riches of others what he himself needs."[43]

What all this means is that for Thoms Aquinas as well as recent Catholic social teachings, ownership of property is not considered an absolute right in situations of scarcity. People are more important than property, the life of the poor more sacred than the liberty of the rich. If a choice must be made, food is more basic than freedom. Such valuations are not likely to be appreciated by North American audiences, for whom "Give me liberty or give me death" is something of a battle cry. The important distinction, of course, is that Catholic social teaching concerning the priority of food over freedom applies to situations of scarcity. It is acknowledged that depriving the rich of their property involves a degree of dehumanization, but it is recognized that this involves less dehumanization than if the poor were allowed to starve. The Catholic Church recognizes the integral nature of the human being and thus the dignity of pneumatic and physical rights. But the fact that they opt decisively in favor of the poor in situations of scarcity reflects a very positive assessment of the physical dimension of human existence, much more positive than post-Enlightenment liberalism and much more positive than most would expect the heirs of St. Paul and St. Augustine to be.

The achievement of the Roman Catholic documents has been to return the focus of the human rights discussion to fundamental assumptions regarding human nature and human dignity. Like the liberals, the Catholics believe that concern for human rights should be based upon a concern to protect the dignity and worth of the human being. Unlike the liberals, Catholics do not define the human being in a dualistic fashion, as essentially a pneumatic rather than physical being. Catholic social teaching has stressed that humanity is an integral being. The physical as well as the pneumatic dimension is endowed with dignity, and they are inextricably related. Thus rights related to physical needs should be accorded the same respect as rights related to pneumatic needs.

BASIC HUMAN NEEDS AND THEOLOGICAL ETHICS

It is not easy to convince the average bureaucrat of the relevance of theology, or even theological anthropology, to the human rights discussion. Gilbert Rist, himself an advocate of human rights as basic human needs, insists that the primary barriers to implementing basic human needs strategy are practical and political. "To be sure, the problems of development are not going to be solved by reflecting on human nature."[44] Theological anthropology does not claim that the problems of development will be solved by reflecting on human nature, but it does claim that they will not be solved without reflection on human nature. As long as liberalism's fundamental assumptions go unquestioned, it is difficult to imagine any fundamental changes taking place in human rights policy and development strategy. A bad tree cannot bear good fruit. The basic human needs critique of liberalism has focused thus far on liberalism's faulty logic. Theological anthropology insists that the critique begin at a more fundamental, almost prerational and mythical, level and that these ontological and anthropological assumptions of liberalism be exposed and critiqued. For example, when liberals state that "it is an insult to one's dignity to have welfare rights at the same time one is subject to arbitrary detention without charge or trial," but that "the converse is not true"[45]—in other words, it is not an insult to one's dignity to be deprived of welfare rights—the anthropological assumptions underlying such a statement should be recognized. The statement implies that dignity resides only in the pneumatic dimensions of human being and such an assumption sharply conflicts with the Judeo-Christian tradition's many affirmations of human physicality.

What has been needed, as a follow-up to Vatican II's call for an integral view of humanity and a broader concept of human rights, is a full-blown ethic of human rights as basic human needs. This would involve showing the theological basis for an integral view of humanity and the affirmation of human physicality. Also of value would be attempts, in the various nations, to translate the theory into practice. In the U.S., this would mean showing how such theory should impact U.S. foreign policy and UN human rights activity. Unfortunately, North American Protestant human rights literature has been quiet on the question of international human rights as basic human needs.[46] U.S. Catholics, inspired by Vatican II and Latin American liberation theology, have shown more interest in the issue. The Woodstock Theological Center's human rights project has produced three volumes on the subject of human rights and basic human needs which are discussed in the next section.

The Woodstock Theological Center's Human Rights Project

Human Rights and Basic Needs in the Americas, edited by Margaret E. Crahan, analyzes political, military, and economic factors affecting basic human needs in Latin America and suggests how U.S. policy could be altered to promote basic needs in Latin America. None of the contributors to the volume are theologians, and the volume does not attempt to address the issue at a theological level. The volume is quite useful in terms of practical applications of basic needs theory.[47]

More oriented toward theoretical questions is *Human Rights in the Americas: The Struggle for Consensus*, edited by Alfred Hennelly and John Langan. A number of the essays critique liberalism's reduction of human rights to civil and political liberties. John Haughey criticizes liberalism's individualist bias, John Langan criticizes liberalism's lack of concern for basic human needs, and Drew Christiansen gives an apologetic for human rights as basic human needs. What is disappointing, at least from the perspective of our present concern, is that none of the critiques is grounded in theological ethics. Haughey offers a Marxist critique of individualism, and Langan and Christiansen rely on John Rawls, Ronald Dworkin, David Miller, and other political philosophers. The Marxist perspective is important, and so is political philosophy in general, but what we expect to be distinctive about this volume, and what we do not get, is a critique of liberalism grounded in Christian theology, particularly theological anthropology.[48]

One portion of the volume contains a debate between the Protestant member of the symposium, Max Stackhouse, and Catholic theologian Monika Hellwig over the lack of biblical and theological material in the volume. Stackhouse argues that "today, many in the churches are looking in the wrong place for the foundations, meanings, and implications of human rights." Stackhouse accuses contemporary Christian theologians and ethicists of focusing "on modes of thought that are rooted in biblical and theological materials" and of avoiding "basic questions of theological anthropology," with the result that "an enormous amount of work by scholars, practice by clergy, and opinion by laity is shaped by nontheological views of humanity." Hellwig responds that since all knowledge comes from God, she is not concerned that biblical and theological sources have not been tapped as directly and as often as they could have. She rightly points out that a critique of liberalism need not be justified on theological grounds in order to be legitimate. She rightly points out that liberation theology has benefited from Marxian social analysis, just as Thomas used Aristotle and Augustine used Plato.[49]

These are valid points, but they make a caricature of Stackhouse's concern. Stackhouse does not argue that Marxian social analysis or Aristotlean logic or notions of the common good have no place in the theological discussion. He does not adjure theologians to rely exclusively upon theological sources and methods. He says simply that theologians should rely primarily upon theological resources since, after all, this is their area of expertise. I suspect that Hellwig may be afraid that Stackhouse's approach would yield more conservative results than the reliance upon Marxism and the basic human needs social thought. If this is the case, one cannot help but note a significant ironic twist. Langan and Christiansen, like Shue, base their argument for basic human rights on the claim that basic human rights are necessary means to higher ends. Langan argues that provision of essential goods is desirable because it enables individuals "to pursue their own plans of life." Christiansen argues that "fulfillment of basic needs offers a foundation for . . . those humanizing goods which make up that good life, things like religion, art, and politics." Basic human needs are not worthy as ends in themselves, but "are rather only the means which allow men and women to begin to lead that [good] life." Christiansen also argues that a U.S. foreign policy committed to promotion of basic human needs would serve as a means toward the realization of such ends as improved U.S. esteem abroad and greater political and economic stability in nations pivotal to U.S. interests.[50]

What is lacking, in these essays and in most others in the volume, is the argument that food and shelter are important as ends in themselves, that God has endowed the physical dimension with as much dignity as the pneumatic, that being in good health would be important even if it were not a prerequisite to the fulfillment of life plans or the exercise of free speech. This shortcoming of the Woodstock project vindicates Stackhouse's concern that a lack of attention to biblical and theological sources, particularly to the insights of theological anthropology, could result in an insufficiently prophetic concept of human rights, as it became more a mirror of its culture than a critic of it.

The third volume to emerge from the Woodstock project is David Hollenbach's *Claims in Conflict: Retrieving and Renewing the Catholic Human Rights Tradition.* Hollenbach was the sole contributor to the Hennelly/Langan volume who probed questions of theological anthropology. His essay for that volume, "Global Human Rights: An Interpretation of the Contemporary Catholic Understanding," like his book, develops a Catholic ethic of human rights based on papal, conciliar, and synodal documents since Leo XIII. One concern of Hollenbach's is to establish the theological affirmation of human dignity as the basis for human rights. He sees this concern as the "unifying thread" through all the recent Church teachings on human rights. "Respect for the dignity and worth of the person," he claims, "is the foundation of all the specific human rights and more general social ethical frameworks adopted by the encyclicals and other Church teachings." "The central theological affirmation at the foundation of the Roman Catholic rights theory," Hollenbach reiterates, "is that the human person is a living image of God." In the Catholic human rights tradition, dignity is something that persons "*have*," not something "granted to persons by the ethical activity of others." Nor can it be taken away. "It is a concrete reality which exists wherever persons exist," and it is independent of the "actions and relations" that help to structure it.[51]

Another concern of Hollenbach's is that church and society do more than make claims concerning human dignity. They must take actions to protect human dignity. Human dignity is at once a transcendental concept and a concrete reality. Unless it is recognized in terms of "particular needs, actions and relationships," it becomes little more than a pipe dream: "Unless the relations between the transcendental worth of the person and the particular material, interpersonal, social and political structures of human existence can be specified, human dignity will become an empty notion." Protecting human dignity involves determining the full range of threats to human dignity. These include the deprivation of both food and freedom. Recent Catholic social teaching has consistently held, says Hollenbach, "that dignity would be violated by any system which denied political freedom in the name of economic rights or which appealed to the primacy of individual liberty as justification for its failure to meet basic human needs." Hollenbach insists upon "an integral theory of human rights." Such a theory includes physical needs such as "life, food, shelter, sexuality and work" as well as pneumatic needs such as "freedom of expression, association, religion, communication." Such a theory also insists that the two are interrelated. Hollenbach cites one study that shows that "violations of civil and political rights increasingly appear to be linked with failure to respect social and economic rights," and another that indicates "more of a causal linkage between economic deprivation and the denial of rights to political participation, freedom from arbitrary arrest and torture, freedom to organize labor unions etc., than the liberal ideology can account for." Hollenbach is thus critical of both doctrinaire Marxism and doctrinaire capitalism for identifying human rights with an all-too-limited domain of human existence. As an American, he is particularly critical of U.S.

foreign policy for being "insufficiently sensitive" to the linkage between economic deprivation and denial of civil and political rights, for advocating pneumatic rights while ignoring basic human needs. He attributes this insensitivity to "the liberal roots of the American understanding of rights," and urges the U.S. to adopt a more integral notion of human rights.[52]

At the root of the liberal understanding of human rights is a pneumatic understanding of what it means to be human. It is for this reason that Hollenbach centers his critique of liberalism on the question of anthropology. There is hardly a page of his book that does not discuss these themes: human nature, human dignity, human needs. What enables Hollenbach to make such a fundamental and radical critique of U.S. policy is his belief, rooted in the Christian doctrine of creation, that the inalienable dignity of the human person pertains to the physical as well as the pneumatic dimensions of human being. "All material reality, including the human body, is a creature of God and thus [is] to be valued as essentially good." Physical well-being is, therefore, essential "for the realization of human dignity," and thus is valid as an end in itself. "Material well-being is not simply instrumental in value," Hollenbach insists. "It is not a means of dignified life. It is, rather, *integral* to the standard of all moral value, human dignity." Such a claim is diametrically opposed to the liberal belief that humans are essentially pneumatic beings and that physical rights, if there are any, can be justified only on the grounds that they are necessary means to enjoy pneumatic rights. Such a claim, rooted in the predominant religious tradition of the West, provides an effectual basis for policy designed to promote and protect basic human needs.[53]

Modern Pneumaticism and Ancient Gnosticism

The reason that Christian theological anthropology offers such an effectual critique of liberalism is that the major points of Christian anthropology were developed in response to a belief system that views human nature in a number of significant ways which parallel the liberal view. Gnosticism, like liberalism, created a sharp dualism between the pneumatic and the physical, deprecating the physical as finite and evil, while praising the pneumatic as eternal and good. In response the early Christians, drawing upon the positive, world-affirming and life-affirming beliefs of Judaism, asserted that human physicality is good and that the spiritual and physical dimensions of human beings are integrally related.[54]

The doctrine of creation emphasized that humans were created in the image of God and that the image of God related to both the physical and pneumatic dimensions. There is a link, it said, between being the image of God and being a physical and, more particularly, sexual, procreative, and technologically oriented being. In the Genesis account, the same sentence that declares that humanity is made in the image of God also defines the image of God as a sexual being ("male and female he created them"). The story then goes on to command humanity to continue the act of creation ("be fruitful and multiply") and to delegate to humanity responsibility for governing over this creation ("and have dominion"). There is also a link between being the image of God and being a pneumatic being. What distinguishes Adam and Eve from the rest of creation, in the second Genesis creation story, is that they are the beings capable of choosing between good and evil. They, like God, are free beings. Even Tertullian, notorious in some circles for his misanthropical tendencies, is able to appreciate the doctrine of creation's affirmations of human physicality and human integrity. The following critique of the gnostic Marcion is apropos to modern liberalism as well.

> The world was made up of all kinds of good things, and gives sufficient indication of the great good in store for him for whom all this was provided. Who really was worthy to inhabit God's works but the image and likeness of God himself? ... Thus goodness spoke; and goodness fashioned man out of clay to make this wonderful structure of flesh, equipped with so many qualities though formed of one material.

Tertullian goes on to praise human life, its responsibilities, and its pleasures, as gifts that God intended all persons to enjoy, developing an ancient version of the modern argument for human rights as basic human needs.[55]

The doctrine of the incarnation insists against the gnostics that the Word became flesh and dwelt among us. He lived the full range of human experience: physical, volitional, emotional. He got hungry and ate, thirsty and drank, grew tired and slept. He was tempted. He got angry on some occasions, happy on others, and sad on others. He was tortured, suffered pain, and died. The doctrine of the incarnation affirms human physicality in that God, the paragon of goodness and spiritual transcendence, is not ashamed to become a physical and emotional being. The doctrine of the incarnation affirms the integral wholeness of the human being in that Jesus Christ, the paragon of true humanity, cannot be divided into a divine and human, spiritual and physical being. The Nestorians did so and were condemned: "If any one in the one Christ divides the persons after their union," Cyril of Alexandria proclaims, "let him be anathema."[56] The reason that such a bifurcation was condemned was that it implied a dualistic anthropology, setting the pneumatic over against the physical. Early Christians insisted that humanity is an integral being and that the physical was as much the temple of God as the spiritual. Such a view carried with it radical moral implications, which the Vatican II documents have recognized and applied to the debate over pneumatic versus physical human rights.

The doctrine of the resurrection insists that Christ not only rose from the dead (a notion the gnostics would have readily accepted) but also that Christ's resurrection was a bodily one. For gnostics, resurrection was spiritual. Indeed, the whole purpose of death was to escape the fetters of the mortal, sinful life in the flesh. By gnostic standards, a bodily resurrection would, instead of being an escape from prison, be a return to prison. By Judeo–Christian standards, the body was not a prison but was the temple of God, life was a good gift to be cherished, and death, not life, was the true enemy. Thus Thomas doubts not the resurrection of Christ but the bodily resurrection—he must *feel* Christ's flesh to believe it. Thus Paul tells the Corinthians that over five hundred people *saw* the resurrected Christ. Thus Paul refuses to identify the resurrected Christ as *either* "spirit" or "flesh," but as an inextricable relation of the two, a *both/and* he calls a "spiritual body." And thus Irenaeus insists to the gnostics that

> what is restored to life is not something other than that which dies; just as that which is lost is not something different from that which is found.... What then was it which perished? Clearly it was the substance of flesh, which lost the breath of life.... The Lord came to restore this flesh to life, that 'as in Adam all die', as possessing merely sensual life, we may live 'in Christ', as having spiritual life, putting away not the handiwork of God but the lusts of the flesh, as receiving the Holy Spirit.

The physical dimension itself is not evil, but it can become corrupted by an evil will. Salvation involves not the shedding of the flesh but its restoration through the redemption of an evil will for a good one. Resurrection symbolizes this redemption: "The flesh which at the beginning was the subject of God's art," Irenaeus says, "will be found capable of receiving and assimilating God's power."[57]

What each of these doctrines seeks to promote is human wholeness (*shalom*). The doctrines of creation, incarnation, and bodily resurrection make the bold claim that God creates, redeems, and raises to new life the whole human being. These claims are asserted against the pneumatic bias of gnosticism. The implication for the contemporary human rights debate over the question of food versus freedom is clear. Christian theological anthropology condemns liberalism's pneumatic bias and urges that rights related to physical needs, like those related to pneumatic needs, be granted the status of inalienable human rights.

CONCLUSIONS TO CHAPTERS 4 AND 5

1. Non-Western nations have condemned the human rights movement's preoccupation with civil and political liberties and lack of concern for basic human needs.

2. Since the election of Jimmy Carter, many in the West have begun voicing the same criticism, resulting in the development of what has come to be known as the basic human needs critique of liberal human rights.
3. While the basic human needs critique rightly recognizes that food is a prerequisite for freedom, it fails to recognize that the satisfaction of physical needs is an important end in itself.
4. The Roman Catholic doctrine of human rights, as worked out around the time of Vatican II, offers a more fundamental and radical critique of liberalism. The Catholic doctrine condemns liberalism's anthropological dualism, which bifurcates humanity into a superior, pneumatic dimension and an inferior, physical dimension. Catholic teaching has developed a more holistic, life-affirming anthropology known as integral humanism. The bases for integral humanism's affirmation of the physical dimension of human existence are the doctrines of creation, incarnation, and bodily resurrection.
5. Our thesis is held to be valid. At the root of the differences between Western and non-Western concepts of human rights are differing concepts of what it means to be human. Christian theological anthropology offers a via media between pneumatic and materialist conceptions of humanity which in turn makes possible a rapprochement between pneumatic and materialist conceptions of human rights.

NOTES

1. Fouad Ajami, *Human Rights and World Order Politics* (New York: Institute for World Order, 1978), 27.
2. Cyrus Vance, "Law Day Speech on Human Rights and Foreign Policy," April 30, 1977, University of Georgia Law School, in *The Human Rights Reader*, eds. Walter Laqueur and Barry Rubin (New York: New American Library, Meridian Books, 1979), 299–300.
3. "Notre Dame Address on Foreign Policy," May 22, 1977 in *James E. Carter: Chronology, Documents, Bibliographical Aids,* ed. George J. Lankevich (Dobbs Ferry: Oceana Publications, 1981), 97; Jimmy Carter, *Keeping Faith: Memoirs of a President* (New York: Bantam Books, 1982), 144.
4. Andrew Young, "A New Unity and a New Hope in the Western Hemisphere: Economic Growth with Social Justice," *Department of State Bulletin,* May 30, 1977, 571, cited in Joshua Muravchik, *The Uncertain Crusade: Jimmy Carter and the Dilemmas of Human Rights Policy* (New York: Hamilton Press, 1986), 93; Angus Deming, "The Push for Human Rights," *Newsweek,* 20 June 1977, 53.
5. Henry Shue, *Basic Rights: Subsistence, Affluence, and U.S. Foreign Policy* (Princeton, Princeton University Press, 1980), 5–7; see also Muravchik, *The Uncertain Crusade,* 89–90.

6. George H. Brand, "Human Rights: Rhetoric or Reality," in *Human Rights: Rhetoric or Reality*, eds. George W. Forell and William H. Lazareth (Philadelphia: Fortress Press, 1978), 15; Norman A. Graebner, "Human Rights and Foreign Policy: The Historic Connection," in *The Moral Imperatives of Human Rights: A World Survey*, ed. Kenneth W. Thompson (Washington, D.C.: The University Press of America, 1980), 54.

7. In addition to the works cited herein, some others include: Attila Agh, "Human Nature and the Concept of Basic Needs," *Dialectics and Humanism* 8 (Summer 1981): 81–94; Philip Alston, "Human Rights and Basic Needs: A Critical Assessment," *Human Rights Journal* 12:19 (1979): 10–67; Gilbert Brown and Shahid Javed Burki, "Sector Policies and Linkages in Meeting Basic Needs," IBRD, Policy Planning and Program Review Department, Basic Needs Paper No. 7 (February 1978); E. William Colgazier, "Basic Human Needs as a Development Strategy," Colombo Plan (Washington, D.C.: November 1978) CC (78) OM STC-D/2; Michael Crosswell, "Basic Human Needs: A Development Planning Approach," AID Discussion paper No. 38 (Washington, D.C.: AID, October, 1978); Sidney Dell, "Basic Needs or Comprehensive Development: Should the UNDP have a Development Strategy?" *World Development* 7:3 (March 1979): 291–308; D.P. Ghai et al, "The Basic Needs Approach to Development: Some Issues Regarding Concepts and Methodology," *International Development Review* 19:3 (1977): 8–16; James P. Grant, *Disparity Reduction Rates in Social Indicators: A Proposal for Measuring and Targeting Progress in Meeting Basic Human Needs*, Monograph No 11 (Washington, D.C.: Overseas Development Council, 1978); Mahbub al Haq, "Basic Needs: A Progress Report," IBRD, Policy Planning and Program Review Department (10 August 1977); International Labour Office, *Employment, Growth, and Basic Needs: A One World Problem* (New York: Praeger, 1977); Franklyn Lisk, "Conventional Development Strategies and Basic Needs Fulfillment: A Reassessment of Objectives and Policies," *International Labour Review* 115:2 (March–April 1977): 171–91; Han S. Park, *Human Needs and Political Development: Dissent to Utopian Solutions* (Schnenkman, 1984); Rodney Peffer, "A Defense of Rights to Well-Being," *Philosophy and Public Affairs* 8:1 (Fall 1978): 65–87; *The Planetary Bargain: Proposals for a New International Economic Order to Meet Basic Human Needs*, Report of an International Workshop convened in Aspen, Colorado, July 7–August 1, 1975 (Aspen Institute for Humanistic Studies, 1975); "The Relationship of Basic Needs to Growth, Income Distribution and Employment: The Case of Sri Lanka," IBRD, Policy Planning and Program Review Department (June 1978); T.N. Srinivasan, "Development, Poverty, and Basic Needs: Some Issues," (Stanford Research Institute, MS, n.d.); Paul Streeten, "Basic Needs and Human Rights," *World Development* 8:2: 107–11; Streeten, "The Distinctive Features of a Basic Needs Approach to Development" *International Development Review* 19:3 (1977): 8–16; Streeten and Shahid Javed Burki, "Basic Needs: Some Issues," *World Development* 6 (1978).

8. For example, prior to writing *Basic Rights*, Shue edited, with Peter G. Brown, *Food Policy: The Responsibility of the United States in the Life and Death Choices* (New York: The Free Press, 1977). Shue and Brown continued their concern for issues related to poverty and the Third World experience by editing the follow-

ing books: Brown and Shue, *Boundaries: National Autonomy and Its Limits* (Totowa, NJ: Rowman and Littlefield, 1981); Brown, Conrad Johnson, and Paul Vernier, *Income Support: Conceptual and Policy Issues* (Totowa, NJ: Rowman and Littlefield 1981); and Brown and Shue, *The Border That Joins: Mexican Migrants and U.S. Responsibility*, (Totowa, NJ: Roman and Littlefield, 1983).

9. The French Revolution is, in some ways, an exception. Economic collapse exacerbated the tension leading to the revolution. See, for example, George V. Taylor's article, "French Revolution," in *Encyclopedia Americana*, International Edition, 1980, vol. 12, 66–72. Even so, the goal of the revolution was to transfer political rights to the middle class: "The Third Estate—bankers, industrialists, businessmen, and professionals—wanted to replace an entrenched aristocracy of parasitic royalty and clergy with a representative government." They wanted "equal rights for all, freedom of the press and speech, representative taxation, accountability of public servants, and the right to property." See Clyde L. Manschreck, *A History of Christianity in the World: From Persecution to Uncertainty* (Englewood Cliffs: Prentice-Hall, 1974), 300.

10. This is the conclusion reached by political scientists Adamantia Pollis and Peter Schwab in their study of human rights in non-Western cultures: "The colonial experience of economic exploitation gave credence to the notion of human dignity as consisting of economic rights rather than civil or political rights. Freedom from starvation, the right for all to enjoy the material benefits of a developed economy, and freedom from exploitation by colonial powers became the articulated goals of many Third World countries." See Pollis and Schwab, "Human Rights: A Western Construct with Limited Applicability," in *Human Rights: Cultural and Ideological Perspectives*, eds. Adamantia Pollis and Peter Schwab (New York: Praeger Publishers, 1979), 9.

11. Shue, *Basic Rights*, ix, 26–27, 34, 32, 183.

12. Ibid., 27.

13. Had the Universal Declaration omitted the reference to "holidays with pay," one wonders whether Cranston would have had any other basis for criticizing economic rights; see Cranston, *What are Human Rights* (New York: Taplinger Publishing Co., 1973), 66–71.

14. Johan Galtung, "The Basic Needs Approach," in *Human Needs: A Contribution to the Current Debate*, eds. Katrin Lederer and Johan Galtung (Cambridge, MA: Oelgeschlager, Gunn, and Hain Publishers, 1980), 101.

15. Gilbert Rist, "Basic Questions about Basic Human Needs," in *Human Needs*, eds. Lederer and Galtung, 242.

16. For example, Dominguez's modified version of Harold Lasswell and Abraham Kaplan's eight basic values. See Jorge I. Dominguez, "Assessing Human Rights Conditions," in *Enhancing Global Human Rights*, eds. Dominguez, Nigel S. Rodley, Bryce Wood, and Richard Falk (New York: McGraw-Hill Book Co., 1979), 33–100.

17. For example, the criteria of the Bariloche Institute of Argentina: food, health care, housing, and education. See Dominguez, 32.

18. Rist, 240.

19. Shue, *Basic Rights*, 65–91.

20. See Louis B. Sohn, "Supplementary Paper: A Short History of United Nations

Documents on Human Rights," in Commission to Study the Organization of Peace, *The United Nations and Human Rights: Eighteenth Report of the Commission* (1968), 105–06, cited in Shue, *Basic Rights*, 158.

21. Shue, *Basic Rights*, 37–38.
22. Richard R. Fagen, "The Carter Administration and Latin America: Business as Usual?" *Foreign Affairs*, 53:7 (1978): 663–68; on the way that the IMF encourages illiberal state capitalism, see William Goodfellow, "The IMF and Basic Human Needs Strategies," Paper prepared for Seminar on "Basic Human Needs: Moral and Political Implications of Policy Alternatives," Woodstock Theological Center, Georgetown University, February 26, 1979, mimeo., cited in Shue, *Basic Rights*, 189.
23. Shue, *Basic Rights*, 40–47.
24. Ibid.
25. Ibid., 39–40.
26. Ibid., 51–53.
27. It is also interesting to note the way that liberal realists have appealed to utilitarian argument to support their position. In essence, their claim is that pneumatic rights are merely negative, and therefore less expensive to protect, and therefore more important and more worthy of being called "natural rights" and "human rights." Following such logic, one might reach such absurd conclusions as that the right to due process, which involves the expensive process of litigation, is less essential than the right of children not to be spanked.
28. Shue, *Basic Rights*, 30. In fairness to Shue it should be pointed out that he resists saying that physical necessities are "means" to pneumatic ends. He says that physical necessities are an "inherent" part of enjoying all other rights (26–27), suggesting an integral view of human nature like that of recent Catholic social thought. Even so, his heavy reliance on logic (the "transitivity principle for rights" [32]) and his silence on the question of human nature suggest a tacit acceptance of liberalism's pneumatic anthropology.
29. *Mater et Magistra*, no 15 in *The Gospel of Peace and Justice: Catholic Social Teaching since Pope John*, ed. Joseph Gremillion (Maryknoll: Orbis, 1976). [Hereafter, all church documents from Gremillion unless otherwise noted.]; *Rerum Novarum*, no. 40 in *The Church Speaks to the Modern World: The Social Teachings of Leo XIII*, ed. Etienne Gilson (Garden City: Doubleday: Image, 1954).
30. *Mater et Magistra*, no. 1; *Pacem in Terris*, no. 3; *Gaudium et Spes*, no. 12; *Dignitatus Humanae*, no. 1; *To the Peoples of Africa*, no. 1.
31. *Mater et Magistra*, nos. 83, 84, 92, 215; *Gaudium et Spes*, nos. 34, 23, 40; *Populorum Progressio*, no. 35; *To the Peoples of Africa*, nos. 9, 17, 36; *Populorum Progressio*, no. 30; *To the Peoples of Africa*, no. 21; *Medellin Documents: Poverty*, no. 11; *Gaudium et Spes*, no. 29.
32. *Mater et Magistra*, no. 215; *Gaudium et Spes*, nos. 40, 41; *Pacem in Terris*, no. 3.
33. John 1.14.
34. *Gaudium et Spes*, no. 22; *Medellin Documents: Justice*, no. 4; *Gaudium et Spes*, no. 26; *Populorum Progressio*, no. 32; *Pacem in Terris*, no 10.
35. *Gaudium et Spes*, no. 14.

36. *Populorum Progressio*, nos. 42, 14; *Medellin Documents: Justice*, no. 4; *Mater et Magistra*, no. 1.

37. *Populorum Progressio*, nos. 15-17; *Gaudium et Spes*, nos. 23-26.

38. *Mater et Magistra*, nos. 23, 146; *Pacem in Terris*, no. 98; *Populorum Progressio*, nos 43-48; *Medellin Documents: Poverty*, nos. 7-11; *Medellin Documents: Peace*, no. 14c; *Populorum Progressio*, no. 1.

39. *Gaudium et Spes*, nos. 14, 41; *Pacem in Terris*, nos. 57-58.

40. *Gaudium et Spes*, no. 14; *Mater et Magistra*, nos. 2-5.

41. *Gaudium et Spes*, no. 63.

42. *Pacem in Terris*, nos. 11-27; *Gaudium et Spes*, no. 26.

43. *Mater et Magistra*, nos 53-55, cf. no. 117; *Pacem in Terris*, nos. 140-41; *Gaudium et Spes*, no. 69; *Populorum Progressio*, nos. 22-24.

44. Rist, 248.

45. Hugo Adam Bedau, "Human Rights and Foreign Assistance Programs," in *Human Rights and U.S. Foreign Policy*, ed. Peter G. Brown and Douglas MacLean (Lexington, MA: Lexington Books, 1979), 37.

46. Lutheran Richard J. Niebanck addressed the food versus freedom issue in a brief essay, "Theology, Politics, and Human Rights," in *Human Rights: Rhetoric or Reality*, eds. George W. Forell and William H. Lazareth (Philadelphia: Fortress, 1978), 31-42. A number of Reformed theologians touched on the question in *A Christian Declaration on Human Rights: Theological Studies of the World Alliance of Reformed Churches* (Grand Rapids: William B. Eerdmans Publishing Co., 1977). See, for example, the essays by Europeans Jan Milič Lochman, "Human Rights from a Christian Perspective," esp. 15, and Jürgen Moltmann, "A Definitive Study Paper: A Christian Declaration on Human Rights," esp. 132-34. American James H. Cone's essay, "Black Theology on Revolution, Violence, and Reconciliation," 64-76, indirectly addresses questions related to basic rights. The World Council of Churches' Commission of the Churches on International Affairs' three dossiers entitled *Human Rights and Christian Responsibility* shows some concern for questions of basic rights, as does the "Human Rights Issue" of the World Council of Churches' *Ecumenical Review* 27:2 (April 1975), which contains a contribution from East Germany entitled "The Meaning of Human Rights and the Problems They Pose," 139-46.

47. Margaret E. Crahan, ed., *Human Rights and Basic Needs in the Americas* (Washington, D.C.: Georgetown University Press, 1982).

48. Alfred Hennelly, S.J. and John Langan, S.J., eds., *Human Rights in the Americas: The Struggle for Consensus* (Washington, D.C.: Georgetown University Press, 1982); see especially the essays by: John Langan, S.J., "Defining Human Rights: A Revision of the Liberal Tradition," 69-101; John C. Haughey, S.J., "Individualism and Rights in Karl Marx," 102-41; and Drew Christiansen, S.J., "Basic Needs: Criterion for the Legitimacy of Development," 245-88.

49. Max Stackhouse, "A Protestant Perspective on the Woodstock Human Rights Project," in *Human Rights in the Americas*, eds. Hennelly and Langan, 144; Monika Hellwig, "The Quest for Common Ground in Human Rights—A Catholic Reflection," in *Human Rights in the Americas*, eds. Hennelly and Langan, 164.

50. Langan, 98; Christiansen, 264, 281.

51. David Hollenbach, S.J., *Claims in Conflict: Retrieving and Renewing the Catholic Human Rights Tradition* (New York: Paulist Press, 1979), 89, 42, 108, 90–91. See 90: "Thus the Roman Catholic tradition answers the question of the foundation of human rights with a single phrase: the dignity of the human person."

52. Ibid., 90–91, 191–95, 200; David Hollenbach, "Global Human Rights: An Interpretation of the Contemporary Catholic Understanding," in *Human Rights in the Americas*, eds. Hennelley and Langan, 15–17, 19.

53. Hollenbach, *Claims in Conflict*, 126, 79.

54. There are, of course, exceptions. But the recent trend in New Testament scholarship has been to emphasize early Christianity's continuity with Judaism and discontinuity with gnostic ontology, epistemology, and ethics. See, for example, Walter Schmithals, *Gnosticism in Corinth: An Investigation of the Letters to the Corinthians* (Nashville: Abingdon, 1971); Robert Jewett, *Paul's Anthropological Terms: A Study of their Use in Conflict Settings* (Leiden: E.J. Brill, 1971); E.P. Sanders, *Paul and Palestinian Judaism: A Comparison of Patterns of Religion* (Philadelphia: Fortress, 1977); .

55. Genesis 1–3; Tertullian, *Adversus Marcionem*, ii.4 in *The Early Christian Fathers: A Selection from the Writings of the Fathers from St. Clement of Rome to St. Athanasius*, ed. and trans. Henry Bettenson (New York: Oxford University Press, 1978), 106. For a scathing critique of Tertullian as a misanthropist, see Friedrich Nietzsche, *The Genealogy of Morals*, First Essay, XV in *The Birth of Tragedy and the Genealogy of Morals*, trans. Francis Golffing (Garden City: Doubleday, 1956), 183–85. For the most part Nietzsche simply quotes Tertullian without comment, letting the polemicist dig his own grave, as it were. Such a method gives a somewhat distorted picture of Tertullian, however. Nietzsche fails to describe the context within which Tertullian writes. Tertullian is not the Grand Inquisitor that Nietzsche implies, but writes as a member of a persecuted minority. His vindictive spirit reflects what has been called "survival language." This does not justify everything he said, but it does take some of the edge off of Nietzsche's attempt to read later ecclesiastical blunders back into Tertullian.

56. Cyril of Alexandria, "The Anathemas of Cyril of Alexandria," no. 3 in *Documents of the Christian Church*, Second Edition, ed. Henry Bettenson (New York: Oxford University Press, 1977), 46.

57. John 20.26–29 ("Put your finger here, and see my hands; and put out your hand, and place it in my side; do not be faithless but believing."); I Corinthians 15; Irenaeus, *Adversus Haereses*, v.xxxi.2 in *Early Christian Fathers*, 98.

6

WESTERN POLITICAL HEGEMONY

Chapters 2 through 5 argued that the West's individualistic, libertarian concept of human rights is inconsistent with Christian theology's assertions that the social and physical dimensions of human beings are as essential elements of human dignity as the individual and pneumatic dimensions. Chapters 6 through 9 will abandon the discussion of the West's "concept" of human rights, and will examine issues related to the historical "movement" for human rights in the West. They will consider two objections to the "way" that Westerners have publicized their concept of rights throughout the world.

The first of these objections involves the question of state sovereignty. Chapters 6 and 7 will consider the claim that the human rights movement, in the declarations, covenants, and conventions of the United Nations and in the foreign policy of President Carter, violated or threatened to violate the sovereignty of the individual nations. I will argue that the doctrine of sin, as interpreted by Reinhold Niebuhr, sheds new light on the issue. Niebuhr's extension of the doctrine of original sin and total depravity to the nation-state shows how the human rights movement's faith in the efficacy of international law is somewhat naive. Humans are sinful beings. It is futile to try to promote human rights around the world without taking this into consideration.

Whereas the first objection involves the question of intervention itself, the second objection involves the "manners" of intervention. Many observers have noted that Western advocates of international human rights have been guilty of such sins as chauvinism, self-righteousness, and hypocrisy. Chapters 8 and 9 will consider these sins from the perspective of

Christian theology. I will show how an increasing number of Western theologians have become sensitive to the cultural, contextual nature of human rights, and how such theological themes as transcendence and humility bear on the discussion. I will argue that an essential part of human nature and dignity is that humans are cultural beings, and that it is "bad manners" to try to universalize, in any direct way, one's own culture's concept of human rights.

OBJECTIONS VOICED BY NON-WESTERN NATIONS

In its zeal to turn Western ideals into international realities, the human rights movement has been guilty of showing insufficient respect for the sovereignty of non-Western nations. That, at least, is the claim of many non-Western opponents of Western human rights initiatives.

The sovereignty issue has arisen in response to Western efforts to promote human rights through intervention—legal, economic, or military— in the affairs of other countries. Examples include efforts to transform the general ideals of the UN Charter and the Universal Declaration into specific, enforceable international laws, efforts by the Carter administration to turn the human rights provisions of the Helsinki agreements into binding covenants that could be interpreted by the majority to the minority, and efforts to "strong-arm" Third World nations through economic and military sanctions against those weaker nations.

Objections to Early UN Initiatives

At the third session of the General Assembly in September 1948, a number of Communist nations expressed concern over the sovereignty question. The representative of the USSR gave three reasons for Soviet disapproval of the draft of the Universal Declaration, the first being its failure to guarantee that the declaration's concern for human rights is not intended to encourage intervention in the domestic affairs of sovereign states. The representatives from the Byelorussian SSR, the Ukrainian SSR, and Poland reiterated this view. The Polish representative added that the draft should specify certain rights of nations, namely, the right to use their native language and to maintain the traditions of their culture. These statements reflected the concerns of both the Soviet satellite nations and of the colonized nations of the Third World. At the plenary session of the General Assembly, December 9 and 10, 1948, in which the Universal Declaration was voted upon and approved, the concerns for national sovereignty were reiterated. The *Yearbook of the United Nations* records the following:

The representative of the USSR repeated his objections to the Declaration, and again stated that the Declaration was directed against national sovereignty and was therefore entirely inconsistent with the principles of the United Nations. The independence and well-being of a nation, he argued, depended on the principle of national sovereignty, and this principle was the sole protector of the smaller countries against the expansionist dreams of more powerful States.[1]

The response of the Western nations to statements such as these was decidedly negative. On several occasions the Soviet delegate proposed amendments to the draft, all of which were voted down by large margins. From the Soviet perspective, the Western nations were the aggressors. They held colonies throughout the world and used them to promote their military and economic interests. By asking that these colonies be given the right to become self-governing nations, the Soviets were voting on behalf of the colonized peoples, who had no real vote of their own. To argue the political independence of the smaller countries certainly was consistent with the United Nations' claim to be concerned about international justice. Of course, it cannot be denied that the primary Soviet concern was to promote its own interests. On the one hand, the Soviets hoped to weaken the Western empires by divesting them of their colonies. On the other hand, the Soviets were trying to avoid becoming colonies, of a sort, themselves—that is, subservient to the Western bloc. As most of the votes in the General Assembly and in the smaller committees indicate, the United Nations was sharply divided between the handful of Soviet bloc nations and the vast majority of Western nations and their satellites and allies. One reason the Soviets sought guarantees of national sovereignty was to prevent the possibility of the Western majority using the lack of civil liberties in the Communist countries as justification for "humanitarian intervention" in their affairs, through the channels of the United Nations and in the name of human rights. In other words, the Communists perceived the human rights efforts of the United Nations to be a camouflage for an attempt of the Western superpowers to dominate not only Third World colonies but also Communist nations as well.

The ambiguity of the Western nations regarding the issue of sovereignty and democracy was dramatized by a conflict which arose at the plenary meeting over the status of the colonized countries. Exactly what happened is difficult to determine. Early UN records reflect a Western bias, and the reporting of this particular discussion contradicts itself. Without speculating as to "the story behind the story," this much seems clear: the Soviet delegation proposed an amendment geared toward promoting the right to self-rule in the so-called Non–Self–Governing Territories. The amendment was voted down by the session, which of course was dominated by Western nations and their allies. The United Kingdom then proposed an amendment to replace Article 3 of the draft, which had specified that the rights of the declaration extended to the persons of the Non–Self–Governing Territories, with a milder statement concerning the rights of these persons. The amendment proposed that Article 3 be deleted and that another statement be added at the end of Article 2 (thus, less conspicuous) which would guarantee the rights of all people but which would not single out colonized areas as areas of special concern (thus no special article dealing with colonized countries and thus no implied criticism of colonialism). The amendment passed by a vote of twenty-nine to seventeen, with ten abstentions. This was much closer than most votes in the General Assembly at that time. A large number of nations that usually supported the Western bloc "crossed over," thus suggesting the divisiveness of the issue and perhaps the injustice of the way that the Western superpowers handled the sovereignty question. As a result of the amendment, Western empires were spared the embarrassment of being singled out by the declaration as "high-risk" human rights violators. The Western democracies had managed to author a proclamation that ostensibly promoted democracy but did not condemn their own efforts to prevent democratic governments from emerging in Asia, Africa, and the Americas.[2]

The only article of the declaration that dealt with political rights, Article 21, was carefully worded to avoid affirming rights to national sovereignty and self-rule. The article grants persons the right to "participate" in the governing of their country. "Participation," of course, is a vague term. Giving colonized peoples the right to elect a nonvoting member of the legislative body of the ruling nation may be construed as "participation," but certainly not as "self-rule." The vast majority of the thirty articles of the declaration pertain to rights which are usually termed as "civil liberties." The preamble makes it clear that these civil liberties are to extend to all people, "both among the peoples of member states themselves and among the peoples of territories under their jurisdiction." What the declaration has done, from the perspective of the colonized peoples, is to give them some rather empty freedoms.

They view themselves as being given the right to speak freely, worship freely, and so on, but as having no political power by which to turn their convictions into actual policies—in other words, the right to "bark" but not to "bite." And they have no economic rights. From their perspective the Universal Declaration gives employers the right to starve workers to death on low wages as long as they do not deny these workers the right to talk about the unjust situation. As the Soviets and later independent Third World nations would charge, such is not democracy but is an insult to true democracy. Pragmatically, it is designed to promote Western interests in two ways, by condoning Western imperialism and by condemning the communist version of democracy, that is geared toward a democratization of economic and political power more than toward democratization of civil liberties.

Objections to Helsinki and Belgrade Initiatives

A second Western human rights initiative in which the question of sovereignty became a central point of contention was the series of discussions between Western and Soviet bloc nations that gave rise to the Helsinki Accords in 1975. As the series of disagreements subsequent to Helsinki would indicate, there is some question as to whether any true accord was ever reached. The West interpreted the Helsinki Final Act as a victory for human rights, the Soviets interpreted it as a victory for state sovereignty or, more particularly, the recognition and sovereignty of the Soviet bloc vis-à-vis the West.

The Helsinki Final Act, adopted August 1, 1975, sought to promote cooperation in a number of areas: science, technology, economics, environmental concerns, humanitarian aid, and security. The section on security, "Declaration on Principles Guiding Relations between Participating States," contained three clauses: "Non-intervention in internal affairs" (VI); "Respect for human rights and fundamental freedoms, including the freedom of thought, conscience, religion or belief"(VII); and "Equal rights and self-determination of peoples"(VIII). The sixth clause prohibited "any intervention, direct or indirect, individual or collective, in the internal or external affairs falling within the domestic jurisdiction of another participating state." On the basis of this clause, the Soviets would object strenuously to subsequent Western support for Soviet dissidents. The seventh clause promoted the Western concern for civil liberties. On the basis of this clause, Western nations would support Soviet dissident activity. The eighth clause reaffirmed the independence and sovereignty of all peoples, their right to political self-determination. On the basis of this clause, the West would argue against the "Brezhnev doctrine," which claimed the right of the Soviet Communist party to control the activities of Communist parties outside the Soviet Union.

Instead of easing East–West tensions, the Helsinki Final Act, replete with conflicting signals, exacerbated them. Two years later at the Belgrade conference, the purpose of which was to review the progress made since 1975 in implementing the Helsinki accords, a number of squabbles surfaced.

On June 11, 1977, Sergi Vishnevsky, senior editor of *Pravda*, accused the West, and particularly the Carter administration, of using the human rights issue as a smoke screen for promoting Western interests: "The anti-Soviet campaign being waged under a false signboard of protection of

human rights is one of the manifestations of invigoration in the West of
forces hostile to socialism." Such an anti-Soviet campaign, he felt, violated
both "the spirit and the letter" of Helsinki. He accused the United States of
trying to use the Helsinki process to advocate its "right to interfere in our
internal affairs." It is "high time," he charged, for the United States to realize that "the Soviet Union shall allow nobody to pose as a mentor and teach
it how it should resolve its internal affairs."[3]

In December 1977 and March 1978, the United States used the
Belgrade forum to attack the Soviet Union for imprisoning human rights
activists whose only crime, according to the United States, was that they
exercised the rights granted by the seventh clause of the Helsinki Accord.
United States delegate Edward Mezvinsky said he was "deeply troubled by
reports of religious persecution and anti-Semitism in the Soviet Union."
Soviet delegate Valerian Zorin accused the United States of "interference"
in Soviet affairs, of using human rights as a pretense for fighting a
"psychological war" against the Soviet Union.[4]

Konstantin Chernenko addressed the Belgrade dispute in an essay entitled "For Lasting Peace and Dependable Security in Europe." After com-
plimenting the Belgrade review conference for continuing the work of
Helsinki toward strengthening European security and cooperation, Chernenko criticizes the efforts of some Western conferees to undermine these
efforts by trying "to introduce into the final document of the conference
provisions aimed at legalizing interference in the internal affairs of the
socialist countries under the farfetched pretext of 'defense of human
rights'." Chernenko repeats this concern for national sovereignty throughout the essay, pointing out that some Western delegates, particularly those
from the United States, went out of their way to turn the meeting into a
debate on the "farfetched" issue of human rights. Such efforts violated
what he considered the main purpose of Helsinki and Belgrade, which was
to promote security and cooperation. Chernenko expresses his satisfaction
that these efforts failed.[5]

The tension at Belgrade was heightened by two controversies which
arose at that time, both of which involved the issue of sovereignty. One was
the growing Western support for Soviet dissidents. The other involved the
growing independence from Moscow of the Communist parties of Western Europe.

Soviet Dissidents

Western support for Soviet dissidents may be attributed largely to the
writing and activities of Alexander Solzhenitsyn. His writing had won him
considerable popularity in the West at the time of his expulsion from the

Soviet Union in 1974. After coming to the West, Solzhenitsyn emerged as a prophetic-apocalyptic figure who commanded the respect of Democrats and Republicans, politicians and labor unions, Americans and British. In his first major speech since coming to the West, delivered June 30, 1975, Solzhenitsyn described the East–West conflict in simple terms of good versus evil, criticized the West for compromising with evil in the name of détente, and urged the West to launch an all-out effort to rid the cosmos from the menace of Communism. After years of Henry Kissinger's "realist" approach to dealing with the Soviets, the stage was set for an enthusiastic reception of Solzhenitsyn's infusion of morality and religiosity into the foreign policy formula. Solzhenitsyn strongly denounced détente and respect of national sovereignty as excuses for avoiding confrontation with this incarnation of evil. "On our planet there are no longer any 'internal affairs,'" he told a Washington audience. "The Communist leaders say, 'Don't interfere in our internal affairs. Let us strangle our citizens in peace and quiet'." Solzhenitsyn's response is an all-out plea for U.S. intervention in Soviet affairs: "But I tell you: *Interfere more and more. Interfere as much as you can. We beg you to come and interfere*" [italics mine]. Solzhenitsyn is vague as to what sort of intervention he would like to see take place.[6]

It is not difficult to understand why the Soviet government would be concerned about the near-messianic popularity of Solzhenitsyn. Solzhenitsyn was warmly received by American labor unions, the United States Congress, and the BBC. His only major rebuff in the West was by President Gerald Ford who, in the interests of détente, did not invite him to the White House.

When Jimmy Carter was elected the following year, one of his first official actions as President was to send a letter to Soviet dissident Andrei Sakharov promising to "continue our firm commmitment to promote respect for human rights." Sakharov leaked the letter to the Western press, and expressed his appreciation for Carter's "expression of support" for human rights activists in Communist countries. Carter had sent signals to the Soviet Union that the United States was taking seriously the advice of its prophet-in-exile, Solzhenitsyn. Wrote one observer of East-West politics, Arpad Kadarkay: "No other American president had intervened so directly in the internal affairs of other countries in defense of their people's rights." Hans Morgenthau accused Carter of being "terribly naive," and predicted that Carter's "nonsense . . . won't do anybody any good." Most other Westerners applauded Carter's confrontive spirit and, once again, it was not difficult to see why the Soviet government would feel its security and sovereignty threatened. Yuri Kornilov, senior commentator for *Tass*, accused Carter of assuming "the role of mentor to the USSR and other socialist countries." Anatoly Dobrynin protested that Carter's letter ignored the principle that human rights matters should be treated as internal, falling within the "competence of States."[7]

Not long after his letter to Sakharov, Carter made a second bold gesture toward the Soviets in the name of human rights by inviting exiled dissident Vladimir Bukovsky to the White House. Once again Carter affirmed his commitment to human rights, and his intention not "to be timid about it." Carter stated that the meeting would help him prepare for the upcoming Belgrade conference. Once again, Moscow expressed concern over its security and sovereignty, protesting Carter's interference in the "internal affairs" of the Soviet Union. Moscow reminded Carter that in 1933, when the U.S. and the USSR had established diplomatic relations, both sides had agreed to "refrain from interference" in each other's internal affairs.[8]

The Sakharov letter and the Bukovsky invitation stirred up dissident activity on both sides of the Iron Curtain. A group of more than six hundred East European intellectuals circulated and signed Charter '77, which advocated intellectual and religious freedom. At the AFL-CIO convention in December 1977, Vladimir Bukovsky and Senator Daniel Patrick Moynihan advocated economic sanctions on behalf of the dissidents. George Meany read a letter from Sakharov which compared the Soviet government to a brontosaurus and urged the AFL-CIO to continue fighting the cause of the dissidents.[9]

One way the Soviet government responded to such Western human rights initiatives was by arresting dissident Anatoly Shcharansky, accusing him of spying for the CIA. The arrest occurred on the eve of delicate Salt II negotiations and a visit to Moscow by Secretary of State Cyrus Vance. Carter came to the support of Shcharansky, thus creating a direct conflict between the Kremlin and the White House. Carter was forced to back down, somewhat, to save the Salt II negotiations. Once again the reaction from Moscow was to express concern over the sovereign right of the state against the Western concern for the sovereign rights of the individual.[10] A. Petrov, writing in April of 1977, sharply condemned U.S. support for Soviet dissidents. In view of the Helsinki Accords' "clear statements" affirming national sovereignty, he asks "how is one to take the attempts by certain Western leaders to patronize people who come out against the socialist system which the Soviet people have established in their own country? . . . Only as intervention in the internal affairs of the Soviet Union and disrespect for the Final Act and its principles."[11]

Two months later Yuri Kornilov, a senior commentator for *Tass*, expressed a similar view:

> It would be interesting to see how the American authorities and the American judiciary would react if anybody outside, or inside, the country undisguisedly tried pressuring them in regard to a criminal case, and especially pressuring at the official level. We imagine that such attempts at pressuring would be rejected outright. But why is something which is in-

admissible for American justice, considered by certain individuals in Washington quite acceptable when it concerns Soviet justice?[12]

What is missing in Carter's concern for human rights, according to the Soviets, was a respect for the principle of national sovereignty, which had been affirmed both in the letter and spirit of Helsinki.

Eurocommunism

The tension of the Belgrade review conference was heightened not only by the growing Western concern for Soviet and East European dissidents but also by the increasingly independent attitude of the European Communist parties. Heretofore the European Communists had been loyal to the Soviet Communist party but, in the spirit of Helsinki with its emphasis on self-determination and national sovereignty, they began to resent interference and domination from Moscow. They wanted the freedom to develop their own indigenous versions of communism, rather than be pawns and clones of the Soviets.

In March 1977, the heads of the Spanish, Italian, and French Communist parties met in Madrid and agreed to the principles of "Eurocommunism"—greater independence from the Soviet Union and adaptation of principles to their own national situations. All three leaders expressed opposition to intervention in the sovereignty of other nations. Santiago Carrillo of Spain, in a bold condemnation of Moscow, announced the Eurocommunists' "rejection of any directing center that tries to intervene in the internal affairs of other parties and other peoples." Carrillo had authored a book in which he developed the concept of Eurocommunism, with its implicit rejection of international Communism directed from Moscow.[13]

The conflict came to a head in November 1977, when leaders of Communist parties around the world were scheduled to gather in Moscow. French leader Georges Marchais boycotted the conference. Carrillo came, but was denied the right to speak. Enrico Berlinguer of Italy spoke and used the opportunity to advocate the autonomy of each national Communist party, with no hierarchical relation to Moscow or anywhere else. Among the West Europeans, only the Portuguese and West Germans expressed loyalty to the USSR. Brezhnev condemned the independent spirit of the Eurocommunists, arguing for a united, international Communism. Brezhnev thus reaffirmed his so-called Brezhnev doctrine, which justifies Soviet intervention into foreign countries—militarily and otherwise—in order to protect "the socialist system" in those countries.[14]

The Soviet stance toward the Eurocommunists negated any public relations gains the Soviets might have made in their earlier defense of the sovereignty of the weaker nations. The Soviets were now seen to have adopted a double standard on the issue of national sovereignty. On the one hand, they had condemned certain Western human rights initiatives on the grounds that they would encourage intervention in the internal affairs of some nations by other nations. Such a stance was morally and politically defensible. But when the Soviets elected to violate the principle of sovereignty with regard to the promotion of their own concept of human rights, that is, international justice according to communist principles, it became obvious that the only principle operative for them was the principle of national self-interest. This does not diminish the theoretical merit of the principle of national sovereignty as a restraint on certain types of human rights activity, as we shall see later in this chapter. It does, however, diminish the Soviet Union's own claim to be an advocate in the world forum of the self-determination of all peoples. Thus, in 1977, when Brezhnev condemned U.S. interventionism in the name of human rights ("the outright attempts by official American departments to interfere in the internal affairs of the Soviet Union," and "we will never tolerate interference in our internal affairs by any country under any pretext," and "the claims on the part of Washington to be able to teach others how to live cannot be accepted by a single sovereign state") and proclaimed Soviet allegiance to the principle of national sovereignty ("the Soviet Union itself does not interfere in the internal affairs of other countries") the hypocrisy of such claims would be obvious to any student of world politics.[15] But Brezhnev had introduced the concept of national sovereignty into the human rights discussion and, as will be argued in Chapter 7, this concept would offer a "realist" check to the international movement for human rights.

Objections from the Third World

The Third World nations' struggle for development and improvement in their relations to the First and Second World nations was a third area in which the issue of sovereignty became a focus of discussion. The nations to the South found themselves in something of a double bind. They needed the economic and military assistance of stronger nations, such as the United States and the Soviet Union, in treading the path of development. But they resented the attempts of the stronger nations to tell them how to run their country. The United States and the Soviet Union tended to force them into alliances with one or the other superpower. It was difficult for these Third World nations to receive economic or military assistance without losing political autonomy.

When President Carter began using human rights criteria as a basis for determining aid and trade policies to Third World countries, he evoked both anger and praise from the Third World. In February 1977, the Carter administration cut aid to Argentina, Uruguay, and Ethiopia because of those countries' poor records on human rights. Carter announced that improved relations between the United States and Cuba would be contingent upon the improvement of human rights conditions within Cuba. Argentina and Uruguay protested to the U.S. State Department that it was trying to interfere in their affairs. Castro was "appalled," wrote Benjamin C. Bradlee, executive editor of the *Washington Post*, who interviewed the Cuban leader for two consecutive days. Castro was appalled because he believed that Cuba's record on human rights was superior to that of the United States, and because he considered the intervention of one country into the internal affairs of another to be the worst type of human rights violation. "What," he asked, "does Cuba have to learn about human rights . . . from the country that mounted an invasion of Cuba and has relentlessly tried to assassinate Cuba's leader for 20 years?"[16] (From the U.S. perspective, individual rights have greater value than communal rights. Thus the United States was justified in interfering with Cuba's communal right to self-determination if to protect civil rights of individual citizens.)

After such a backlash from Third World leaders, Carter was forced to reassess his human-rights oriented foreign policy. It became clear that, while many in the Third World appreciated Carter's concern for human rights both in his own country and abroad, they did not appreciate the way that the United States and the Soviet Union failed to respect the independence and sovereignty of the smaller nations. Even though the domination was, theoretically, for moral rather than economic reasons, such a noble end did not justify such an ignoble means. To the smaller nations, interference could not be justified for any reason. So Carter attempted to assure these nations that his concern for human rights would not lead him to interfere in the affairs of other countries. "America's concern for human rights does not reflect a desire to impose our particular political or social arrangements on any other country," Carter told a NATO ministerial meeting on May 10, 1977. In a similar vein, when Rosalynn Carter visited Brazil in June 1977, she received a cool reception because of concerns she had expressed for missionaries tortured by the Brazilian government, and for Brazil's plans to develop a nuclear power industry. She attempted to mollify the situation by stating that even though her husband had a "deep, deep commitment to human rights," this would not affect his "recognition of the individuality and . . . the sovereignty of each of the countries of the hemisphere." Even so, she visited prisoners of conscience, and the United States continued to oppose Brazil's development of a nuclear power industry, leaving the Brazilians to question whether the expression of concern for independence and sovereignty was to be taken seriously.[17]

There were other reasons for questioning the United States's expressed concern for sovereignty and human rights. As a number of observers would point out, Carter seemed less willing to confront strategic allies, South Korea for example, than to confront those whose military and economic cooperation was more expendable. Commented New Zealand Prime Minister Robert Muldoon:

> If the Carter administration says: "Here's a small country in South America which is infringing upon human rights, we will stop the assistance we're giving them until they behave themselves," but then says: "Well, South Korea is infringing civil rights but the strategic position is so important that we can't move," then that's a form of selective application which in my view is immoral.[18]

From the perspective of the smaller countries the United States seemed overly timid in taking security risks in the name of human rights.

Another area of hypocrisy, in the eyes of much of the world, involved Carter's willingness to intervene in the sovereign affairs of nations on behalf of political dissidents but not on behalf of impoverished peasants. The West "thinks it is legitimate to intervene in the politics of Third World societies by lecturing them on how they should treat their dissidents, but pleads the principle of 'nonintervention' when the issue of Third World poverty comes up," observes Fouad Ajami. In regard to the former issue, the West advocated global norms or, rather, global adherence to Western legal norms. In regard to the latter, it advocated national norms. Poverty and hunger were treated as local issues, matters of positive law. But civil and political rights were considered inalienable, universal, matters of natural law, thus transcending national boundaries. Ajami calls this "a strange contradiction." Certainly the need for and right to food is more basic than the need for and right to civil and political liberties.[19]

Something else clouding the whole question of human rights and national sovereignty was the fact that in many types of human rights violations in the Third World, intervention was already involved as a cause of the problem—apartheid in Namibia, homelessness in the West Bank, and poverty in Western colonies and former colonies still dominated by Western economic and military interests. What was needed to protect human rights in these countries was a recognition of their right to self-determination. If a foreign country has violated that right it is arguable that, in the name of the sovereign rights of the people there, foreign nations have a duty to intervene in the "intervention" and restore that land to its people.[20] What is certainly clear is that if a nation finds itself interfering in the affairs of another nation and causing human rights violations in that nation, then the intervening nation has the obligation to stop intervening and to make amends for the injustices incurred.

When President Carter began speaking so passionately for human rights, many Third World nations did not hear his words because the actions of the United States spoke more loudly. The United States was interfering in dozens of countries throughout the Third World and in such a way as to promote human rights abuses of every kind—covert CIA operations, unfair economic practices of U.S. corporations abroad, sale of torture devices to repressive regimes, partnerships with corrupt governments, and so on. So Carter's human rights campaign came across as ambiguous in yet another way. While the United States verbally advocated the cause of rights around the world, its actual policies had promoted and continued to promote human rights abuses throughout the world.

To summarize: Second and Third World nations have complained that, in many of the efforts to promote international human rights, their sovereignty has not been respected. The occasions most often cited are the drafting the Universal Declaration of Human Rights, the discussions at Helsinki, and the foreign policy initiatives of the Carter administration. What remains is to examine the activities and literature of the Western human rights movement to determine whether these objections are well-founded.

THE ANATOMY OF WESTERN POLITICAL HEGEMONY AND ITS INFLUENCE ON THE HUMAN RIGHTS MOVEMENT

A survey of the early history of the movement reveals two facts relevant to the concern for sovereignty by Second and Third World nations. One fact is that the United Nations was dominated in the early years by Western nations and Western interests. Most of the early debates and controversial votes divided along East–West lines, with the West winning by a large margin because of the control it exercised over Third World governments. The cold war struggle was quite evident on this unlikely battlefield, the floor of the United Nations, as it attempted to draft a Universal Declaration of Human Rights. It is easy to see why the Communist nations felt their sovereignty threatened. They constituted a minority voice in what purported to be a world forum.

The second fact is that there was significant support among Western human rights advocates in the late forties and early fifties for turning the United Nations into some sort of world government. With the Soviet bloc constituting a minority voice in the organization, and with Soviets continually being outvoted by an opposition unified against them, it is easy to see why Communist nations, and any other nations that wished to avoid alignment with the West—such as Moslem nations and former colonies moving toward independence—would feel threatened by any talk of turning the United Nations into a governing body.

The term "world government" was seldom used in the UN debates. However, the idea of world government was continually the focus of discussion. Most often it surfaced in the discussion of whether the articles of the Universal Declaration should be considered "ideals" or "laws." "Ideals" would express the aspiration of the United Nations, but there would be no legal sanctions against those nations which did not choose to live up to the ideals. "Laws" would express the standards set by a social contract between the members of the United Nations. Failure to live up to these international laws would not be considered simply lack of zeal for a nice ideal, but violation of a law. Procedures would be set up to punish such violators. In the case of international human rights ideals, the sovereignty of the nation is not really threatened. Its cultural integrity is questioned—[this aspect will be discussed in chapters 8 and 9] but there is no threat of legal sanction. In the case of international human rights laws, national sovereignty is threatened. A supranational body is set up to enforce laws to which all nations must bow and bend. If the majority of the members of the United Nations ally themselves with the Western bloc against the smaller Eastern bloc, there is little question who will be doing most of the bowing and bending.

From September 24 to December 7, 1948, the United Nations' Third Committee discussed the draft of the International Declaration of Human Rights that had been prepared by the Commission on Human Rights. The first two weeks of the discussion were devoted to general philosophical issues. A philosophical issue that dominated the discussion was, of course, the question of national sovereignty.

Eleanor Roosevelt, the American delegate who chaired the Commission on Human Rights, stated that the Declaration was an important step toward international human rights. This was, however, merely the first step toward implementing the objectives of the UN Charter. The next step would involve drafting a covenant on human rights which, unlike the Declaration, would take the form of a treaty, or social contract. Its articles would be positive laws rather than natural law ideals and, as such, would be instituted in such a way as to be legally binding.[21]

The Norwegian representative agreed that the purpose of the Declaration was to establish moral standards rather than legal obligations. But, like Roosevelt, he pressed for something more than vague ideals. He said that matters of human rights transcend state boundaries, and states that violate international human rights standards have no grounds for objecting when other states intervene in the name of human rights. Since human rights transcend state boundaries, he believed that the domestic jurisdiction clause of the Charter and Declaration should not be interpreted as putting significant limitations upon the implementation of international human rights objectives.[22]

New Zealand argued that the Declaration should not be approved until provisions were made to make it legally binding. A number of other states agreed that the declaration was an imperfect one, and that ideally it, or a subsequent convention (treaty), should be made legally binding. Until it became possible to draft such a document, however, they agreed that the Declaration should be approved as drafted.[23]

The representatives of Bolivia, Panama, and Brazil, unlike the others, interpreted the Charter and Declaration in legal terms. They argued that the purpose of the documents was to establish positive legal obligations and thus to provide secure protection against human rights violations.[24]

The Union of South Africa, Poland, and the USSR argued that the Declaration should not be approved because it had already gone too far in infringing upon the sovereignty of states. South Africa argued that the Declaration had gotten too specific in stating not only what general principles should be upheld but how concretely those principles should be interpreted and implemented. Such specificity and concreteness left little room for individuality among the various nations.

Poland and the USSR argued that the Declaration failed to guarantee that the sovereignty of the states would be respected. In a somewhat contradictory vein, the USSR and a number of East European nations argued that because the Declaration was so "abstract" it was worthless in terms of making any effective human rights guarantees and, thus, there was little reason to approve it. While this position may seem hypocritical, it may also be interpreted as a realistic appraisal of the problem of international human rights. On the one hand, if a bill of rights is to be effective, it must be expressed in terms of positive law. On the other hand, any attempt at positive law at the international level is bound to fail, since the first principle of the law of nations is a respect for each nation's sovereignty and an unwillingness by each to surrender that sovereignty.[25]

On December 9 and 10, 1948, the General Assembly discussed the Declaration for the final time prior to approving it. The same arguments were repeated. Canada regretted that the wording of the document was vague and imprecise. South Africa regretted that the wording was too precise and did not give individual states more freedom in applying its principles to their particular situations. The USSR regretted that the articles on slavery and the right to education were not specific and concrete enough. East European states reiterated the USSR's concern that such an abstract set of standards had little value in terms of effectiveness.[26]

To conclude: The sovereignty question was a major philosophical issue in the drafting of the Universal Declaration of Human Rights. Western insensitivity to its importance gave the smaller Soviet bloc cause for worry over the possible consequences of an attempt to universalize Western notions of human rights. Practically every nation that entered the discussion alluded to the sovereignty question in one way or another. Western bloc nations usually alluded to it indirectly, by arguing that the ideals should be expressed more concretely and less abstractly, more as enforceable laws than as moral ideals. The underlying assumption of such statements is that the United Nations had the legal as well as the moral authority to pass laws to which the nations of the world would be subject. Soviet bloc nations, and a few others such as the Union of South Africa, expressed the philosophical viewpoint that no political body had the authority to intervene in the internal affairs of nations and the practical concern that the United Nations might attempt to use human rights as a smoke screen for interfering in the affairs of less powerful nations.

NATIONAL SOVEREIGNTY AND HUMAN SIN

The thesis of this section is that a major source of conflict in the human rights movement has been caused by the conflicting demands of national sovereignty and human sin. At first glance these two concepts, one political and the other theological, may not seem to be related or in conflict with one another. Among Western human rights advocates, however, there has been a sharp division on this issue. Many of those who have affirmed national sovereignty have played down what theologians refer to as sin. Those conscious of the propensity of persons and nations to do evil, to act in their own self-interest, have for this reason expressed little respect for the sovereignty of nations. The exception to this rule, as chapter 7 will point out, is Reinhold Niebuhr. Niebuhr's concept of depravity is so radical that, somewhat paradoxically, it makes him a respecter of national sovereignty. He believes that political bodies are incapable of being much else than sovereign, self-interested entities. For Niebuhr, the choice is not sovereignty "or" sin, but sovereignty "and" sin. His is a "both/and" rather than an "either/or" solution. The following analysis of moral idealism and legal realism will describe the impasse created by these "either/or" approaches and thus will lay the groundwork for discussion of Niebuhr's "both/and" solution to the problems of sovereignty and sin.

In the debate among Western advocates of universal human rights, those who have shown respect for national sovereignty, but little awareness of the limitations imposed by sin, have come to be known as "moral idealists." Those who have shown greater awareness of the propensity of nations to maximize self-interest, and thus a great interest in holding tight reins on nations, are known as "legal positivists." To show the contrast between legal positivists and the moral idealists, I will refer to legal positivists as "legal realists." The debate between the moral idealists and the legal realists has been the most divisive of debates among Western advocates of international human rights. The debate has centered around the differences between natural law and positive law, assumptions of a natural state of goodness versus a natural state of evil, and solutions to human rights problems based upon national development versus solutions based upon international law.

Moral Idealism

Jacques Maritain is, in many ways, a good example of a moral idealist. He claims to be aware of the danger of too naive a view of sin, but seems more concerned about avoiding the opposite problem—too cynical a view of the human potential for progress. He sees himself as proposing a via media between the extremes of pseudo-idealism and pseudo-realism, with the former promising too much and delivering too little, and the latter promising too little and ignoring the transcendent dimension of humanity. Maritain believes that his somewhat qualified notion of progress offers a middle way between "both the illusory notion of necessary progress, conceived after the manner of Condorcet, and that denial or dislike of progress which prevails today among those who have lost faith in man and freedom, and which is in itself a principle of historical suicide."[27]

Interestingly enough, Niebuhr also views himself as offering a middle way between cynicism and idealism. But for Niebuhr, the problem is the idealism which dominates the human rights movement rather than any cynicism that would detract from it. Even though Niebuhr and Maritain view themselves as moderates between the two extremes, they would certainly view each other as extremists. Maritain is precisely the sort of moral idealist that sours Niebuhr towards liberalism. Niebuhr takes such a pragmatic approach for a man of religion that he must be one of those Maritain has in mind when distressing about "those who have lost their faith in man and freedom."

At times Maritain seems to be preaching directly at Niebuhr. Rather than blaming "sin" for all the evils of the world, Maritain argues that they be attributed to the youthfulness of the human race. He cites Teilhard de Chardin's statement that "humanity is still *very young.*" These are problems that, with time and experience and the development of wisdom, can be corrected. Writing in 1942, Maritain counsels those in the West who have lost their faith in humanity to consider the war as a temporary thwarting, rather than as the end, of human progress. "If we take as our perspective the entire history of life and humanity, wherein we must employ a scale of duration incomparably greater than that to which we are used in our ordinary experience, we recover faith in the forward march of our species."[28]

Another point on which Maritain locks horns with the realists, and especially Niebuhr, is over the question of whether force or freedom should be the basis for unifying a broken world. He sharply condemns the realists' reliance upon external, coercive force ("coercion" and "force" are two of Niebuhr's favorite terms) rather than the internally unifying forces brought about by "the progress of moral conscience." In his defense he cites Teilhard:

> Coercive unification only gives rise to a surface pseudo-unity. It can assemble a piece of machinery, but it cannot bring about any basic synthesis; and, as a result, it does not engender any growth of conscience. It materializes, in fact, instead of spiritualizing.

There is a unifying force associated with freedom, also, but it holds things together from within, through attraction to a transcendent center, rather than from without, through external pressure. Maritain does not deny the need for external coercion but sees freedom as a higher way. Love between men and nations is the ultimate goal, and freedom is a prerequisite for love.[29] As Niebuhr will argue later on, justice, despite all its negative connotations regarding the necessity of force, is a prerequisite for love. The promotion of internal, spiritual freedom can and should be the concern of educational and religious bodies but the primary concern of states and societies of states, according to the realists, should be the protection of human rights through legal and/or political channels.

On the subject of utopia, Maritain's moral idealism continues to express a concern for imperfection but not for the more radical notion of sin. Maritain does not believe that utopia is something that will be attained in history but he does believe that progress is made by striving toward it in freedom, all the while promoting love and community. "The establishment of a *brotherly city* where man shall be free from misery and bondage," he writes, is an ideal which "constitutes a 'limit' attainable at infinity, and we must strive towards it all the more vigorously because its realization can be only approximate here below."[30] Niebuhr believes that a better way of handling the impossible-to-reach ideals is not to grit one's teeth and try harder but to distinguish between the ideals one dreams about and the goals one strives for. To do otherwise is to set one's ideals too low or one's goals too high. The former reflects cynicism, the latter pride, or ignorance of the human condition. Maritain's confusion of ideals and goals is like a person who, after falling flat on his or her face after attempting to fly, deals with this failure by "trying harder" rather than by setting a more realistic goal. Niebuhr and other realists are content to aim lower, at establishing more moderate levels of order and justice. In an atmosphere of order and justice, some love and community may develop but this is "icing on the cake," as it were. The realists' problem with Maritain's approach is that by aiming too high, Maritain is in danger of achieving nothing in terms of concrete, historical progress. Ironically, the children of darkness might achieve more real progress in the area of human rights than the children of light.

Nowhere is the difference between moral idealism and the various forms of realism more evident than in Maritain's comments on human nature. Maritain states that his belief in political progress toward a utopian ideal is based upon what he calls "the reality of human nature." The realists also claim to base their political philosophy on the reality of human nature. Maritain's is an essential reality, however, and the realists' is an existential one. The sort of sin that Maritain does discover in human existence is no cause for great human concern (or, for that matter, divine concern). It can be fixed, he says in one unfortunate analogy, as easily as a piano can be tuned. More easily, in fact, since humanity "is endowed with intelligence" and thus is capable of "tuning" itself—"it is up to him to put himself in tune with the ends necessarily demanded by his nature." The piano analogy betrays some rather sanguine assumptions regarding human nature, sin, and redemption.[31]

According to Maritain, the locus of the problem of international human rights is not the self-interested nature of people and nations, as the realists would claim but a lack of a common "philosophy of life" between the various peoples and nations of the world. Maritain identifies the problem as a cultural one, one that can be solved through dialogue rather than through force. There is, once again, a naively optimistic dimension to this analysis of the problem but that is not the whole story. Maritain argues effectively that the attempts of legal realists to enact positive international human rights laws will be of little use as long as the peoples of the world do not agree on a "scale of values," a "philosophy of life." Laws are based on moral values, and moral values must be understood and shared before laws can be shared. In a statement more pessimistic than one might expect from a moral idealist, Maritain pointedly criticizes the naive optimism of the legal realists(!) "On this point," he says in regard to the achievement of positive international human rights laws, "I should not venture to express more than the most guarded optimism. For to reach agreement, no longer merely on the definition of human rights, but on arrangements for their exercise in daily life, the first necessity . . . would be agreement on a scale of values."[32] Maritain's point is that the legal realists ignore the divergences among cultures and nations and naively assume that they can successfully apply Western legal standards to the rest of the world.

On this point Niebuhr and Maritain come close to converging. Both believe that there is something unrealistic about using international laws to solve human rights problems. For Maritain it is unrealistic because of cultural differences. Problems can be solved, however, if peoples and cultures will sit down and discuss their differences. Maritain believes that because a universal natural law exists, such a discussion will reveal there are some common bases for international law beneath the surface differences. But this will take considerable dialogue.

For Niebuhr, there is a political problem that runs deeper than the cultural one. It is a problem that would exist even between nations that shared similar cultures. It is a problem that will never be "solved" and thus is a reality that must be lived with. It is a problem that is inherent in the power structure of nation-states and, for that matter, any other corporate bodies. It is the problem, or rather the reality, of national sovereignty. Nations, if they are to be nations, must be sovereign. There is no such thing as a "nonsovereign nation." Such an expression would be a tautological surd, a contradiction in terms.

Legal Realism

Whereas moral idealists appealed to natural law in an effort to elevate humanity toward a universal moral ideal, legal realists attempted to establish positive laws and positive means of enforcement in an effort to restrain humanity from sinking too far into the depths of its depravity.

International jurist Hersch Lauterpacht expressed the view that the United Nations should move (1) in the direction of turning human rights ideals into positive, international laws and (2) from recognition of sovereign nations to the recognition of a sovereign world government. The problem of human rights violations, he said, "cannot be solved except within the framework and under the shelter of the positive law of an organized Society of States." Lauterpacht cites Immanuel Kant as the prophet of such an international governing body. Without positive laws and an authority to enforce them, universal human rights remains a "vague phrase" and a lofty ideal rather than an enthroned reality.[33] The barriers to universal human rights, Lauterpacht believes, are twofold. One is the excessive respect given to natural law by many of the advocates of human rights. The other is the excessive respect given to state sovereignty.

Lauterpacht argues that natural law has little to do with international human rights. International protection of human rights, he says, is "independent of any doctrine of natural law and natural rights." What is needed is not eloquent ideals and "high-sounding phrase" but "specific rules of law and effective legal remedies." Those who advocate an International Bill of the Rights of Man, he said, "would do well to steer clear of any elusive and illusory conceptions of the law of nature and natural rights."[34] One reason for Lauterpacht's skepticism is that bare statements of natural law principles lack force. The other is that they lack clarity.

They lack intrinsic force because they are backed up only by appeals to conscience and to the public opinion of the world. If the nations of the world are serious about international human rights, Lauterpacht argues, they should do that which would bring about the fulfillment of such an ideal. The only thing he believes capable of bringing about such a state of affairs is "an International Bill of the Rights of Man ... conceived, not as a declaration of principles [natural law], but as part of positive law, as a part of the constitutional law both of States and of the Society of States at large."[35]

The other reason for Lauterpacht's skepticism is that bare statements of natural law lack clarity. As ideals, they are often expressed in terms so general, abstract, vague and even contradictory, that it is difficult to determine what it is that they are advocating. This is particularly true of international human rights declarations and treaties. Often the urge to reach an agreement—any agreement—is so great that precision is sacrificed for the sake of "unity." The wording is sufficiently vague to allow each party to the "agreement" its own interpretation of what was "agreed" upon. Such agreements, Lauterpacht believes, have little value. They are "innocuous" and "ineffectual." Language is slippery. Its capacity "for evasion or concealment of thought is infinite." This is particularly the case with "the language of international intercourse," and thus Lauterpacht prefers the precise language of the legal profession.[36]

The single most barrier to the achievement of universal human rights is, in Lauterpacht's opinion, the nations' insistence on their rights to sovereignty. International human rights "cannot be achieved at a nominal price." The price of international human rights is a "radical" innovation: the "surrender ... of the sovereign rights of the State." "It is clear, therefore, that the International Bill of Rights of Man, conceived as one of the bases of the future international order, cannot be accepted without a substantial sacrifice by States of their freedom of action."[37]

Lauterpacht criticizes the Dumbarton Oaks Proposals for trying to have the "cake" (international human rights) and eat it (state sovereignty), too. "By making human freedoms a matter of international interest," the proposals assert the right of interference. In the same breath, however, the proposals assert the principle of noninterference—"the system of government upon which these freedoms depend is not of effective international concern." Lauterpacht prefers to assert the right of interference. He proposes an International Bill of the Rights of Man that would become "an effective and enforceable part of International Law and of the Organization of the United Nations." By implication, Lauterpacht is suggesting that the United Nations become an international governing body—"The direct consequence of that assumption is that the highest executive organ for the Organization, namely, the Council, must assume responsibility for its ultimate enforcement." The problem with the Dumbarton Oaks Proposals was that they conferred "no executive powers of enforcement" upon the United Nations so that it could "bear the general responsibility for the protection of human rights and fundamental freedoms." The Dumbarton Oaks Proposals were afraid of challenging the nations' right of sovereignty. Lauterpacht is not, because he views sovereignty as essentially a bad thing, especially in the twentieth century, when the "unbridled sovereignty" of certain states created "international anarchy" and threatened to destroy "both the rights of man and the heritage of his civilization."[38]

In view of the destructive capacities of Germany, Italy, Japan, and their allies, Lauterpacht has no interest in supporting the principle of national sovereignty. His reaction is understandable. World War II might have been "nipped in the bud" if Western democracies had not been so reluctant to interfere in the affairs of the Axis nations. It is also understandable, however, that the Soviet bloc would be concerned about such strong advocacy of interventionism. As already pointed out, the Soviet bloc constituted a minority within the United Nations and was a likely victim of such intervention. Chapter 7 will critique Lauterpacht's argument for world government from the perspective of Niebuhr's theologically informed realism. Because Niebuhr's view of sin is so radical, he offers a more "realistic," more effective, solution to the problems that national sovereignty and human sin pose for international human rights.

NOTES

1. United Nations, *Yearbook of the United Nations 1948–49* (New York: Columbia University Press in Cooperation with the United Nations, 1950), 528, 532, 534.
2. Ibid., 534.
3. Sergi Vishnevsky, *Pravda,* June 11, 1977, reprinted in *Human Rights and American Diplomacy: 1975–77,* ed. Judith F. Buncher (New York: Facts On File, 1977), 253.
4. "U.S. Assails Russia on Human Rights Violations," *Los Angeles Times,* 13 December 1977, sec. 1, 5; Jonathan Rollow, "U.S., Soviets Trade Sharp Charges at U.N. Rights Meeting," *Washington Post,* 8 March 1978, A24.
5. K.U. Chernenko, "For Lasting Peace and Dependable Security in Europe," in *Speeches and Writings,* 2nd ed. (New York: Pergamon Press, 1984), 61–72.
6. Alexander Solzhenitsyn, *Warning to the West* (New York: Farrar, Straus and Giroux, 1981), 48.
7. Arpad Kadarkay, *Human Rights in American and Russian Political Thought* (Washington, D.C.: University Press of America, 1982), 209–10.
8. Ibid., 210–12.
9. Ibid., 209–12.
10. Ibid., 212–13.

11. A. Petrov, "And What Is the Final Act?" *Moscow News, Supplement*, 26 March–2 April 1977, 14, cited by George H. Brand, "Human Rights: Rhetoric or Reality" in *Human Rights: Rhetoric or Reality*, eds. George W. Forell and William H. Lazareth (Philadelphia: Fortress Press, 1978), 11.

12. Yuri Kornilov quoted by Angus Deming, "The Push for Human Rights," *Newsweek*, 20 June 1977, 53.

13. James M. Markham, "Red Chiefs at Madrid Parley Skirt Issue of Soviet-Bloc Repression," *New York Times*, 4 March 1977, A4.

14. *New York Times*, 4 November 1977, sec. 1, 1; Eugene Kamenka and A.E.-S. Tay, "Human Rights in the Soviet Union," *World Review* 19:2 (1980): 52.

15. Leonid Brezhnev, "Speech to the Sixteenth Trade Union Council," 1977 reprinted in *The Human Rights Reader* eds. Walter Laqueur and Barry Rubin (New York: New American Library, Meridian Books, 1979), 309.

16. Bernard Gwertzman, "Carter and Mondale See Bukovsky, A Soviet Dissident," *New York Times*, 22 March 1977, A4; Benjamin C. Bradlee, *Washington Post* article, 6 March 1977, reprinted in *Human Rights and American Diplomacy*, ed. Buncher, 185–86.

17. Jimmy Carter, NATO address, 10 May 1977, reprinted in *Human Rights and American Diplomacy*, ed. Buncher, 180; Rosalynn Carter, remarks to Foreign Minister Antonio Azeredo da Silveira, 6 June 1977 reprinted in *Human Rights and American Diplomacy*, ed. Buncher, 183.

18. Robert Muldoon, Associated Press interview, 11 June 1977, reprinted in *Human Rights and American Diplomacy*, ed. Buncher, 253.

19. Fouad Ajami, *Human Rights and World Order Politics* (New York: Institute for World Order, 1978), 31.

20. Nigel S. Rodley makes this point in discussing exceptions to the United Nations Charter's domestic jurisdiction rule (Article 2(7)). See Rodley, "Monitoring Human Rights Violations in the 1980's," in *Enhancing Global Human Rights*, eds. Jorge I. Dominguez, Nigel S. Rodley, Bryce Wood, and Richard Falk (New York: McGraw-Hill Book Co., 1979), 121–22.

21. United Nations, *Yearbook*, 527.

22. Ibid.

23. Ibid., 527–28.

24. Ibid., 527.

25. Ibid., 528–29.

26. Ibid., 532–34.

27. Jacques Maritain, *The Rights of Man and Natural Law*, trans. Doris C. Anson (New York: Charles Scribner's Sons, 1949), 38, 109–10.

28. Ibid., 58, 30. Maritain does not go as far as those who believe that human progress is necessary and linear. He likes to use the term "thwarted" (in the sense of "frustrated," not in the sense of "defeated") to refer to his own concept of progress. The movement toward progress is a "thwarted movement," he says, as if to suggest that for every step forward there may be a half step backward. "The thwarted progress of humanity moves in the direction of human emancipation, not only in the political order but also in the economic and social order, in such a way that the diverse forms of servitude ... may be abolished by degrees, as human history approaches its term." Such progress, which in the opinion of

this writer could be described more accurately as "gradual" than as "thwarted," occurs at all levels—institutional and personal. It involves "not only the transition to better states of organization, but also . . . to a better awareness of the dignity of the human person in each of us, and of the primacy of brotherly love amid all the values of our life. In this manner," Maritain concludes, "we shall advance towards the conquest of freedom (30-33)." This certainly is not a very radical view of evil. Evil is treated as more of a nuisance than anything else. It slows down progress, but does not stop it. At least Maritain is aware that there are barriers in the road to progress, small though they may be. Sometimes it seems that Maritain, who so liberally uses such high-sounding expressions as "the dignity of the human person," "the primacy of brotherly love," and "the conquest of freedom" (whatever that means), is more concerned about how human rights conditions should be in some abstract utopia that does not exist than about human rights in time and space and history, under the conditions of sin.

29. Ibid., 30-33.
30. Ibid., 107-08, 47.
31. Ibid., 47-48, 60-61.
32. Maritain, "Introduction," *Human Rights: Comments and Interpretations*, ed. UNESCO (New York: Allan Wingate, 1950), 17; Maritain, "The Meaning of Human Rights" in Brandeis Lawyers Society, *Publications*, vol. 2 (Philadelphia, 1949), 23.
33. H[ersch] Lauterpacht, *An International Bill of the Rights of Man* (New York: Columbia University Press, 1945), v-vi.
34, Ibid., 3.
35. Ibid., 50.
36. Ibid., 38-39.
37. Ibid., 82.
38. Ibid., 214, 40.

7

FROM GLOBAL HEGEMONY TO NATIONAL SOVEREIGNTY

Reinhold Niebuhr seldom used the term "human rights," but the issue was a preoccupation of his during the decades of the forties and fifties. Though less optimistic than many Western supporters of the United Nations, he still believed that gradual progress could be achieved through this instrument of international order. For Niebuhr, however, progress in the area of international human rights would be a by-product of progress in the area of world order. Efforts to improve international human rights through direct means—international courts of justice, international armies, majority rule in the UN—would prove counterproductive. Such direct approaches would ignore two inevitable features of nation states—their sovereignty and their sinfulness. Attempts to turn the United Nations into an international governing body could only produce conflict because minority nations would resist the extrinsic control of the majority and because no nation could be expected to transcend its own self-interest in ruling on matters of international justice. It would be naive to expect sovereign, sinful nations to function together as an impartial international agency of justice.

Such pessimism did not, however, make Niebuhr the full-fledged cynic that he is often accused of being, and that some of his disciples may have become. Niebuhr believed that progress in international human rights was possible through approaching the matter indirectly, through the gradual process of building bonds of mutual trust between nations. Such trust could not be established through high-sounding declarations or legislative fiat. It could only be nurtured over time by nations communicating regularly, cooperating in small ways, and gradually developing mutual trust. The structure of the United Nations provided just the atmosphere in which this trust could be nurtured, as long as the United Nations resisted the temptation to become an executive, legislative, and judicial body. If this were to happen a majority coalition would inevitably develop to further its own interests at the expense of the minority. Instead of becoming an instrument of international order, peace, and justice, the United Nations would become an instrument of discord, war, and injustice.

This, in a nutshell, is Reinhold Niebuhr's view of the problems of Western political hegemony and of the United Nations as an instrument of international human rights. I will now attempt to explicate Niebuhr's position more fully. First, I will develop a Niebuhrian critique of the three major approaches to human rights at the time of the United Nations' formation: moral idealism, legal realism, and cynical realism. Second, I will show how Niebuhr's solution is a middle way between a number of unacceptable extremes. Finally, I will describe Niebuhr's own vision for achieving international human rights and peace within the limitations imposed by national sovereignty and human sin.

PROBLEMS WITH MORAL IDEALIST, LEGAL REALIST, AND CYNICAL REALIST APPROACHES

As chapter 6 observed, the two leading advocates of international human rights in the late forties and early fifties are fittingly described as the moral idealists and the legal realists. Moral idealists believed that the purpose of the United Nations should be to get the nations of the world to agree to a common set of human rights ideals. The Universal Declaration of Human Rights, ratified December 10, 1948, was the culmination of this effort. The legal realists believed that only by translating these ideals into enforceable international laws could universal human rights be realized. Niebuhr believed that neither understood the limitations imposed upon international human rights efforts by national sovereignty and human sin.

Moral Idealism

One of Niebuhr's criticisms of the moral idealists was that they romanticized about the future. In 1942, he accused them of expecting some sort of miracle to occur at the end of the war that would make nations act differently toward one another than they had ever acted before. Up to this time the Allied Nations had failed to cooperate militarily or politically. Washington dominated the military decision-making and Great Britain, drawing upon its imperial network and the diplomatic skills of Churchill, dominated the political scene. The United States and Great Britain had seldom sought advice from any of the other nations, yet the moral idealists naively believed that this unwillingness to cooperate would miraculously disappear after the war. Niebuhr accused idealists of divorcing the future from the present and assuming that powerful nations would give up their power once the war ended. If cooperation were to be the norm after the war, Niebuhr suggested that it be the norm during the war. For example, he suggested that Britain and India let the United States, the Soviet Union, China, and many smaller nations help them solve the problems of independence for India.[1]

Niebuhr compared the efforts of sentimentalists to escape into a utopian future to an errant husband who, "finding difficulty in working out the day to day conditions of happy marital life, beguiled his leisure by writing a book on The Ideal Marriage." Such sentimentality, he said, "is not Christian idealism."[2] He urged Christians to develop an idealism that is realistic about the future and related to the actual problems of the present, not lost in starry-eyed utopian dreams. Otherwise, human rights becomes a matter so eschatologically removed from the present as to have no bearing upon the present. From a Niebuhrian perspective, eschatological hopes should be expressed in proximate ways that can press upon the present as well as judge the present from afar. It is ironic and tragic, but those with the highest and most absolute moral ideals have the least to offer in terms of translating those ideals into the present temporal dimension. The children of light must learn to express their human rights ideals in terms that take into consideration the limitations posed by the present and abiding sinfulness of nations.

Niebuhr cautioned against the Christian impulse toward perfectionism—"the Christian answer to a problem is not simply the most ideal possible solution which the imagination can conceive." The Christian faith teaches not only high ideals but also "the recalcitrance of sin on every level of moral and social achievement," and so the Christian should not fall victim to "the alternate moods of illusion and disillusionment which harass the world of idealists and secularists."[3] In 1944, moral idealists opposed peace initiatives and proposals for the establishment of a United Nations on the grounds that the initiatives and proposals aimed too far below their ideals. Niebuhr remarked that, by their standards, nothing short of "a perfect constitutional system" would be acceptable. He reminded perfectionists that creating a democratic United Nations is "the most difficult task mankind has ever faced" and that such a task cannot be completed overnight—"we cannot expect to do more in our generation than to lay minimal foundations." Niebuhr observed that, ironically, moral idealists are arguing for the same thing as the cynical realists who, for opposite reasons, are seeking the same end, that is, "to evade international

commitments." Niebuhr considered both groups, the idealistic internationalists and the cynical nationalists, to be "irresponsible."[4]

Niebuhr's second criticism of the moral idealists concerned the self-
righteous pride that accompanied their idealism. He considered this pride a
major cause of the rise of anti-American sentiment around the world,
which in turn inhibited the progress of international human rights initiatives sponsored by the U.S. Writing in 1954, he pointed out that some of
this animosity is due to their sin of "envy" rather than any sin of our own.
They envy, or covet, the power and wealth of those who have more than
they do. But the "basic cause of anti-American animus," Niebuhr alleged, is
due to the American sin of pride—"the pride and arrogance of a nation as
powerful as we are and as certain of its virtue as we have come to be."
Drunk with our victory in the Second World War, we Americans have
come "to combine the pride of power of Babylon with the pride of virtue of
Israel." Because this problem in international politics is "basically a
religious one," Niebuhr recommended a religious solution—that the United States "moderate the arrogance of a self-righteous nation."[5]

Such self-righteous pride is not only a sin in and of itself, but it begets a
number of other sins, such as quietism, fanaticism, and militarism. When
their unrealistic demands for universal rights are not met, idealists are
more likely to throw up their hands in prideful resignation than to develop
more realistic suggestions for small steps that can be taken toward international order and justice. They might retreat into smaller communities of
persons who share their idealism rather than adapt their ideals to the larger
community. The same self-righteousness that begets quietism is also capable of begetting fanaticism. The nation that views itself as good and its
enemy as evil—forgetting about God's judgmental stance toward all—
might go to fanatical extremes in its efforts to promote goodness in the
world. That nation should be aware of its own shortcomings and of the way
that sin and finitude inhibit all efforts at goodness, and it should seek more
modest goals.[6]

Niebuhr often pointed out that evil is as likely to result from prideful
idealism as from an intentionally evil will. Pride blinds the idealists to the
limitations of themselves and of their notions of human rights, and such a
blinded idealist is capable of using the most destructive of measures if for a
cause to which he or she is absolutely committed. Even the atrocities of
Hitler and Stalin, Niebuhr observed on numerous occasions, were committed not because of a desire to do evil but because of a commitment to do
good that was blinded by self-righteousness. "It is very important to realize," Niebuhr wrote in 1951, "that most of the evil in this world is not due
to malice, but to an idealism of men who have effaced the distinction between God and man." The cruelty of even the most totalitarian regimes, he
argued, is not caused by malice, "primarily," but finds its roots in "a mon-
strous pretension."[7]

The third shortcoming of the moral idealists was closely related to the other two. They used absolutist and chiliastic terms to describe the future of the world. Both Soviets and Westerners, Niebuhr observed, viewed the future in terms of "win or lose" rather than some sort of "draw." Both had a "one world or none" philosophy that reduced international conflicts to "good" versus "evil" rather than to a conflict between shades of grey. Such a philosophy ignored the fact that East–West conflicts were far from being resolved, with neither side showing much interest in resolving them. Such a philosophy militated against the compromise and "patience" necessary to resolve conflicts between nations. Instead it encouraged "blindness" and "hysteria," and preached a "dogma of an irreconcilable conflict between the capitalist and communist world."[8]

The slogan "one world or none" was quite popular among Western human rights idealists in the forties. Ironically, such a slogan created more despair than hope, more division than unity. Since there was little hope of achieving one world in the foreseeable future, Niebuhr said, "the logical conclusion . . . is that we are fated to have no world at all," and such logic "drives us to despair." What began as an overly optimistic statement of hope resulted in an overly pessimistic feeling of despair. The other unintended result, disunity, was brought about in a number of ways. Such a slogan tended to divide the world according to those who favor one world and those who would rather maintain a balance of power between a number of sovereign states. Those who believe in one world are put into one camp, those who do not are put into the other. "This absolute division of the world into two warring camps in the name of 'one world' is a nice indication of the absurdity of pure logic in human history," Niebuhr commented. Another way it encouraged disunity was by creating a division among Western idealists themselves. Some wanted to create one world by granting the Communists their demands, while others, such as McCarthy, wanted to create it by subduing Communism. Still others wanted to set up a "world government" and, if the Soviets or anyone else did not want to participate, "these idealists [seemed] ready to bring on another world war in the name of world government."[9]

The irony and tragedy of such a strong idealism, then, is that believing too strongly in international peace and human rights can result in just the opposite—international discord and violence. Niebuhr's counsel to moral idealists was that they learn to be patient, resist the temptation to turn a human rights initiative into the battle of Armageddon, and avoid expressing their ideals in absolutist terms. Their sin was the sin of pride, which had "no understanding of the limits of human powers, of the ambiguity in all human virtues, of the partial character of all human wisdom and of the precariousness of all human achievements." They must learn to live by faith, realizing that people and nations, unlike the realms of science and nature, are free, unpredictable, and uncontrollable. No human action was

capable of guaranteeing universal human rights. No nation could be co-
erced into adopting a certain standard of human rights. Thus, Niebuhr
believed, a "now or never" attitude was bound to be counterproductive.
Reform could only come in small, relatively undramatic steps.[10]

Legal Realism, or "Constitutional Idealism"

From Niebuhr's perspective, legal realists made many of the same mistakes as the moral idealists. They aimed too high—at the immediate
realization of the ideal rather the gradual development of trust between
and reform within nations. They could be self-righteous concerning Western concepts of human rights. Like the moral idealists, they could appeal to
natural law as the basis for international human rights. The main difference between the two, from the legal realists' perspective, was that the
legal realists translated these natural laws into positive laws that could be
interpreted and enforced by an international governing body. Legal realists
recognized the limitations of education, communication, and understanding. They believed that laws backed by force were necessary if human
rights ideals were to become human rights realities.[11] Legal realists thus
felt they had adopted a more "realistic" approach to the international
human rights situation. From Niebuhr's perspective, however, legal
realists were no more realistic than the moral idealists. Instead of calling
them "legal realists," he called them "constitutional idealists" to emphasize their similarities with the moral idealists. These legal realists, or
constitutional idealists, made several false assumptions concerning the
way that national and international communities are formed and maintained. Each of these misconceptions was based upon a failure to interpret
the insights of the Enlightenment and of the eighteenth century revolutions in light of the Judeo-Christian notions of history and sin.

One misconception of the legal realists was that constitutions could
create community. "Governments cannot create community, whether
national or international," Niebuhr pointed out on numerous occasions.
They can only "perfect" the community that already exists.[12] The failure of
legal realists to create a world community resulted not from poor statecraft
but from a naive assumption that world community could be created "by
legal, constitutional, and governmental means," as though the complex
problems of universal human rights could be dealt with "in purely logical
and constitutional terms." Such an assumption ignores the fact, "which
history attests on every page," that while governments may be able to "perfect the order and justice of a community," they "cannot create a community." Laws and police and courts of law are efficacious only within
communities that generate and respect them. They are useful only "to sup-

press *incidental* recalcitrance *against the will of the community"* [italics mine].[13] Communities, whether local, national, or international, must be built slowly through the gradual development of trust between persons, institutions, or nations. Trust develops historically, not in the abstract. Thus "abstract commitments to ideal and impossible world constitutions" are not nearly as important as many idealistic Americans made them out to be. "World community must gradually grow through acts of mutual loyalty."[14]

Community creates government, then, and not vice versa. Legal realists thought that if the statecraft were better—the laws more just, the means of enforcement more defined—that community could be created. Niebuhr believed that community, or "social tissue," must be a "given" that wise statecraft could "cut, sew and redesign ... to a limited degree" but could never create. "No group of individuals has ever created either government or community out of whole cloth."[15] A better understanding of sin, closer attention to historical patterns in relations between nations, and less respect for the power of an idea to become an historical reality simply on the virtue of its merit (in the abstract) would have helped the constitutional idealist be more realistic about the international human rights situation.

Niebuhr believed that the American faith in the ability of constitutional solutions to solve political problems stems from our perception of how the United States came into being. We believe that our nation was created by constitutional fiat, and "we think it our special business to ask the world to do in macrocosm what we so successfully accomplished in microcosm." Such a view ignores the fact that there were forces of cohesion present prior to the drafting of the United States Constitution. "The fear of a common foe, the shared experiences of the battlefield, a very considerable degree of similar culture"—these experiences were the "organic," "historical," factors that created community. The Constitution merely perfected it, creating "a more perfect union." A social contract cannot create a community *ex nihilo.* It can merely shape the community that already exists.[16]

The other misconception of the legal realists was that the cohesion of an international community was analogous to the cohesion of a national community. The two are so different, Niebuhr said, as to be a difference "of kind rather than degree."[17] Efforts to replicate in the global macrocosm what happened in the American microcosm were thus doomed to fail. The difference between national and international community involved several factors, political and social, that constitutional idealists did not understand.

The political factor concerns the extent to which nations must protect their sovereignty if they wish to survive as nations. Constitutional idealists naively believed that nations would "abrogate or abridge their sovereignty" for the sake of a global constitutional order, apparently unaware that "no such explicit abnegation has ever taken place in the history of the world."[18] The idea of creating a universal constitutional sovereignty completely disregards the peculiar nature of corporate entities. If nations relinquish their sovereignty, they cease to be nations. Constitutional idealists naively believed that a diplomat representing a nation at an international conference could and would offer to relinquish that nation's autonomy to the other nations of the world. Constitutional idealists would have regarded such a diplomat as a champion of international peace and justice; however, that diplomat's own nation would have regarded him or her as a traitor.

In 1944, Niebuhr supported the Dumbarton Oaks Proposals because they aimed at more modest goals than the formation of an international governing body. They recognized the fact, attested throughout history, that powerful nations are "not likely to abridge their sovereignty in favor of a great world system."[19] The following year, when the United Nations Charter was being formulated, a major debate developed over the insistence of the more powerful nations that they be given veto power in the General Assembly. Constitutional idealists objected that this would strip the UN of its power as an international governing body. The nations viewed the veto as the means of protecting their autonomy.[20] Niebuhr observed that if the majority of the United Nations voted to change something in a minority of the nations, and if the minority did not have the power of the veto, then the minority would be faced with two options, neither of which would promote world community. If they acquiesced, then what would the power to which they had acquiesced become other than a totalitarian world government? As the majority recognized its power over the minority, it would become a tyrannous regime indeed.

In the forties this would have meant the formation of a Western-controlled majority coalition that would have tried to impose its will upon the Communist nations. Most likely the Communist minority would not acquiesce but would defy the ruling of the majority. At this point the majority could either back down from its position, which would be tantamount to dissolving the United Nations, or it could attempt to use coercion to enforce its decision, which would be tantamount to declaring World War III. Without the veto power today, the most likely scenario would be a power play of Third World nations against the nations to the North.

One social factor ignored by constitutional idealists (and also moral idealists) concerns the natural forces of cohesion that hold a nation together and hold nations apart. "National and imperial communities all have ethnic, linguistic, geographic, historical, and other forces of social unity," Niebuhr argued, whereas universal communities have no common culture or language or geography or history "to create the consciousness of 'we'." Even in an ethnically pluralistic nation like the United States, there are still the bonds of a shared language, geography, history, and religion, as well as a common love for freedom as defined by Western liberalism. The world community has no such forces of cohesion. The bonds that give individual nations their unity also give them their autonomy—what makes community possible on the national scale makes community impossible on the international scale.[21]

Another social factor that constitutional idealists (as well as moral idealists) misunderstood is the effect of improved technology, communication, and transportation upon international relations. A naive appraisal might suggest that these advances would improve the relations between nations. Improvements in technology could be shared among nations and promote the advancement of all. Improvements in communication and transportation could bring the nations of the world "closer together," as it were. Technology could, in short, transform the world into a global community. This scenario would be true except for one factor that idealists consistently ignored—namely, that the nations of the world do not view themselves as mere members of a global family but as autonomous units whose self-preservation is based upon the degree of sovereignty that can be maintained against the forces of disintegration. Advances in technology, Niebuhr argued, do not usually lead to greater cooperation but to greater competition, as each nation's survival is dependent on its ability to maximize its resources for its own self-interest. Rather than improving relations between nations, the shrinking size of the world is as likely to "change the ocean barriers of yesterday into the battlegrounds of today." Rather than improving upon the instruments of communication and transportation which draw peoples together, advances in technology are as likely to "increase the deadly efficacy of the instruments of war" which drive peoples apart.[22] By ignoring the role of sin in the relations of nations, idealists failed to recognize the way that technological improvements (which are capable of drawing the peoples of the world together) become, tragically and ironically, the means by which the peoples of the world are pulled apart.

What has been shown thus far is that both the moral idealists and the legal realists, or constitutional idealists, were too unrealistic for Niebuhr's tastes. They had such a strong confidence in the possibility of the new, or such a great ignorance of the lessons of the past, that they failed to consider the decisive influence of human sin and national sovereignty upon efforts to secure international human rights. Blinded by "pride and pretence," they had a strong confidence in their own ability to create a new world order, forgetting "the fact that they are creatures of God with only limited power" to do so. Blinded by a facile optimism, they replaced clear and realistic thinking with wishful thinking, operating on the fallacious assumptions that "the desirability of world order proves the attainability of world government"[23] and that the best solution to a problem is the most utopian solution imaginable. Their ambitions may have been praiseworthy and their motives sincere, but their actions would bear no good fruit because they ignored the presence of sin and sovereignty in the structure of nations and empires.

Cynical Realism

Another option, on the other end of the idealist-realist spectrum, was that of the ultra-realists or, as Niebuhr called them, the cynical realists. Like Niebuhr they believed that concerns for power and survival are the primary bases upon which states must act. Unlike Niebuhr, they were unwilling to allow moral considerations to be even a secondary consideration of states as they formulated foreign policy.

One of Niebuhr's criticisms of the cynical realists was that they failed to appreciate the possibility of progress in the international political arena. He had chided the idealists for having too optimistic a view of the possibility of the new—of a world in which nations would put the establishment of global peace and justice before concerns for their own needs. Niebuhr criticized the realists for just the opposite problem—having too cynical a view of the possibility of moral considerations being a factor in the way nations operate and of nations breaking out of the old destructive patterns of behavior. Whereas the idealists failed to ameliorate international problems because their solutions were impractical, the realists, Niebuhr said, "usually do not go far enough in meeting new problems and situations." Their solutions were practical but insufficiently idealistic to offer any significant improvement to the situations they wished to address. Unlike the idealists who seemed oblivious to the lessons of history and the limitations imposed by sin, realists "are so conscious of the resistance in history to new ventures . . . and are so impressed by the force of the perennial problems of politics, which manifest themselves on each new level of history, that they are inclined to discount both the necessity and the possibility of new political achievements."[24]

The second shortcoming of the cynical realists, in Niebuhr's view, was that they failed to recognize the importance of justice in international relations. Whereas Niebuhr accused idealists of failing to appreciate the importance of power in international relations, he now accused certain realists of being too cynical in their exclusive preoccupation with power as the only basis for the actions of nations.

At the time of the first meeting of the United Nations Assembly in 1946, Niebuhr criticized Western nations for dealing with the controversies over Soviet intervention in Iran and Western intervention in Indonesia in too cynical a manner. Western nations refused to submit their actions to an impartial investigation, which the Soviet delegation had demanded, all the while calling for the Soviet Union to do the same with regard to their intervention in Iran. Such a policy was in keeping with the ultra-realist, or cynical, view that nations should try to maximize their own interests and not attempt to be virtuous, objective, or consistent. "By rejecting the Russian demand," Niebuhr commented, "we have increased the cynicism [with] which these international issues are bound to be considered by many critics." Here realism has clearly gone beyond the bounds of prudence and even self-interest. Niebuhr elaborates:

> If the West is critical only of relations in the Russian zone and Russia only of those in the West, we prove thereby that we have not yet established an insrument of impartiality which bridges the gap between Russia and the West. For the moment we have gained only a parliamentary, rather than military, expression of the conflict between Russia and the West.[25]

This controversy indicates how the short-term interests of the West have obscured the long-term interests of everyone that there be East–West stability, mutuality, and peace. Here Niebuhr called for fairness and objectivity, not because he cherished justice as an abstract moral ideal that should be forced upon every international conflict but because of his historically grounded fear—that if the Soviets and the Western powers did not settle up in a way that treated both sides with equal respect and equal skepticism, then the efforts of the United Nations to promote global human rights were more likely to cause a global war. Niebuhr expressed a concern about justice, not out of sentimentality and not with illusions that nations really would like to be fair, if only shown how. Niebuhr believed a certain measure of justice to be essential to achieving world order (stability) which, in turn, was essential to achieving greater degrees of justice and peace between nations and greater respect for human rights within nations.

Niebuhr's concern here, in one sense, was not so much a plea for greater idealism but for a more prudent realism, a realism that recognized the situations in which the establishment of justice in the international arena may prove mutually beneficial in the long run. Some of the more Machiavellian cynics were shortsighted in considering only the immediate impact of efforts to maximize national self-interest and Niebuhr disassociated himself from this form of realism. "The business of statecraft," he said, was not simply to maximize self-interest but "to find the point of concurrence between the national interest and the wider good." Niebuhr wondered whether it was possible, in the modern world, to assure one's own security apart from considering the security interests of the other nations. While he agreed that "each nation's concern for its own security is inevitable," he believed that each nation must attempt to do so within the framework of a "common program of collective action" or else "a new period of world anarchy is bound to ensue."[26]

Niebuhr's third criticism of the cynical realists was that they failed to appreciate the importance of world community. Niebuhr did not hold as high a hope for the United Nations as did the idealists but he did not regard the United Nations with as much skepticism as the cynical realists. Even though Christians should be aware that sin will tarnish everything good that people try to do, Niebuhr believed that Christians should also work for world community and world peace. The Judeo-Christian concept of history suggests, he said, that there is a unique divine imperative "in every new historical situation." In 1942, Niebuhr believed "the creation of some form of world community, compatible with the necessities of a technical age," to be "the most compelling command" of that time. A year later he reiterated his view concerning the importance of world community. "The paramount problem" of the day, he said, was "the creation of some kind of world community."[27]

A fourth criticism that Niebuhr leveled at the cynical realists was that, in their appreciation of the virtue of power, they failed to appreciate the power of virtue. Niebuhr agreed with their claim that power is the principal variable in the international relations formula, that the manipulation of power is the essence of politics. But he was not so cynical as they in the way that he conceptualized power. For the cynical realists, power consisted of political, economic, and military strength, and perhaps also an intangible usually referred to as "the will of the people." Niebuhr considered the moral virtue of a nation to be yet another source of power. "Some of our strength is actually derived from our virtue," he wrote in 1946. "A proper regard for moral aspirations is a source of political prestige," he wrote in 1942, and "this prestige is itself an indispensable source of power." Sounding more like the moral idealists he disdained than like the hard-core realist he is usually accused of being, Niebuhr could say in 1946 that he believed that, if the United States is a virtuous nation, "the smaller nations will flock to us because they trust us a little more, just a little more." In the next breath, however, he warned against placing too great a reliance upon the power of virtue, pointing out to moral idealists that a great deal of the power of the United States is derived from its military strength: "from the atomic bomb and the threat of it."[28]

Niebuhr's fifth criticism of the cynical realists was that they failed to appreciate the need for constitutional guarantees as aids to the creation of a just world order. Even though Niebuhr is better known for his criticisms of the constitutional idealists, who put too much faith in positive law as a means of establishing international human rights, he also chided the cynical realists for failing to recognize the meritorious aspects of constitutional guarantees. Even though constitutional measures did not, in the international arena, express positive laws, they did express publicly the policy guidelines for nations party to the agreement. Niebuhr believed that such expressions, and the diplomatic processes which led to their formulations, could help maintain just and peaceful relations between the lesser and greater powers and between the superpowers.

In 1943, Niebuhr expressed concern "that immediate steps . . . be taken to give constitutional guarantees and rights to the smaller nations, to the dependent peoples and to the defeated nations in order that the relations of the nation may achieve justice as well as order." Niebuhr harbored no illusions that words inscribed on pieces of paper would be sufficient to guarantee a just world order but he had difficulty conceiving how the more powerful nations could be persuaded to respect the sovereignty of the less powerful nations apart from guarantees expressed in constitutional form.[29]

In a review of Leopold Schwarzschild's *Primer of the Coming World*, a 1944 book which presented the cynical realist critique of efforts to establish a world government through constitutional reform, Niebuhr argued that, while words inscribed on paper cannot create a world government, neither can any sort of world community be created without some words being inscribed on paper. Schwarzschild was correct, Niebuhr believed, in holding that "no present formula for a constitutional world order could preserve the peace if one of the three great powers should not desire its preservation." But Schwarzschild was "wrong in thinking that 'only their will and self-restraint' can preserve the peace." Even if they did have a desire for peace, Niebuhr argued, "they would not be able to do so if they could not find at least quasi-constitutional forms for their partnership and for the regulation of their relations to other powers."[30]

NIEBUHR'S MIDDLE WAY

It should be obvious by now that Niebuhr's approach to human rights was less idealistic than the moral and constitutional idealists but less cynical than the cynical realists. He tried to incorporate the positive insights of both extremes. One appreciated the potentialities of human goodness, while the other realized the limitations brought about by human sin. One aspired that virtue and law become the modus operandi for international relations, the other was aware that power and self-preservation are the fundamental determinants of national behavior in the international arena. Niebuhr viewed the international situation from the perspective of neoorthodox theology's despair concerning the human condition but hope in the ultimate triumph of God. Niebuhrian realism is clearly a via media between a number of unsatisfactory extremes.

Between Historical and Idealist Approaches

First and foremost, it is a middle way between historical and idealist approaches to human rights. History attests to the human propensity to sin and to the propensity of nations to act according to self-interest. The idealist tradition attests to the human potential to transcend nature and sin's limitations. The problem with the idealists is their tendency to view human rights issues solely in abstract terms. Their solutions to human rights problems are well suited to an ideal world that only exists in their minds, but have little bearing on the way things actually are.

"On the whole," Niebuhr writes in 1942, "the task of world organization must be attempted from the standpoint of historical realism" because, to put it bluntly, "no historical process has ever, even remotely, conformed to the pattern which the idealists have mapped out for it." Instead of conforming their ideals to historical reality, idealists hope that history will somehow miraculously conform to their projections of how things ought to be. Even so, Niebuhr is careful to disassociate himself from the cynical extreme of historical realism. "It must be added immediately, however, that the truth does not lie simply on the side of the realists." Were it not for "an admixture of the temper and the insights" of the idealists, "there could be no genuine advance in social organization at all." What is needed, then, is the historical realists' understanding of the importance of power in politics combined with the idealists' sense of "the urgency of a new situation."[31]

Niebuhr astutely observes that sentimental idealism and callous cynicism are two extremes that feed upon one another. When utopian dreams are thwarted, sentimental idealists often become cynics and thus go from one bad extreme to another. This was what happened in the period between the two world wars. A postwar idealism turned to a mood of disillusionment, isolationism, and cynical irresponsibility when the League of Nations failed to materialize into a world democracy. "Cynicism is, in fact, the usual reaction of disappointed sentimentalists," Niebuhr concludes. "It is always wrong to interpret political tasks purely in terms of either ideal ends or of purely egoistic ones," because "no political program ever completely lacks the inspiration of the one and the corruption of the other." He urges churches to preach the dual messages of sin and hope to mitigate the tendency of Christians to build their optimism upon sand. In a reproof directed at idealistic Christian liberals, Niebuhr argues that every Christian knows, "or ought to know," that there is a big difference between

Christianity and secular utopianism. "An adequate Christian political ethic is not established merely by conceiving the most ideal possible solution for a political problem," but by dealing human nature's "realities" as well as her "ideal possibilities." A Christian should not be surprised or disillusioned when human rights are abridged by human recalcitrance but should try to work for universal human rights "within the limits" set by this recalcitrance. A middle way between idealism and cynical realism must be encouraged, Niebuhr believes, because a slow progress is the only progress possible.[32]

Between Order and Justice

Second, Niebuhrian realism offers a middle way between approaches to human rights that emphasize the primacy of order and approaches that emphasize the primacy of justice. Generally, Niebuhr leans toward viewing order as the precondition for justice. But he often argues that an unjust order, a tyranny, is not much of an order because it is the precondition of anarchy. The resolution of the apparent inconsistency seems to be in distinguishing between various levels of justice. Niebuhr does not consider grossly unjust orders worth preserving. He does, however, prefer slightly unjust orders to egalitarian systems devoid of the order necessary to prevent a disintegration into anarchy and injustice.

During the early years of the United Nations, Niebuhr urged Western nations to respect the sovereignty of the Soviets and to avoid forcing them into accepting Western standards of human rights. Niebuhr believed that an attempt to put international justice before international order would only create friction and make it more difficult for nations to reform their human rights policies. Niebuhr believed that the United Nations should strive to build a world order in which nations felt secure. Only if they felt their sovereignty respected, their borders protected, and their economy prosperous could they turn to matters involving human rights. Unlike Western nations (which seem more willing to risk national and personal security, as well as the material well-being of many citizens, for the sake of civil, political, economic, and religious freedom) most non-Western nations prefer to establish higher levels of security and well-being before trying to secure the "luxury" of liberal human rights. Niebuhr urged Western leaders to show respect for the Soviet Union's sovereignty and urged U.S. leaders to give economic aid to the war-torn countries of Western Europe and the developing nations to the South. Only in this indirect manner could universal human rights be promoted by the Western democracies.[33]

As one who leaned toward the primacy of order, in 1943 Niebuhr called for Anglo-Saxon nations to unite against the Nazi effort to destroy the present world order. He feared, however, that realists would take this Anglo-Saxon hegemony and turn it into an imperialism not much better than the imperialism of the Nazis. To the realists Niebuhr says that in creating an hegemony which will attempt to assert its influence upon the world, the Anglo-Saxon nations must strive for "justice as well as order." On the one hand, order must be the first priority—power must be centralized to the point that the alliance is able to be strong and effective. Even though the ultimate objective is the creation of a just order (the creation of "something like a federation of the world or a league of nations") such an order "must be brought into being by considering first how the creation of a power and authority at its center may check the tendency toward disintegration." On the other hand, power must be sufficiently decentralized to create a just order as well as a powerful one. "A proper equilibrium" between the nations must be developed, Niebuhr maintains, in order to "check the tendency toward domination from the center."[34]

The following year, Niebuhr addressed the relationship between order and justice, and its relevance to the global situation, even more explicitly:

> The two basic requirements for world peace are order and justice. Minimal order in the world can be established only by the preponderant power of the great nations who now have the effective strength to bring the war to a successful conclusion. This order can be made just only if it is prevented by constitutional forms from becoming oppressive to the small nations.
>
> Thus the two basic requirements of peace—order and justice—demand in the context of current events a stable three- or four-power accord on the one hand and on the other a broader accord of all the nations. Idealists are afraid that the great powers may achieve a partnership at the expense of the small powers and thus fasten a super-imperialism upon the world. But there is a greater danger that they will not reach a significant accord at all [and therefore that anarchy will result]. To do so, they must arrive at agreements on how the continents shall be organized which will obviate the fears that one side is trying to organize the world against the other. If they are to succeed in doing this at all they must do it by drawing the smaller powers into the accord. A genuine European agreement, for instance, cannot leave out France. There is therefore less danger that the powers will organize a super-imperialism than that they will reach only superficial agreements which will fail to guarantee a stable peace.[35]

Niebuhr's middle way between order and justice, then, is a middle way between overly centralized power and overly decentralized power. In the long run, a stable, moderately just arrangement is preferable to an unstable though highly just arrangement. Order serves as the precondition for justice and human rights.

Between Isolationist and Imperialist Approaches

Third, Niebuhrian realism offers a middle way between approaches to human rights that are isolationist and approaches that tend to be imperialist. In the two decades following World War I, the United States had retreated into an isolationist posture that Niebuhr found irresponsible for a nation as powerful as the United States. Such a retreat had, he believed, created a power vacuum that the Axis powers filled. Thus U.S. isolationism contributed in some measure to the rise of the Axis powers and the destabilization of Europe. With the advent of World War II, a new sentiment began developing in the United States. The new attitude was one of wanting to get more involved in global affairs. Niebuhr applauded the new realization that America was no longer as isolated or incapable of rendering assistance as it once had been and praised the new willingness to get involved in the affairs of the world beyond the oceans. What he found disturbing, however, was the manner in which Americans wanted to participate. Rather than participating as a member of an alliance of nations, submitting to the decisions of the alliance, Americans wanted to intervene on their own terms. They wanted a solo performance, not a cooperative effort. Niebuhr was critical of both this "isolationist imperialism," as he called it, and the earlier simple isolationism. He suggested a third alternative—participation in efforts to nurture international community.[36]

A number of factors had contributed to the isolationist sentiment in America, including past foreign policy, geography, power, youth and innocence, and the failure of the League of Nations. The United States had been formed as a rebellion against extrinsic control by a foreign power. American foreign policy had respected the sovereignty of other nations and, as formulated in the Monroe Doctrine, had asked other nations to do the same. It was considered "out of character" for the United States to intervene in the affairs of other nations—or, at least, other continents. Such a policy seemed credible in principle although, as Niebuhr would point out, such a policy was capable of turning into an irresponsible isolationism. There are ways to participate in the global community without violating other nations' sovereignty, he said. There are ways to be involved without being imperialistic.

It is a bad thing to intervene, uninvited, in the affairs of other nations. It is also a bad thing to insulate oneself from the problems of the rest of the global community. In America's youth the insulation had been more a matter of circumstance than choice. The Atlantic and Pacific Oceans insulated the United States from the problems of Europe and Asia. With the development of air transportation and the rise of a global communications network, Niebuhr believed that technology had taken away nature's insulation. The Atlantic Ocean now gave the United States little more security than the English Channel gave Britain, Niebuhr said in 1943. In fact, one might add that it had now become a liability in the sense that it gave most Americans a false sense of security; thus, Americans had difficulty realizing how "near" the European war was to the American continent.[37]

Another contributing factor was America's military and economic strength. In earlier days, the United States could bow out of global dramas on the legitimate grounds that it had not yet established political hegemony, economic infrastructure, and military muscle sufficient to make its influence in international affairs a factor worth reckoning. By the twentieth century, the major regional disputes had been settled, a strong central government had coalesced, and America had become an industrial giant, an agricultural cornucopia, and a military stronghold. Americans continued to justify their isolationism, but for the opposite reason. This new sense of power, along with the supposed geographic isolation from the European theater, gave Americans a sense of security that made involvement with the efforts of other superpowers to establish international order seem unnecessary.

Niebuhr observed that because of America's strength and isolation, "our survival is not at stake in the same [immediate] sense that it has been for Russia, Britain, China and the smaller nations." These factors "make the establishment of a system of mutual security less urgent for us than for other nations." Niebuhr believed that this rise to power, when coupled with the shrinking size of the world, should give Americans a new sense of responsibility rather than reinforce their old sense of isolation and uninvolvement. No longer could the United States image itself as a young nation, impotent and innocent. The concomitant of power is responsibility, and Niebuhr (sounding more like an idealist than the cynical realist he is often made out to be) called in 1943 for the United States to wield its power in a responsible manner, in a manner that seeks to build a just world. Niebuhr believed that, unfortunately, most of the idealists of this period still lived in the past, still viewed the United States as too young and too innocent to dirty its hands in the affairs of the world. Niebuhr believed that America had "come of age," and should accept the responsibilities of a mature nation. America had "gone through too much experience," as Niebuhr put it, "to make the isolationism of 1920–40 a live option."

Niebuhr viewed the American posture as at once humorous and hypocritical. The United States had developed a "tremendous preponderance" of economic and military power, which everyone seemed to be aware of except the United States itself. America still clung to its image as an innocent youth isolated from the European center of global power. When the isolationist–oriented U.S. acted in an uncooperative manner in the international arena, the destructive impact on other countries could be quite significant. For example, Americans "are outraged by what we call the power politics of the European nations, but the European nations recall that the aviation conference broke down because we refused to allow any international checks to be placed upon our air power." When criticized for such behavior, Americans revert back to the childhood image. "We assume an air of injured innocence," believing that "America has a vantage-point of international virtue from which it can survey, and be offended by, the power politics of Russia and Britain upon the Continent." We act oblivious, he said, to the fact that America has "grown up" and entered the world of power politics as well.[38]

America had indeed passed from innocence to experience. Sentimental longing for a lost youth was simply a mechanism for avoiding facing up to the responsibilities of adulthood. Niebuhr loathed those Christians (and other idealists) who preferred "immoral irresponsibility and inaction to the moral taint which is involved in all poltical [sic] action." Such sentimentalism (which preferred a perfect solution or none at all) was a major factor in U.S. failure to support the League of Nations. The failure of the League of Nations, in turn, reinforced the isolationist tendency of the sentimentalists—they refused to believe any longer in the possibility of nations working together to create a more just world.[39]

By 1942, Niebuhr can state, with a fair degree of confidence, that most Americans, excepting the most obdurate of the liberals, have accepted America's passage into experience and international responsibility. "It is probable, though not certain, that we have learned the necessity of participating responsibly in building a community of nations." It was possible, of course, that Americans would revert back to their "psychosis of fear, disillusionment, and withdrawal from the world," but he did not consider such a reversion likely.[40]

The new problem to emerge in the forties, as Niebuhr saw it, was a growing sentiment toward "isolationist imperialism." Americans had seen the need to become a more active participant in international affairs, from considerations of both self-interest and morality. The influences of their independent, isolationist past, however, and their new awareness of their preponderant strength among nations combined to cultivate an attitude among Americans that their participation not be dictated by extrinsic influences. Americans sensed their power to influence international politics and their ability to protect themselves against the Axis powers. Unlike the European nations, they did not feel the necessity to align for purposes of survival. They wanted to stay out of encumbering alliances and help out as they saw fit. They wanted now to wield their power in the world, but to do so without entering into international commitments.[41]

Niebuhr considered such a manner of participation to be almost as irresponsible as the former isolationism. This had been the pattern of U.S. involvement during World War I and the postwar period. The United

States took a responsible role in the war and then after the war refused its "continuing responsibility" to help build a just world order. Because so powerful a nation as the United States shirked its responsibility, Niebuhr considered the United States culpable for the development of conditions leading to World War II.

No longer could the United States play the role of a "lone ranger" that refused to participate in structures of international order that would carry over into peacetime. Niebuhr believed that the cooperation needed to win the war should lay the groundwork for an alliance of nations that would continue to serve as the basis for international order and justice in peacetime. Because of Niebuhr's belief that order is the prerequisite for justice and peace, Niebuhr saw winning the war as no guarantee against the repetition of human rights abuses. Winning World War I had not prevented the rise of Nazism. For the United States to participate in putting out the fire, without helping rebuild the building, was to fall short of its responsibility as a world citizen. This generation, Niebuhr says, can lay the foundation for future international peace and justice. This is "the most difficult task mankind has ever faced." It will become "quite impossible" to achieve this task "if the nation which now has more power that [sic] any other, throws itself and its power into the world community in times of crisis and withdraws its power irresponsibly after the crisis." For "the mark of maturity among men and nations," Niebuhr concludes, "is willingness to assume *continuing responsibility* [italics mine]."[42]

Niebuhrian realism should be viewed as a via media between a naively idealistic and a cynically realistic approach to human rights. It incorporates the idealist concern for global responsibility with the realist concern for respecting national sovereignty. It encourages Western nations not to isolate themselves from the problems of the world, however, it also encourages them not to intervene in other nations' affairs. It encourages a middle way—ongoing international involvement based upon mutual commitments to establish world order, nurture international community, and thereby develop an atmosphere in which respect for international human rights can be cultivated. Niebuhrian realism believes that nations do and must act out of self-interest. It also believes, however, in the dignity of persons created by God and urges nations to find areas in which promotion of human dignity can coincide with national interest. Niebuhr did not expect nations to sacrifice their own power and self-interest and become charitable entities. He did believe that creative statesmen and stateswomen could discover ways in which promoting international order and justice would promote national security and well-being.

INTERNATIONAL HUMAN RIGHTS WITHIN THE LIMITATIONS IMPOSED BY NATIONAL SOVEREIGNTY AND HUMAN SIN

What, specifically, can Niebuhrian realism offer to help promote universal human rights? Niebuhrian realism suggests that progress is possible only when proponents of universal human rights (1) regard nations and individuals—the two players in the human rights drama—in historical, realistic terms, and (2) promote universal human rights in a cautious, indirect manner.

Regard Nations As Sovereign and Persons As Citizens

Viewing the nation in historical, realistic terms suggests that efforts to promote the rights of individuals must be within the limitations imposed by the sovereign rights of nations. Both Soviet and Third World nations have complained (on numerous occasions) that they feel their national sovereignty threatened by Western human rights initiatives. The legitimacy of this concern has been reinforced by Western nations who, when forced to choose, opted to protect their own sovereignty, not international human rights. Examples include the unwillingness of the United States to have its air power controlled by a committee of Allied Nations in World War II, the unwillingness of Western nations to give up their veto power in the United Nations' General Assembly, or, more recently, the unwillingness of the United States to submit to international courts of law on issues such as the rights of Salvadorean refugees, the U.S. to mine Nicaraguan harbors, and U.S. military vessels to sail in Canadian waters.

The Judeo-Christian tradition emphasizes history, rather than abstract reasoning, as the source of truth. History certainly attests to the self-interested behavior of nations. The notion that nations will submit to transnational laws—be they natural laws or positive laws—is conceivable in the abstract but without historic precedence. With the weight of historical evidence against the possibility, the historical realist is forced to conclude that there is something about the nature and structure of nations that makes them incapable of acting against their self-interest. Niebuhr discovered that the doctrine of total depravity explains this phenomenon rather well. Sin is so pervasive in a fallen world that it affects the behavior not only of individual human beings but also of human institutions. Under the conditions of sin nations must act to promote their self-interest or else they will be swallowed by other nations acting to promote their self-interest.

Such an analysis also suggests that Western nations must recognize the extent to which their promotion of international human rights is a self-interested act. They would not and could not advocate universal human rights if such advocacy involved national self-sacrifice. This suggests why the human rights movement has chosen to emphasize liberal notions of human rights—to promote them is to promote Western values, Western interests, and thus Western power. Such an analysis further suggests that Western nations should recognize that promoting international human rights without respecting other nations' sovereignty is bound to do more harm than good. Other nations recognize that Western nations are acting in a self-interested fashion and resent the use of moralism to cloak such power plays. Also, other nations feel threatened when told what to do by enemy nations or more powerful nations. Niebuhrian realism suggests that any efforts to promote international human rights be made within the insurmountable bounds created by national sovereignty rather than by acting as though national boundaries did not exist or were not important.

An historical, realistic view of the individual suggests that the human rights movement view individuals not only as abstractions of humanity called "persons" but also in their historical role as citizens of particular communities and nations. The Western liberal tradition has viewed persons in such abstract terms that the rights granted by the movement are not to real people but to abstractions of real people. The rights granted by the articles of the Universal Declaration of Human Rights, for example, are granted, supposedly, to everyone. In reality, they are granted to no one because they are granted to people as persons rather than as citizens. In a fallen world, only persons as citizens may or may not have rights.

In their abstract status as persons, people may be said to have rights before God which no nation can, in an ultimate sense, take away. But history teaches that under the conditions of existence nations can and do take away these rights which God is said to have granted. Humans may be created as persons, and one may speak in a theological and philosophical sense of people as persons to describe what is the essence of being human. The Universal Declaration of Human Rights may speak of the dignity of persons and the rights that should accrue to them because they are persons, however, it can never grant them these rights simply because they are persons. All it can do is state what rights should accrue to them as persons. The Universal Declaraton is, therefore, not a list of rights per se, but of ideals— of what should be the rights of all persons if they lived in nations that recognized the full implications of their status as persons.[43] Humans may be created by God as persons but, under the conditions of sin, humans exist necessarily as citizens, as members of sovereign political entities. Any rights that a person gains under these conditions of sin are gained only through the executive, legislative, and judicial actions of their own nations. Abstract declarations, even though they claim to have universal status, fail to offer persons as citizens any substantial human rights.

Although statements of international ideals may be effective in challenging nations to change their laws, any progress in human rights must eventually be the fruit of changes at the national level.

Because our existential status is as citizens rather than as persons and because nations are the largest political entities capable of exercising executive, legislative, and judicial authority, there can be no such thing as fully authoritative "international laws." The broadest laws that can pertain to citizens are national laws. There can be international ideals toward which nations may or may not choose to strive. There can be religious laws and natural laws that pertain to persons as persons or as devotees to a particular belief system, depending upon the universality claimed by the laws. The only guarantees of human rights that can have any effective legal status, however, are those imposed by a body that has the power and authority to enforce them. For this reason, Niebuhr encouraged Western advocates of international human rights to recognize the limitations of abstract statements of principle and to do that which is most likely to bring about greater respect for human rights at the national level. This leads to the other major contribution that Niebuhrian realism can make to the human rights movement.

An Indirect Approach Is Best

Niebuhrian realism suggests that, in the effort to secure universal human rights, the shortest distance between two points may not be a straight line. Do not aim at achieving universal human rights, it advises, but at creating a more stable world order. Because nations are sovereign entities, there is nothing that can be done at the international level to guarantee human rights. Certain things can be done, however, to foster an environment in which universal human rights are more likely to be realized. Creating a more stable world order encourages the development of international community. It cannot create a respect for human rights in nations around the world but it can remove many of the barriers that stand in the way.

Because the path to international human rights must be indirect, Niebuhr seldom discussed the subject in a direct manner. He devoted his efforts more toward the creation of a stable world order, not because this was his ultimate end but because this was a prerequisite for universal human rights, and because this end could be attained through a direct approach. Niebuhr considered it counterproductive to talk about universal human rights. Too many idealists had already said too much, arousing false hopes among their followers and arousing the ire of non-Western nations. Idealists became cynics as they discovered that the wheels of justice turn ever so slowly, and non-Western nations resisted Western human rights efforts as they detected the moral self-righteousness and hypocrisy of Western nations. Thus Niebuhr preferred the Dumbarton Oaks Proposals, which tried to establish the prerequisites to universal human rights, to documents such as the Universal Declaration of Human Rights, which dealt with international human rights problems in a direct manner.[44]

Niebuhrian realism suggests that creating a more stable world order involves the proper use of power. Nations that wish to promote world order and create an atmosphere in which concern for human rights is most likely to develop must have the proper mixture of "strength" and "weakness" to contribute to a stable balance of power. Western nations should avoid being so weak that a power vacuum is created that encourages aggressive nations to become imperialistic. Western nations should avoid being so strong or interventionist themselves that they make other nations feel so insecure as to become aggressively self-protective. Human rights initiatives that show insufficient respect for the sovereignty of nations do in fact promote conditions unfavorable to human rights as non-Western nations interpret Western initiatives as threats to their security or well-being.

Creating a more stable world order also involves taking advantage of the economic, sociological, psychological, religious, and cultural forces of cohesion. As long as a reasonable balance of power can be maintained, then the more positive forces of cohesion can be nurtured. Niebuhr considered the increasingly interdependent world economy as a piece of "social tissue" that should be exploited for purposes of global community. He considered the disparity between the minority "haves" and the majority "have-nots" to be a source of global disharmony, but potentially a source of harmony if Western nations would recognize that their long run interests coincided with the interests of the poorer nations of the world. Poorer nations needed economic assistance. Wealthy nations needed both resources and assurances of security from the more populous nations to the South. Promoting the well-being of the nations to the South seemed to help promote the military security of the nations to the North. Another source of cohesion, in Niebuhr's view, was the fear of annihilation—particularly nuclear annihilation—shared by many of the nations of the world. Such a threat of global disaster had the capacity, Niebuhr believed, to promote cooperation among nations, if only they would realize that their long term interests were mutual.[45]

Another source of global community was the moral sense, shared by persons in all nations throughout the world, that they have a duty to each other that transcends their duties to their respective nations. Niebuhr considered this to be the "most important factor in the social tissue of the world community." He hastened to add that such unity is motivated by cultural and religious values and is not a political unity because nations can never transcend their structure as autonomous political units. Even so, a more universal and pervasive sense of moral "ought-ness" among citizens can have the impact of encouraging their governments to try harder to discover ways of promoting their own interests so that they have a constructive rather than a destructive impact on the global community as well. Nations whose citizens have a sense of duty to the global as well as to the national community are more likely to find ways of promoting the national good andthe global common good at the same time. In areas such as the gap between the rich and the poor and the threat of nuclear annihilation, it should not be so difficult to see that these are concerns that nations must solve together or be dissolved by them.[46]

I hope that this chapter has helped dissolve the misconception that Reinhold Niebuhr was not interested in the United Nations and international human rights. Although the literature on Niebuhr reinforces this impression, Niebuhr's own writings and activities in the forties and early fifties indicate a commitment to the United Nations and international human rights. Despite his many criticisms of idealistic internationalism, Niebuhr's attitude toward the United Nations and international human rights was much more positive than what one might expect given his reputation, in many circles, as a cynical cold war realist. With U.S. support for the United Nations currently waning, such a positive attitude from a self-proclaimed "tamed cynic" merits our consideration.

Chapters 8 and 9 will explore other ways of creating a global atmosphere in which international human rights may be nurtured. The proponents of contextual theology have suggested that cultural barriers are as inviolable as national barriers but that reform across cultural barriers is still possible if done, as Niebuhr suggested—regarding political barriers—in an indirect manner. They urge Western nations to stop using confrontive methods such as international declarations, laws, and boycotts to promote universal human rights. They urge Western nations to focus their efforts on setting a good example at home and to utilize the give and take method of intercultural and interreligious dialogue.

CONCLUSIONS TO CHAPTERS 6 AND 7

1. Non-Western nations have expressed fears that the drive for international human rights poses a threat to their sovereignty.
2. Westerners are divided into three camps. Moral idealists believe that international human rights will be achieved by getting the nations of the world to agree to a common set of moral ideals. They view the United Nations as a forum in which to resolve conflicts between nations

through discussion and debate. Legal realists, whom Niebuhr called constitutional idealists, believe that international human rights must come through more coercive methods. They advocate the development of international law. They favor turning the United Nations into a world government to enforce international human rights legislation. Ultra-realists, or cynical realists, as Niebuhr called them, believe that nations must act in their own self-interest and that moral considerations have no place in the political arena. They oppose any efforts to promote international human rights.

3. Niebuhr agrees with the ultra-realists that nations must act in their own self-interest but he believes that promoting virtue can, at times, promote self-interest. Niebuhr likes the moral idealists' and legal realists' concern for international peace and justice, but both fail to appreciate the extent to which national self-interest inhibits international efforts in this direction. The concern for national sovereignty prevents negotiation and legislation from being effective means of securing international human rights.

4. Since it is impossible to secure international human rights through direct methods, Niebuhr recommends an indirect approach—that efforts be focused toward creating an atmosphere in which justice and peace can be nurtured. Niebuhr believes that such an atmosphere requires a stable international order because only as nations feel secure militarily, stable politically, and prosperous economically will they give human rights the consideration that they merit. It is in the interest of powerful, stable, and prosperous nations such as the United States to promote the development of these conditions throughout the world.

5. Our thesis is held to be valid. At the root of the international conflict over human rights is a question addressed by theological anthropology. The theological notion of sin, applied to corporate political bodies, suggests that the non-Western concern for national sovereignty is a legitimate one. Whether they admit it or not, nations act to promote their own self-interest, and non-Western nations are wise to beware of the wolves in sheep's clothing advocating universal human rights. Christian theological anthropology offers a via media between optimistic and pessimistic assessments of humanity and the possibility of achieving global human rights, pointing to both the limitations imposed by sin and the potential inherent in the divine promises.

NOTES

1. Niebuhr, "Common Counsel for United Nations," *Christianity and Crisis* [hereafter *C&C*] 2:16 (5 October 1942), 1–2. Two weeks later Niebuhr praised the

"historical realists" for having a more continuous view of the relation between future and present time. "They are right in looking to the mutual commitments made by the United Nations in war as the real source of possibly wider commitments for the future." (See Niebuhr, "Plans for World Reorganization," *C&C* 2:17 (19 October 1942), 4.) Even though these commitments were less democratic than we might like, Niebuhr considered them more indicative of what the starting point of international order and justice might be than the thoroughly utopian dreams of the moral idealists. Three months later he praised a group of American churchmen who were idealists in every sense of the word except that they did not maintain a continuous view of time. The churchmen, headed by Bishop McConnell, had called for the immediate democratization of the United Nations Council. Their statement, Niebuhr observed, "recognizes the unity of history and makes no absolute distinction between the experience during war-time and the responsibilities which must be assumed after the war." Nations, he believed, are not likely to be more responsible and more just after the war, "when immediate pressures and perils are removed," than "under the urgencies of the conflict." Any changes in the power structure of the Council should take place during the war, rather than waiting and believing they will happen quite naturally once the war is over. Niebuhr viewed the ecclesiastical statement as a refreshing break from the habit of most idealists, religious and otherwise, "of planning for peace without reference to the experience of the war." (See Niebuhr, "The United Nations and World Organization," *C&C* 2:24 (25 January 1943), 1.) In September of 1944, with the Dumbarton Oaks conference underway with its efforts to create a permanent United Nations organization, Niebuhr praised the conference's efforts to make wartime cooperation the basis of peacetime cooperation. "The experiences of mutual accord and accommodation, gained in war time and under pressure of immediate necessities," Niebuhr urged, should become "the cornerstone of a permanent and genuine form of world order." (See Niebuhr, "Democratic Goals and World Order," *The New Leader* 27:39 (23 September 1944), 5.)

2. Niebuhr, "World Community and World Government," *C & C* 6:3 (4 March 1946), 6.
3. Niebuhr, "Plans," 6.
4. Niebuhr, "The Basis for World Order," *The Nation* 159:17 (21 October 1944) 489.
5. Niebuhr, "A Plea for Humility," *The Messenger* 19:21 (16 November 1954), 7, Niebuhr, "A Plea for More Humility," *The Messenger* 20:7 (5 April 1955), 6-7.
6. Niebuhr, "The Conflict Between Nations and Nations and Between Nations and God," *C & C* 6:14 (5 August 1945), 2-4.
7. Niebuhr, "Creating a New World Order," *The Lutheran* 34:8 (21 November 1951), 10. On self-righteousness and war, see Niebuhr, "Editorial Notes," *C&C* 6:15 (16 September 1946), 3.
8. Niebuhr, "Editorial Notes," *C & C* 6:9 (27 May 1946), 2.
9. Niebuhr, "One World or None," *C&C* 8:2 (16 February 1948), 9-10; Niebuhr, "The Myth of World Government" *The Nation* 162:11 (16 March 1946), 313.

10. Niebuhr, "Creating," 10; Niebuhr, "The Future Can't Be Controlled," *The Lutheran* 34:17 (23 January 1952), 11.
11. Niebuhr, "The Theory and Practice of UNESCO," *International Organization* 4:1 (February 1950), 3-11, esp. 5.
12. Niebuhr, "Is World Government Possible?" *The Messenger* 11:16 (6 August 1946), 6.
13. Niebuhr, "The Myth," 312.
14. Niebuhr, "The Moral Implications of Loyalty to the United Nations," *Motive* 16:1 (October 1955), pp. 19-20 [reprinted from *The Hazen Pamphlets*, no. 29, Edward W. Hazen Foundation, New Haven, July 1952]; see also Niebuhr, "The Churches and the United Nations," *Christianity and Society* [hereafter *C & S*] 18:1 (Winter 1952-53), 3-4.
15. Niebuhr, "The Illusion of World Government," *Foreign Affairs: An American Quarterly Review* 27:3 (April 1949), 386, 381.
16. Niebuhr, "The Myth," 313; see also Niebuhr, "Is This 'Peace in Our Time?'" *The Nation* 160:14 (17 April 1945), 382-84; Niebuhr, "Democratic Goals," 4; Niebuhr, "The Illusion," 379-81; Niebuhr, "World Community," 5.
17. Niebuhr, "The Myth," 313.
18. Niebuhr, "The Illusion," 380.
19. Niebuhr, "Dumbarton Oaks," *C & S* 10:1 (Winter 1944), 3-4; Niebuhr, "The United Nations," *C & S* 12:1 (winter 1946) 3-4; Niebuhr "Revision of the United Nations Charter," *C & S* 13:3 (Summer 1948), 8; Niebuhr, "The Churches and the United Nations," *C & S* 18:1 (Winter 1952-53), 3-4; Niebuhr, "Conversation: On the International Affairs Report from the Evanston Assembly of the World Council of Churches," *C & S* 20:2 (Spring 1955), 7-8.
20. Niebuhr, "The Myth," 312.
21. Ibid., 313-14.
22. Niebuhr, "The Illusion," 379.
23. Niebuhr, "Creating," 10; "The Illusion," 380.
24. Niebuhr, "Plans," 4. The Judeo-Christian understanding of history is that history attests not only to the sinfulness of humanity but also to the uniqueness and particularity of every situation. In the more Idealist world views, events and persons tend to be understood as manifestations of archetypes, with no uniqueness of their own, and thus no possibility of doing anything truly new. In the Hebrew way of thinking, history is regarded as linear, progressive, unfolding. Each moment is a new one—each person, place, and thing unique. There is not only the possibility of the new, there is the inevitability of it. The presence of sin limits the degree of goodness and perfection present present in the new, but the ongoing creative activity of God guarantees that new things will happen and that the goodness of God offers the hope that what is new will be good. Thus the author of Isaiah is moved to proclaim, as spokesman for the Lord, "Behold, I am doing a new thing; . . . Do you not perceive it?" (43.19). And thus the notion that "there is nothing new under the sun" suggests that the author of Ecclesiastes is a critic, not an advocate, of the Hebrew concept of history (1.9).
25. Niebuhr, "World Community," 2.
26. Niebuhr, "The National Interest and International Responsibility," *Social Action* 21:6 (February 1955), 26; Niebuhr, "Democratic Goals," 4.

27. Niebuhr, "Plans," 6; "American Power and World Responsibility," *C & C* 3:5 (5 April 1943), 2. It must be emphasized that Niebuhr did not call for the forma- tion of a world "government." This would be impossible, assuming his views concerning national sovereignty to be correct. But he did believe that nations must communicate with one another, search for areas of mutual interest, and begin to develop mutual trust. If the United Nations could promote this, it would make an important contribution toward the development of inter- national order and human rights.

It should also be pointed out that Niebuhr's use of the term "creation" with reference to the world community is slightly misleading. Niebuhr had problems with the idea that community can be created by fiat. Communities evolve by the slow process of persons being drawn together according to pat- terns influenced by kinship, linguistic, geographic, and economic factors. Communities evolve and then create governments, he said. Governments can- not "create" communities, Niebuhr wrote with regard to the constitutional idealists' faith in the ability of positive law to create a society ex nihilo. Despite the apparent inconsistency here, it seems more likely than not that Niebuhr was really asking for the creation of structures that would nurture and facili- tate the development of international community which, he would say, already exists in kernels of communication, cooperation, and trust between various nations, but which needs a great deal of nurturing. An institution such as the United Nations could provide an atmosphere in which a more perfect com- munity might develop.

28. Niebuhr, "The Conflict," 3; Niebuhr "Plans," 4.
29. Niebuhr, "The United Nations and World Organization," 2; see also Niebuhr, "Democratic Goals," 4-5; Niebuhr, "The San Francisco Conference," *C & S* 10:3 (Summer 1945), 3-4; Niebuhr, "Moral Implications," 19.
30. Niebuhr, "Realist's Eye View" [a review of Leopold Schwarzschild's *Primer of the Coming World*], *The Nation* 159:4 (22 July 1944), 106.
31. Niebuhr, "Plans," 3-4.
32. Niebuhr, "American Power," 3; Niebuhr, "World Community," 5; Niebuhr, "Democratic Goals," 5.
33. Niebuhr, "The Churches," 3-4; Niebuhr, "Is This 'Peace?'" 382-84.
34. Niebuhr, "The United Nations and World Organization," 2.
35. Niebuhr, "The Basis for World Order," *The Nation* 159:17 (21 October 1944), 489.
36. Niebuhr, "Moral Implications," 17; Niebuhr, "American Power," 3.
37. Niebuhr, "American Power," 2-3.
38. Ibid.; Niebuhr, "Will America Back Out?" *The Nation* 160:2 (13 January 1945), 42.
39. Niebuhr, "American Power," 3.
40. Niebuhr, "Thoughts on 'World War III?'" *The Nation* 155:2 (11 July 1942), 32.
41. Niebuhr, "American Power," 4.
42. Niebuhr, "The Basis for World Order," *The Nation* 159:17 (21 October 1944), 489.
43. Maurice Cranston argues this point in Cranston, *What Are Human Rights?* (New York: Basic Books, 1962). Niebuhr wrote the Preface for the 1962 edition. Even though he certainly could not have agreed with Cranston's libertarian

bias or his faith in positive law, Niebuhr liked Cranston's criticisms of the moral idealists.

44. Niebuhr, "The Theory and Practice of UNESCO," esp. 10; Niebuhr, "Is This 'Peace?'", 382-84.
45. Niebuhr, "The Illusion," 383, 386.
46. Ibid., 387.

8

WESTERN CULTURAL HEGEMONY

When more powerful nations try to coerce less powerful nations to change some aspect of their policy, a foreseeable consequence of such action is insecurity on the part of the less powerful nations. They feel endangered politically and militarily. They cry out that their national sovereignty is being threatened. In addition to feeling threatened as a nation, it is also understandable that they would feel threatened, or offended, as a culture. A culture's collective ego is bound to be bruised by being told that its values are inferior to the values of another culture. As chapters 6 and 7 addressed the question of national sovereignty, chapters 8 and 9 will address the question of cultural integrity—whether one culture has the right to tell another culture how to behave and what principles should govern interchange between cultures. Chapters 6 and 7 considered the political aspects of the international human rights movement. Chapters 8 and 9 will consider the movement's impact on the cultural psyche.

Chapter 8 will examine the inveterate American urge to dominate, both historically and in terms of its deleterious effects upon the human rights movement. Chapter 9 will argue that this urge to dominate is rooted in a particular way of defining the human being—in abstract, universal terms rather than in historical, cultural terms. Western liberals speak of "human rights" and "the rights of man" rather than "the rights of French Canadians" or "the rights of working mothers." In chapter 9, I will argue that this aversion to defining humanity and human rights in culturally specific terms conflicts with the Judeo-Christian traditional preference for the particular over the universal, the historical over the abstract.

OBJECTIONS VOICED BY NON-WESTERN NATIONS

Non-Western nations have accused the human rights movement of hypocrisy, moral chauvinism, cultural imperialism, and cloaking cold war propaganda in moralistic disguise. The rhetoric from both sides has been excessive. The task of the ethicist is to separate veritable wheat from polemical chaff.

Objections from the Soviet Bloc

From the Soviet perspective, as well as from the perspective of a number of other non-Western nations, President Carter's human rights efforts suggested an air of moral superiority that, at the most visceral level, was quite offensive. Leonid Brezhnev accused Washington of trying "to teach others how to live." One of the *Tass* senior commentators, Yuri Kornilov, complained that Carter had tried to become a "mentor" to the socialist world. Another Soviet press release, responding to U.S. criticism of Soviet failure to comply with the Helsinki Accords, barked that the U.S. "has no moral right to teach other countries about human rights."[1] These complaints indicate not simply a disagreement with Western concepts of human rights but an objection to claiming universality for any one particular understanding of human right to the exclusion of all others.

"Great powers have a high sensitivity about their prestige," says Roy Medvedev, a longtime critic of Soviet human rights violations who nevertheless has managed to stay in the good graces of Soviet Communist Party. "The diplomatic successes of Kissinger are partly explained by the fact that he tried not to offend the prestige of the USSR." Jimmy Carter's repeated condemnations of Soviet human rights policy did offend the Soviet Union, and for this reason Medvedev expressed doubt, in the summer of 1977, that Carter's actions would "cause any improvement in the plight of dissidents in the USSR." It might even backfire. "It is known to me," Medvedev writes, "that during the period of the noisiest campaign in defense of the right of Soviet people to emigrate, one of the working groups preparing the text of the new Soviet constitution," to avoid the impression of having conceded to Western pressure, "decided to cross out [an] article on the right of free exit from the USSR."[2] In addition to raising the question of whether the children of darkness might do more good than the children of light, Medvedev's comments indicate that nations, like persons, are easily offended by unsolicited criticism, particularly when it impugns their moral character. Nations, like individuals, are likely to respond by retaliating—trying to prove that the accuser is as immoral as the accused. The Soviet Union has pointed to two areas of U.S. hypocrisy.

One is that the United States does not take human rights, at home or abroad, as seriously as it pretends to. "Neither the U.S. situation nor its actions and policies in the world give any justification for such pretensions," Brezhnev stated in 1977. When the newly elected Carter snubbed the Soviet Union by receiving dissident Vladimir Bukovsky at the White House and by writing dissident Andrei Sakharov (the voice of "democratic" Russia) a letter promising to "continue our firm commitment to promote respect for human rights," the *Literary Gazette* retaliated by pointing out Carter's unconcern for American "dissidents." The Soviet journal reported that several weeks prior to meeting with Bukovsky, Carter had received a letter from James Baldwin on behalf of American political prisoners known as the Wilmington Ten and the Charlotte Three, detailing the unjust, inhumane treatment given them in the courts and prisons of North Carolina. Was it not supremely hypocritical, the journal asked, for Carter to respond so promptly to Sakharov's letter but not to reply at all to Baldwin's? The following year, when the U.S. delegate to the United Nations Human Rights Commission, Edward Mezvinsky, accused the Soviet Union of religious persecution and anti-Semitism, the Soviet delegate Valerian Zorin retaliated by pointing to the racism, inhumane prisons, and the inhumane use of the death penalty in the United States. Yuri Kornilov pointed out the hypocrisy of a nation building a neutron bomb and then preaching about "love of peace and love of man." "How can one pose as a champion of human rights and at the same time brandish the neutron bomb that threatens the lives of millions of people?" Konstantin Chernenko accused the United States of "hypocrisy" on two counts. First, he charged that the United States has serious human rights problems of its own in such areas as unemployment, lack of medical care for the poor, racial discrimination, organized crime, and violence. Second, he pointed to the failure of the United States and several West European countries to ratify a number of United Nations covenants intended to promote implementation of the Universal Declaration of Human Rights. He said they do not back up their lofty words with concrete actions—"the international covenants on human rights, which have been ratified by all the countries of the socialist community, are to this day not recognized by those who are the most vociferous about human rights."[3]

A second area of U.S. hypocrisy involves the way that the United States has used the human rights issue as an ideological weapon for fighting cold war political battles. Soviet press and politicians have accused the United States of using human rights to fight a "psychological war" with the Soviets (Zorin); of "using the most ludicrous and wild concoctions borrowed from the stock in trade of reactionary bourgeois propaganda" and of launching a "propaganda campaign" which consists of nothing but "rhetoric around a myth" (Kornilov); of using the human rights issue to "sow mistrust and suspicion between peoples" (Sergi Vishnevsky, senior editor of *Pravda*); of launching "a campaign of slander over the farfetched problem of 'human rights'" (Chernenko); of encouraging the "renegades [dissidents] . . . who maliciously slander Soviet reality" by praising the activities of such renegades as the "defense of human rights" (Andropov); and of trying to use human rights propaganda "to undermine the solidarity of the socialist community" by trying to create the illusion of "internal opposition" (Brezhnev).[4] The real U.S. concern, these Soviets believe, is not for the rights of human beings but for maximizing U.S. power and influence around the world. The United States should be honest about its imperialistic and Machiavellian interests rather than disguising them in propaganda about love and human dignity. The other U.S. concern, these Soviets believe, is to divert attention away from the injustices of "bourgeois society," as though one form of hypocrisy could be covered up by another.

Objections from the Third World

This response—a sense of being offended, followed by resentment and retaliation by accusing the accuser of being hypocritical—is also characteristic of the Third World reaction to U.S. human rights initiatives. Islamic scholar Rashid Ahmad Jullundhri resented the insinuation that Christianity and Western culture offered a higher view of human dignity and human rights than Islam. He pointed out that during the medieval period Islamic nations were more democratic and Christian nations more authoritarian. Present human rights atrocities in Moslem nations, he wrote in 1978, should not be attributed to the Islamic religion, which is very affirming of human dignity and human rights, but to "colonial legacies" left over from the days of Western-Christian rule. For example, the current practice of lengthly detention without trial is "absolutely against Moslem law," but was introduced during the colonial period and has been continued by a secular ruling class unsympathetic to Moslem principles of human rights.[5]

Africanist Dunstan Wai also resented the insinuation that Western notions of human rights were superior to those in non-Western societies. Traditional African societies had complex, humane structures of justice. The current disrespect for human rights in many African nations, he says in 1978, "is not at all in accord with the spirit and practice of traditional political systems" but is an aberration "facilitated by colonial legacies and reinforced by the agonies of 'underdevelopment.'" The current "repression, exploitation, and violence is no less than the past brutality of the colonists," and the methods of terror and torture were introduced by the colonial governments and passed on to their successors. The instability and poverty which inflame these problems result largely from the colonial experience. Rather than condemning African peoples for human rights problems on their continent, Wai believes that Western peoples should recognize their own role in creating this problem. To create a horrendous situation in a foreign country and then to condemn the people in that country because of the horrendous situation there is a supreme act of hypocrisy.[6]

In the Western hemisphere, Fidel Castro said he was "appalled" by the patronizing element in U.S. human rights initiatives. "The United States does not have anything to show us," he said in December 1977, after Carter expressed concern over human rights conditions in Cuba. He pointed out U.S. hypocrisy in assuming the role of the world's leader in the moral sphere. "We have no prostitution, no gambling, no racial discrimination," he said on one occasion. On another, he added to the list, Vietnam, Watergate, U.S. support for "every totalitarian regime in Latin America," and American "businessmen [who] regularly bribe public officials of other countries." He resented U.S. failure to acknowledge Cuban achievement in literacy and public health. Launching a polemical counteroffensive, he suggested that, "in the field of human rights, Cuba might be "better off than the United States." Brazilian Foreign Minister Azeredo da Silveira, incensed by U.S. exaggeration of the Brazilian torture of two missionaries, counterattacked by pointing out that at about the same time Chicago police had "killed two demonstrators and injured 133 during a Puerto Rican demonstration." He asked why the United States was so hypocritical, applying one standard at home and another abroad—"One cannot protect human rights in a cockeyed fashion, looking only to one side."[7]

Within the United Nations, the United States does not have the reputation of being a champion of human rights. The United States has not ratified many of the human rights covenants that it once fought so hard to secure. The United States does not devote much effort and expertise to the work of the United Nations' Human Rights Commission. The Soviet Union and other nations assign their top people to long-term appointments with the commission. The United States typically assigns inexperienced political appointees to hold the job for short periods of time. This weakens the U.S. capacity to contribute to the commission and suggests to the rest of the world that the United States is not serious about human rights. It also makes the U.S.'s lofty appeals for international human rights sound rather hypocritical. Even the conscientious American delegate who tries to do some good within the commission is likely to be outmaneuvered by the more seasoned delegates from other countries.[8]

THE ANATOMY OF WESTERN CULTURAL IMPERIALISM AND ITS INFLUENCE ON THE HUMAN RIGHTS MOVEMENT

Had the integrity of non-Western cultures been violated by the human rights movement? Did they have just grounds for feeling offended or were they camouflaging their own shortcomings with rhetoric? Certainly there is a polemical element to their response but, as a number of Western scholars, journalists, and politicians have recognized, there was also an element of truth as well.

United Nations Human Rights Initiatives

With regard to the early efforts of the United Nations, a number of factors give credence to the claim that the human rights movement has been a veiled attempt of Western cultures to dominate non-Western cultures. All the meetings to form the United Nations, to write its charter, and to write the Universal Declaration of Human Rights were held in the United States. The United Nations headquarters was, of course, located in New York City. Most of the persons active in drafting the Universal Declaration were from the West, particularly France, Canada, New Zealand, Australia, and the United States. Eleanor Roosevelt served as the first president of the Commission on Human Rights.[9]

A number of Western scholars have commented that the Universal Declaration has a distinctively Western character. Adamantia Pollis and Peter Schwab state that the West "dominated" the early UN leadership, that the United Nations' concept of human rights is rooted in Western culture, and that the declaration assumes that "Western values are paramount and ought to be extended to the non-Western world." Pollis and Schwab refute the claim that the concern for similar types of rights in the charters of the Organization of American States and the Organization for African Unity suggest that the Universal Declaration is truly universal. This only proves, they say, that Latin American and African countries were dominated by colonial power and influence at the time that these charters were adopted.[10]

Promotion of human rights in the United Nations has been motivated largely by extra-moral factors. The concern to condemn Fascism has been widely recognized and accepted. Just as much a factor, if not more so, was the role that the Universal Declaration played in waging the cold war against Communism. "The ideological conflict with Soviet communism," comments political scientist John T. Wright, was a significant factor giving "impetus to the quest for the protection of human rights." "The Declaration was ratified," comments sociologist Marnia Lazreg, "while the Cold

War was under way and the economy of the United States was in full expansion." The principles of the declaration thus "fulfill an ideological function in the struggle between socialism and capitalism." The declaration also served a "legitimizing" function within the capitalist nations. At a time when Western nations (and particularly the United States) faced a number of crises (civil rights, Vietnam, the energy crisis of 1973 and the rise in oil prices, urban decay, rising unemployment and food prices, Watergate) the legitimacy of the capitalist economic system and the liberal political system was undermined. One way to restore this legitimacy was to wave the banner of universal human rights. In this way, the United States was able to reestablish itself as the moral leader of the world.[11]

Amnesty International and Freedom House

With regard to the nongovernmental organizations, such as Amnesty International, the International Commission of Jurists, and Freedom House, there is also evidence to substantiate the claim that human rights initiatives aimed at cultural domination rather than cultural reconciliation. One of the leaders of Amnesty International, Nigel S. Rodley, has identified Amnesty's Western orientation and Western constituency as factors contributing to the ineffectiveness of Amnesty and the International Commission of Jurists. They emphasize civil rather than economic or social rights. Most of their members and leaders are Western. Political scientist Richard H. Ullman concurs: "it is precisely their concentration on civil and political liberties that makes organizations like Amnesty International or the International Commission of Jurists seem to the citizens of poor countries like political agents of the industrialized West." Political scientist Ibne Hassan observes that Amnesty International is strong in liberal nations (the United States, West Germany, The Netherlands, The United Kingdom, and Sweden) and weak elsewhere. Most of Amnesty's "members, " he says, are from the First World and most of Amnesty's "clients" are from Second and Third World countries.[12]

Political scientists Harry M. Scoble and Laurie S. Wiseberg point out Amnesty's reluctance to criticize First World nations for the role they play as an ultimate cause of human rights problems in the Third World. Amnesty's definition of human rights is "static" rather than "dynamic," it deals "with the consequences of political repression and never comes to grips with the underlying causes." An examination of underlying causes would reveal the sins of Western colonialist nations. To turn the spotlight upon these Western nations would "alienate" a large portion of Amnesty's constituency, so Amnesty is reluctant to do so. It is easy to understand why non-Western nations would view Amnesty as a Western organization attempting to foist Western values upon the rest of the world.[13]

Much more insidious, in the eyes of the non-Western world, is a U.S. human rights organization known as Freedom House. Each year since 1973, Freedom House has issued the "Comparative Survey of Freedom," which ranks each nation on a scale of one (most free) to seven (least free). Not surprisingly, the United States is rated a "one" and the Soviet Union a "seven." The survey and its accompanying "Map of Freedom" are highly influential because their quantitative results can provide quick and easy measurements of human rights performance. Media personnel looking for news stories, government agencies trying to make policy decisions, and social scientists looking for data to analyze have all found the survey useful. What concerns non-Western observers, and the more critical Western scholars, is that the bases for Freedom House's quantifications are seldom scrutinized. Scoble and Wiseberg have done such a study and concluded that the survey is "rigged" [my term, not theirs] to favor the United States and U.S. allies. Rather than developing broad criteria to measure freedom, the survey judges nations according to whether they do things the way the United States does them. For example, political participation is measured on the narrow basis of whether a general election is held and whether there are two or more political parties, despite the fact that there are a number of other ways to organize a society to maximize political participation. By Freedom House standards, Tanzania achieves a poor rating, despite the success and fairness of its innovative one-party system. Yugoslavian workers' councils, West European worker self management programs, and other attempts to promote political participation that is different from general two-party elections go unrecognized—even though these experiments attempt to give ordinary persons control over the decisions that most directly affect them. To cite an extreme but not atypical example, the Freedom House approach assumes that it is feasible for a nation of illiterate peasants who, through a violent struggle, have just gained independence from economic and political domination to establish immediately a Western-style democracy. Such an assumption, Scoble and Wiseberg comment, runs contrary both "to our knowledge of the sociology and psychology of political attitudes" as well as to "the early decades of the U.S. party system."[14]

Changing Attitudes in the West

In recent years, both the United Nations and Amnesty International have taken steps to alter their image as "political agents of the industrialized West." The United Nations has become very critical of the First World—so much so that the United States has withdrawn much of its support for the organization. In December 1977, the Czechoslovak Communist Party newspaper *Rude Provo* accused Amnesty of being "anti-Communist," of engaging in "'demogogical attacks' against Socialist countries over the violation of human rights, while almost overlooking abuses in the United States, Britain or West Germany." In response to such criticism, Amnesty "adopted" eighteen American political prisoners, expressed concern over the death penalty, and accused the U.S. of torturing some of its prisoners and fabricating charges against political activists. The *Washington Post* reported that "the Carter administration's campaign to highlight human rights violations around the globe" had taken "an ironic reverse bounce—a new look at the abuses of the rights of Americans." Some conservative journalists and politicians criticized Amnesty for creating the illusion that human rights abuses were as bad in the West as in Communist and Third World countries. President Carter responded more positively: "We welcome the scrutiny and criticism of ourselves as part of the normal dealings between nations." Assistant Attorney General for Civil Rights, Drew S. Days III, reiterated "it is important to acknowledge that we have some problems." "The action of Amnesty International and the Soviet Union's awareness of human rights violations in this country," he told a group of black attorneys in Alabama, "mean that further success in our own human rights campaign abroad may hinge on how forthrightly and firmly this administration addresses such domestic problems."[15]

Unfortunately, such concessions and attempts at domestic reform were too few and too late to compensate for the negative reaction engendered by U.S. human rights initiatives. Many U.S. journalists, politicians, and scholars have agreed with non-Western critics that an unstated objective, or at least an inevitable consequence, of the human rights movement is Western cultural hegemony.

Hypocrisy

One indication of this, they say, is that the United States has failed to do at home what it has asked others to do abroad. If the United States were truly concerned about human rights for their own sake, rather than as a means to political ends, would it not try especially hard to realize human rights at home where there is some possibility of success, rather than abroad where political and cultural barriers make matters more complicated?

One American who raised this question at the time that Congress began placing human rights restrictions on foreign aid, was Senator Charles Goodell in a book entitled *Political Prisoners in America*, published in 1973. Goodell delineated abuses of civil and political rights in America, ranging from imprisonment of Quaker pacifists during the Revolutionary War, to the Palmer Raids of 1919, to the abuses of the McCarthy era, to J. Edgar Hoover's harassment of civil rights leaders, Vietnam protesters and radical political groups such as the Weathermen and the Students for a Democratic Society.[16]

In 1975, the U.S. Senate Intelligence Committee launched a probe into the Federal Bureau of Investigation's intelligence activities of the previous twenty years. It made a number of shocking and embarrassing discoveries. The investigation revealed that the FBI's COINTELPRO operations had involved wiretapping, letter opening, fake letters to destroy reputations and break up families (and organizations), threats, bribing witnesses, and other illegal measures to harass, discredit, and destroy organizations that Hoover considered subversive. These organizations included the Ku Klux Klan and the Communist Party, USA, in the fifties, and the Vietnam Veterans against the War and civil rights and black power groups, in the sixties and seventies. Former FBI officials and attorneys general testified that the FBI had used "unlawful and reprehensible" methods that "served no public purposes" to carry out what seemed to be Hoover's personal vendetta against Martin Luther King. These methods included bugging King's motel rooms and threatening King's life. Former Attorney General Nicholas Katzenbach testified that he had been "shocked and appalled" upon discovering "the extent of the FBI's attempt to intimidate, to harass and to discredit Dr. Martin Luther King."[17]

On December 11, 1978 (the twenty-fifth anniversary of the signing of the Universal Declaration of Human Rights) a coalition of black attorneys, civil rights activists, and the United Church of Christ's Commission on Racial Justice submitted a petition complaining of human rights abuses in the United States to the United Nations Commission on Human Rights and Sub-Commission on Prevention of Discrimination and Protection of Minorities. Three areas of concern were delineated. One was that minorities and political dissidents were being prevented from exercising their civil rights. The petition listed U.S. political prisoners, including Church of Christ minister the Reverend Ben Chavis, the Wilmington Ten, the Charlotte Three, and a number of Native American activists. The petition submitted evidence that the FBI had "framed" a number of these political prisoners, using illegal methods such as bribing convicts to testify against political prisoners and trumping up false criminal charges against political prisoners. The petition contained a letter sent by Wilmington Ten supporters to President Carter, pointing out that a State Department spokesman had admitted that the case was "an embarrassment," and asking Carter "to speak out for the human rights of the Wilmington Ten as you have done for those you have felt were persecuted in other lands." "It is well and good to speak to the human rights of those in other lands, " the letter reiterated, "but attention must be paid at least equally to those who suffer deprivation of those same rights in our own country." The peition also contained a letter from Chavis to Carter saying that while "it may be embarrassing to admit that there are in fact political prisoners in our country . . . , it has become extremely hypocritical of you to remain silent about the domestic violations of human rights while proceeding to proclaim a selective foreign policy based on human rights." The letter then asks, in a manner reminiscent of the questions raised by non-Western critics, "Should not the protection of human rights begin at home?"

A second area of concern for the petitioners was that the U.S. criminal justice system favored whites and middle-class persons in its method of determining the seriousness of various crimes. They cite the example of a poor, black person brought to trial for stealing a couple of hundred dollars versus the case of a white executive tried for "embezzling" a couple of hundred thousand dollars. The former's likelihood of conviction, they said, is ninety percent, the latter's is twenty percent. If convicted, the black will be sentenced to eight to eleven years, the white to two to four years.

The third concern of the petitioners was that the United States had taken land from Native Americans and Mexican Americans, had enslaved African Americans, had colonized Puerto Rico, and had never offered any compensation for these injustices. As a result, poverty, malnutrition, and unemployment among these U.S. minorities is much worse than among the rest of the population. If the United States were truly concerned about human rights, the coalition maintained, it should begin by rectifying its own injustices.[18]

A number of other Americans chimed in their complaints of human rights abuses by the U.S. government toward minorities and political radicals. Some complaints were more polemically motivated than others. The International Indian Treaty Council, representing ninety-seven tribes, presented to the Soviet mission at the United Nations a list of human rights violations by the United States against Native Americans. They cited violations of treaties, discrimination against their cultural and religious traditions, and lack of economic and social rights. The U.S. Ambassador to the United Nations, Andrew Young, told a French reporter that U.S. prisons hold "hundreds, perhaps even thousands of people whom I would call political prisoners." Some called for Young's impeachment. Congressman John Conyers came to his support. "Simply by reading the morning paper each day," he said, one can see "violations of constitutional and civil rights by the nation's highest officials (and) the FBI and the CIA." The *Washington Post* carried a series of articles on U.S. injustices toward minorities. The articles alleged that Hoover had approved of numerous illegal actions against various groups, and that an FBI informant may have murdered civil rights workers in Alabama in the sixties.[19]

Political sicientist Fouad Ajami points toward the Carter administration's failure to act aggressively toward human rights abuses at home as a major weakness, moral and political, of the Carter human rights campaign. Until the summer of 1967, he says, most Northerners believed that racism was a Southern problem. It took violent, destructive race riots in Northern cities to change that perception. Ajami says that "the same tendency can now be observed in Western pronouncements on human rights." Western discussions of human rights make it sound "as though all is well in the house of the West," and as though human rights abuses only take place in the Communist and Third World countries. Unfortunately, it is easier for Westerners to "see" repression and brutality in foreign (and oftentimes enemy) lands, but it is "much harder to look into their own society, to puncture its myths and claims, to honestly confront the human and social costs of its own arrangements and evaluate the drift of its own history." Ajami concludes with a statement of Stanley Hoffman's, that "well-ordered crusades begin at home." If the United States is serious about human rights, it should demonstrate that seriousness by doing at home what it has asked others to do abroad.[20]

Self-righteousness

A second major theme emerged in the American responses to the charge that the human rights movement sought cultural domination. Not only had the United States failed to accomplish at home what it had asked others to do abroad but the United States had also evinced a self-righteous, chauvinistic, attitude. Such an attitude reflected cultural insensitivity and, these American observers commented, gave non-Westerners just cause for concern that the human rights movement would violate the integrity of non-Western cultures. The U.S. Secretary of State, Cyrus Vance, recognized this problem in a speech to the University of Georgia Law School. "Have we steered away from the self-righteous and strident, remembering that our own record is not umblemished?"[21]

Most countries do not claim to base their foreign policy on moral concerns. The United States often does and thus is more vulnerable to the charge of being self-righteous. President Carter's insistence that America assert itself as the moral leader of the world created problems that many Americans felt could have been avoided simply by setting lower standards for other countries and setting higher standards at home.[22]

One evidence of American self-righteousness is the use of religious language to describe the human rights movement. Carter's human rights initiatives were often referred to in evangelical terms. "Crusade" has been used to describe Carter's actions, and "sermons" has been used to describe his speeches on behalf of universal human rights. Theologian J. Bryan Hehir cites "moralism" and "messianism" as symptoms of an American need "to cast our policy objectives in universal moral terms rather than in the more modest categories of national interest and the necessities of power." George Keenan complains of the American tendency, exemplified in the human rights movement, of claiming "to know with such certainty what other people want and what is good for them in the way of political institutions." Such messianism results in Americans trying "to impose their own values, traditions and habits of thought on peoples for whom these things have no validity and no usefulness." Their zeal blinds them to the limitations of Western-style democracy and to the positive elements of non-Western values. Hence the fear that self-righteousness will lead to cultural domination is a legitimate one.[23]

Another evidence of American self-righteousness is American blindness to the fact that much of the motivation for promoting human rights abroad is to create pride at home. The human rights movement served as a catharsis for Americans bruised by Vietnam and Watergate, and embarrassed by the frankly cynical foreign policy of the Kissinger era. It gave them a reason to believe that America would, to quote President Carter, "regain the moral stature we once had." A newly elected Vice President Mondale expressed hope that this new American role would help Americans start "feeling good" once again. Columnist Anthony Lewis said that, "after the dark years in which many of us became ashamed of the things done in America's name, it simply feels good to hear a president denounce torture and inhumanity in the most direct way." The implication of such statements is that the United States was not concerned about human rights as an end in itself but as a means of boosting the American ego. This is self-righteousness. Non-Westerners had just cause to be offended by this moral pretension and to fear that the human rights movement might prove to be a wolf in sheep's clothing.[24]

A number of Western social scientists have concurred with non-Western critics that there has been an air of self-righteousness associated with the American efforts to promote universal human rights. This self-righteousness may have blinded human rights advocates to the faults of the American system and to the virtues of non-Western cultures. It may have given human rights leaders a false sense of self-assurance which resulted in a number of impolitic actions, as Kenneth W. Thompson has suggested, pointing to the "stridency and half-considered actions" in the first months of the Carter presidency. It may have contributed to the "parochial view of human conditions of Third World societies," as Abdul Aziz Said, Professor of International Relations at The American University, Washington, D.C., has observed. Fouad Ajami, of Princeton's Center of International Studies, pointed toward self-righteousness as a major problem of the American psyche and particularly of the Carter human rights campaign. Such self-righteousness can become the human rights movement's own worst enemy—"A heavy dosage of Western self-righteousness can . . . undercut prospects for a successful struggle against authoritarianism." From the Third World perspective, this "ethnocentric and 'imperial' mentality" says that "America is the center of the world," and "the rest of the world, the Third World in particular, is but a mere periphery." It says that "America calls the tune, while others are expected to follow." Ajami believes that "U.S. self-righteousness is particularly problematic" with regard to First World–Third World relationships. Westerners may need reminding, he says, but non-Westerners will remember, "that a human-rights rhetoric of sorts was very much a part of the mythology and the ideological baggage of Western colonialism. Even when colonizing others, Europeans were fond of justifying their alien rule as a way of promoting human rights."[25]

American activists trying to promote justice at home have complained that their task has been made more difficult by a smug sentiment that all is well here, that injustice is something that only takes place in foreign lands. There is a prevailing attitude that says, to use the idiom, "it ain't broke, so don't fix it." Those who believe it is "broke" and needs "fixing" thus encounter a great deal of resistance. One such example is the coalition of lawyers, civil rights activists, and United Church of Christ members, who petitioned the United Nations concerning human rights abuses in the United States. According to attorney Lennox Hinds, their spokesperson, the group "expressed outrage and frustration at their inability to pierce the domestic cocoon of smug, unexamined self-righteousness that shields the American legal system from examination, and encourages increasing and unconscionable abuse." Perhaps the single-most flaw in the American character is the sin of pride. It is an idolatrous pride that refuses to admit that America is not the moral leader of the world. Such pride blinds Americans to injustices at home even while focusing a telescopic lens upon injustices abroad.[26]

Cold War Politics

A third theme to emerge from the American response to non-Western concerns regarding Western cultural hegemony was that the U.S. motive for promoting universal human rights had involved more self-interest and less compassion than the U.S. rhetoric would suggest. One bit of evidence that has been cited frequently is Carter's double standard toward strategic allies and less strategic nations. In the Philippines, Indonesia, South Korea, and the Western Sahara, Carter was reluctant to cut military assistance despite severe human rights abuses. In fact, U.S. military assistance was used to perpetuate the human rights abuses that Carter condemned elsewhere. Special Consultant to the House of Representatives, John Salzberg, has confirmed that U.S. military aid played a "substantial" role in Indonesia's illegal occupation of East Timor and continued to be used to suppress liberation fighters there. Other observers have noted that the Carter adminstration tended to approve health projects in repressive countries aligned with the United States, using the argument that such aid would lead to the promotion of human rights. The Carter administration tended to disapprove of proposed health projects in left wing nations. New Zealand Prime Minister Robert Muldoon criticized the Carter administration's "selective application" of its human rights criteria for foreign aid, calling it "immoral." More pragmatic observers might not agree that selective aid is immoral. Most nations readily admit that they act in their own self-interest. What may be immoral, however, is to camouflage the U.S. concern for self-interest with false claims to loftier motives. If the United States had been as concerned with univeral human rights as the rhetoric would suggest, the United States would have attempted to promote human rights among her strategic allies and not just against her cold war enemies.[27]

Another bit of evidence that the United States has been motivated less by compassion than by self-interest is the U.S. failure to ratify many of the UN human rights treaties. The United States has opposed UN resolutions to grant equal rights to Indians in South Africa (1948) and self-determination to native peoples (1952). In 1960, ninety-seven nations voted to denounce apartheid as a crime against humanity. The United States was not one of those ninety-seven. Nor did the United States support a 1963 measure to condemn the use of mercenaries by colonial regimes against native peoples. In 1972, the United States refused to support a bill affirming the rights of native South Africans. The United States has never ratified the major human rights covenants, including the Covenant on Civil and Political Rights; the Covenant on Economic, Social and Cultural Rights; the Convention on the Prevention and Punishment of the Crime of Genocide. Carter supported the ratification of these measures but too many others feared a loss of American independence in the world forum if the United States became a part of the process. The U.S. was willing to initiate but it was not willing to participate. As a result, the United States has grown increasingly isolated from the international discussion of human rights and it has not submitted to the international processes for promoting and protecting human rights. In the eyes of much of the world, the United States and Carter were relative "latecomers" to the human rights movement. It seemed odd that this "latest convert" would suddenly want to proclaim itself as the "new archbishop." The United States should not be surprised, Ajami notes, that so many would voice "strong objections and a large measure of skepticism."[28]

All this evidence gives weight to the contention that Western human rights initiatives have as much or more to do with cold war power struggles than with the protection and promotion of truly universal human rights. The human rights movement may very well be just another means for Western political and cultural domination. This is the view of the World Council of Churches' Commission on International Affairs, which asserts that "human rights have been used as a Cold War ideological weapon and a means to strengthen domination." This is also the view of social scientists Lazreg and Ajami. The U.S. effort to promote human rights is, in Lazreg's opinion, "a moralistic ideology that satisfies extra-moral needs." These extra-moral needs include the need for ideological weapons to gain supremacy in West–East and North–South struggles. The U.S. effort to promote human rights is so laden with hidden political agenda that, in Ajami's opinion, "it is often difficult to tell where the West's accustomed antagonism toward the Soviet Union ends and where genuine concern for human rights begins." The United States sponsored human rights campaign appeared to Ajami to be little more than a waging of "the cold war through other means." Détente became a bad word once again, and once more it became respectable to speak harshly of the Soviet Union. Ajami feared that a confusion of political and moral objectives would cause the human rights campaign to lose its moral credibility in the eyes of the world—"Precisely because it is such a worthwhile struggle, it would be negligent and irresponsible to entangle this cause too deeply in cold-war politics." If the United States truly cares for the plight of the Soviet dissidents, Ajami suggests, then it should give the struggle to free them "the dignity and the seriousness that it merits." To do anything less "demeans them, ourselves, and issues raised by this cause." To do anything less also renders the persuasive value of U.S. diplomatic measures on behalf of the dissidents less effective.[29]

Evidence has been presented to justify the claim that the human rights movement seeks the cultural and political domination of the non-Western world. The more ethereal aims of the movement have been overshadowed by hypocrisy, self-righteousness, and cold war politics which offend and alienate non-Western nations and cultures. What remains to be answered are questions concerning the ultimate cause of the problem and what should be done to resolve it. What is it "deep within the American psyche" that yearns to foist American notions of human rights on the rest of the world? In the remainder of this chapter, and in chapter 9, I shall argue that deep within the American psyche are notions of American and human identity that shape our urge to dominate other cultures.

FACTORS CONTRIBUTING TO THE AMERICAN URGE FOR CULTURAL DOMINATION

American Cultural Identity: A "Redeemer" Nation

Americans do not view theirs as a culture among other cultures, but as a culture above other cultures. This identity was born at the time the Puritans settled the American continent. It had been hoped that the Reformation would transform the European continent into the kingdom of God. When this failed to materialize, Puritans focused their hopes on the other side of the Atlantic. God's plan, they now believed, was to usher in the new age in a completely new world. Reforming the old structure had proved more difficult than expected. Starting over, as with Noah after the purifying flood, now seemed a better strategy. The discovery of a new world afforded the opportunity for such an experiment. The New World was a pristine wilderness, reminiscent of the Garden of Eden. It was a reminder of the innocence and goodness that preceded the Fall and a challenge to recreate the world without reenacting the Fall. Puritans believed themselves chosen by God to carry out what Samuel Danforth called an "errand into the wilderness," to settle what Edward Johnson called "the place where the Lord will create a new heaven and a new earth." In this new place and through these chosen people God would, as Jonathan Edwards had put it, "renew the world of mankind."[30]

God's promise to Abraham was that through his progeny all the peoples of the world would be blessed. Puritans believed that God had bestowed on them a similar calling, to be a people through whom all the other nations and cultures would be redeemed. It is hard not to strive to be righteous when one has been granted such a high and holy calling. It is hard not to be self-righteous as well. According to Israel's prophets, self-righteousness, moral chauvinism, and pride were the temptations that "went with the territory" of being a chosen people. America's prophets and critics have made the same observation. Unfortunately, the temptation to self-righteousness is greatest when trying hardest to make the world righteous. Self-righteousness blinds do-gooders to their own faults, making them less effective in doing good as other nations resent their hypocrisy. Such is the morphology of the "cycle of righteousness": a concern for global righteousness inspires not only altruistic actions but also self-righteous attitudes, which ignore declining standards at home while promoting inflated expectations abroad. The unfortunate result is double standards, intercultural tensions, and less righteousness at home and abroad.

America the Righteous Example

The early settlers had a solution to this problem. They envisioned America as a nation and culture through which the rest of the world would be redeemed. This would happen not through American action abroad but by undergoing the sort of redemption at home that would inspire imitation. America was to be a righteous example that others would want to imitate, not a righteous empire[31] that would force others to imitate it. As America grew stronger, however, the possibility of being a righteous empire offered a new way of being the nation and culture through whom the rest of the world would be redeemed. America could focus less on her own sanctification and could police the rest of the world. These contrasting visions of America as a redeemer nation—one as a righteous example and the other as a righteous empire—serve as the basis for the American debate over how Western cultures can best promote human rights among non-Western cultures.

America as a righteous example is the America envisioned by John Winthrop, William Penn, and Thomas Jefferson. Winthrop reminded New Englanders that their role was to be "a city set on a hill." Such a city, Jesus had said, could not be hidden. Because of its location it could not help but serve as an example. Whether it was a positive or negative example was a matter for New Englanders to decide. Puritans were not the only ones who believed that American had been chosen as a light to the nations. Penn wanted his "holy experiment" to be "an example . . . to the nations." Jefferson, writing from Paris in 1787, described America as a "primitive and precious model of what is to change the condition of man over the globe," and exulted that "the disease of liberty is catching." For him liberty was not something that America could preach to the rest of the world. It could be caught, not taught. Those wishing to receive it would have to be the ones to take the initiative.[32]

On a number of occasions the young American nation resisted the temptation to move from righteous example to righteous empire. George Washington advised against helping in the French Revolution on the grounds that "no nation is to be trusted further than it is bound by its own interest." Any nation pretending to do otherwise was fooling either itself or others. Secretary of State John Quincy Adams advised President James Monroe not to support the Greek revolution against the Turks on grounds that the United States was not to be a crusader for righteousness, only an example of it. "She goes not abroad in support of monsters to destroy," he said. "She is the well-wisher to the freedom and independence of all," but is "champion and vindicator only of her own." Like Jefferson, he believed that freedom, by its very nature, had to be caught rather than taught.

Otherwise the fundamental maxim of U.S. policy "would insensibly change from liberty to force," and the United States might become "dictress of the world." On the same issue a Virginia congressman, Alexander Smyth, also argued against American intervention on grounds that the best thing the United States could do to promote global justice and democracy was to do everything in its power to make the "experiment" at home successful. "The cause of freedom, the hope of mankind, depends on the ultimate success of the hitherto successful experiment in the science of government, now making in the United States. When we consider the importance of the interests confided to us," he argues, "it must appear unpardonable wantonly to hazard the success of that experiment." Likewise, Virginia Congressman John Randolph told the House of Representatives that it is not for the United States "to go on a crusade in another hemisphere" even if for such dear principles as "liberty and Religion."[33]

Historian Norman A Graebner concludes that until the election of President William McKinley in 1896 there was not a single effort by anyone in a position of power and responsibility to encourage American involvement in democratic revolutions abroad. The success and failure of these movements "hinged on conditions purely indigenous." Prior to McKinley, American statesmen were not concerned with crusading overseas but with "the creation of a society in America that was worthy of emulation." America was to be a pace setter, a standard toward which others would strive.[34]

From Righteous Example to Righteous Empire

Beginning with McKinley, however, this image took on more negative connotations. America the righteous example was seen as a passive, isolationist well-wisher, capable of helping others but unwilling to do so. America was viewed as preoccupied with its own righteousness and insufficiently concerned with the global situation. A new vision of America was born—America the righteous empire. Instead of passively waiting for others to imitate America the righteous example, America the righteous empire would crusade for democracy and peace throughout the world.

America the righteous empire was the America envisioned by McKinley and Woodrow Wilson. McKinley had held to an ostensibly purer idealism, believing that America should help other nations for their own sake. With Wilson and World War I the universalization of democracy was seen as a way of promoting U.S., British, and French concerns for stability and peace. Wilson believed that our principles and our interests conveniently coincided. Both viewpoints had their problems. McKinley claimed to be concerned only about helping other countries for their own sake. He colonized the Philippines to teach them Christianity and democracy. What he gave them was economic dependence and political corruption. His real reason for colonizing them was for our sake, not theirs. Wilson claimed to make moral principles, and especially the principle of democracy, the cornerstone of his foreign policy. Yet at Versailles he opposed efforts to promote racial equality and self-determination of colonized peoples.[35]

Both images presuppose that America is to be the nation and culture through whom the world will be redeemed. It is only a matter of tactics. Should America serve as a righteous example, or should it try to build a righteous empire? Should it be an introverted pace setter or an extroverted crusader?

American Notions of Human Identity

Deep within the American psyche there are, in addition to these notions of American cultural identity, notions of human identity which also shape our urge to dominate other cultures. Westerners tend to view humans in abstract rather than historical terms, and thus to view human rights in universal rather than cultural terms. This is the second factor contributing to the American urge for cultural domination. The Western proclivity for abstraction, I will argue in chapter 9, both contributes to and detracts from universal human rights.

The question of human identity has been touched on in the political science literature. Lazreg has pointed out the Western tendency to view humanity in "abstract" rather than historical, cultural, empirical terms, to detach humans from their "concrete life experiences" and cultural settings. The Universal Declaration of Human Rights, she said, gave precedence to "human" rather than "citizen" rights, and gave the impression of trying to incorporate "all human beings across nations and cultures into an abstract universal community of which the U.S. government is the champion." When "detached from the sociopolitical and economic life situations of concrete individuals or groups," human rights become "ideological" and "cease to be viewed historically" and culturally. Kamenka and Tay have also commented on this Western predilection for abstraction, as have Ajami, Said, and Pollis and Schwab. "To argue that human rights has a standing which is universal in character is," according to Pollis and Schwab, "to contradict historical reality." "While the pursuit of human dignity is universal," Said writes, "its forms are designed by the cultures of people." Viewing persons in abstract terms results, he says, in masking "parochial" Western notions of human rights in universal language, thus ignoring "the cultural realities and present existential conditions of Third

World societies." Universal human rights means, according to Ajami, that "foreign societies are to be measured, not by their own criteria or norms, but by America's [supposedly] 'timeless and abstract' ones."[36]

The question of human identity can be addressed more directly and extensively by theological anthropology. The question of abstract versus historical notions of human identity and universal versus cultural notions of human rights has been addressed by such theologians as Max Stackhouse, James Sellers, Raimundo Panikkar, and Robert A. and Alice Frazer Evans, and by participants in numerous dialogues, such as those recorded in *The East-West Encounter over Human Rights: Its Religious and Sociological Context* (sponsored by *Soundings* and edited by George R. Lucas, Jr. and James E. Will), *Human Rights in Religious Traditions* (sponsored by the *Journal of Ecumenical Studies* and edited by Arlene Swidler), and *Human Rights and Christian Responsibility* (The World Council of Churches). In the next chapter, we will examine the insights of these theologians in an effort to determine how the American attitude toward other cultures might be transformed from domination to respect, from a desire for hegemony to a respect for the integrity of non-Western cultures.

NOTES

1. Leonid Brezhnev, "Speech to the Sixteenth Trade Union Council," in *The Human Rights Reader*, eds. Walter Laqueur and Barry Rubin (New York: New American Library; Meridian Books, 1979), 309; cited by Angus Deming, "The Push for Human Rights," *Newsweek*, 20 June 1977, 53; cited in "U.S. Assails Russia on Human Rights Violations," *Los Angeles Times*, 13 December 1977, pt. I, 5.
2. Roy Medvedev, "Loyal Opposition" (excerpts from 1977 essay on human rights), *Newsweek*, 20 June 1977, 48.
3. Brezhnev, "Speech," 309; Arpad Kadarkay, *Human Rights in American and Russian Political Thought* (Washington, D.C.: University Press of America, 1982), 211; Jonathan Rollow, "U.S., Soviets Trade Sharp Charges at U.N. Rights Meeting," *Washington Post*, 8 March 1978, A24; Yuri [Juri] Kornilov, cited by Fouad Ajami, *Human Rights and World Order Politics* (New York: Institute for World Order, 1978), 1; Konstantin U. Chernenko, *Human Rights in Soviet Society* (New York: International Publishers, 1981), 141–43.
4. Valerian Zorin, cited in Rollow, A24; Kornilov, cited in Deming, 53; Kornilov, cited in Ajami, 1; Sergi Vishnevsky, article in *Pravda*, 11 June 1977, in *Human Rights and American Diplomacy: 1975–77*, ed. Judith F. Buncher (New York: Facts on File, 1977), 253; Chernenko, "For Lasting Peace and Dependable Security in Europe," 1978 in *Speeches and Writings*, 2d ed. (New York: Pergamon Press, 1984), 66; Y.V. Andropov, "Under the Banner of Lenin, Under Party Leadership," 22 February 1979 in *Speeches and Writings*, 2d ed. (New York: Pergamon Press, 1983), 206–07; Brezhnev, "Speech," 308–09.

5. Rashid Ahmad Jullundhri, "Human Rights and Islam," in *Understanding Human Rights: An Interdisciplinary and Interfaith Study*, ed. Alan D. Falconer (Dublin: Irish School of Ecumenics, 1980), 36–42.

6. Dunstan M. Wai, "Human Rights in Sub-Saharan Africa," in *Human Rights: Cultural and Ideological Perspectives*, ed. Adamantia Pollis and Peter Schwab, (New York: Praeger Publishers, 1979), 115–21.

7. "News in Brief," *Los Angeles Times*, 13 December 1977, pt. I, 2; Benjamin C. Bradlee, article in *Washington Post*, March 6, 1977 in *Human Rights and American Diplomacy*, ed. Buncher, 185–86; interview published in Brazil, 12 June 1977, in *Human Rights and American Diplomacy*, ed. Buncher, 183.

8. Rollow, A24.

9. Egon Schwelb, *Human Rights and the International Community: The Roots and Growth of the Universal Declaration of Human Rights, 1948–63* (Chicago: Quadrangle Books, 1964), 25–26; Sean MacBride, "The Universal Declaration—30 Years After," in *Understanding Human Rights*, ed. Falconer, 9–10.

10. Pollis and Schwab, "Human Rights: A Western Construct with Limited Applicability," in *Human Rights*, ed. Pollis and Schwab, 4–8.

11. John T. Wright, "Human Rights in the West: Political Liberties and the Rule of Law," in *Human Rights*, ed. Pollis and Schwab, 22; Marnia Lazreg, "Human Rights, State and Ideology: An Historical Perspective," in *Human Rights*, ed. Pollis and Schwab, 32–33, 37–39.

12. Nigel S. Rodley, "Monitoring Human Rights Violations in the 1980's," in *Enhancing Global Human Rights*, eds. Jorge I. Dominguez, Nigel S. Rodley, Bryce Wood, and Richard Falk (New York: McGraw-Hill Book Co., 1979), 146; Richard H. Ullman, "Introduction: Human Rights—Toward International Action," in *Enhancing Global Human Rights*, eds. Dominguez et al, 10; Ibne Hassan, "Amnesty International as a Human Rights Organization," Ph.D. dissertation, New York University, 1977, 65, 71–72, 264–67.

13. Harry M. Scoble and Laurie S. Wiseberg, "Problems of Comparative Research on Human Rights," in *Global Human Rights: Public Policies, Comparative Measures, and NGO Strategies*, eds. Ved P. Nanda, James R. Scarritt, and George W. Shepherd, Jr. (Boulder: Westview Press, 1981), 150.

14. Ibid., 152–55.

15. "Czech Newspaper Attacks Human Rights Group," *Washington Post*, 18 December 1977, A29; Sinclair Ward and John Jacobs, "Are These America's Political Prisoners? Examining Amnesty International's Charges Shows Mixed Picture," *Washington Post*, 8 January 1978, D1, D4; "Amnesty International Cites Abuse of Rights in American Prisons," *Washington Post*, 1 February 1979, A13; Scoble and Wiseberg, 149–50.

16. Charles Goodell, *Political Prisoners in America* (New York: Random House, 1973).

17. U.S., Congress, Senate, *Supplementary Detailed Staff Reports on Intelligence Activities and the Rights of Americans*, S. Rept. 94–755, 94th Cong., 2d sess., 1976, *Final Report of the Select Committee to Study Governmental Operations with Respect to Intelligence Activities*, bk. 3.

One threat on King's life was relayed by Hoover's assistant, Cartha DeLoach, through NAACP Executive Secretary Roy Wilkins. An excerpt from

DeLoach's memorandum, dated November 27, 1964: "I told him [Mr. Wilkins] . . . that if King wanted war, we certainly would give it to him. . . . I told him the ammunition was plentiful . . . [162]."

18. Lennox S. Hinds, *Illusions of Justice* [Subtitle: Human Rights Violations in the United States (Iowa City: School of Social Work, University of Iowa, 1979), see esp. xi, 173, 183–84, 188, 204, 249, 254, 44, 33.

19. *New York Times*, 17 June 1977 in *Human Rights and American Diplomacy*, ed. Buncher, 253; *Le Matin*, July 12, 1978 in Hinds, i, 1; Hinds, i–ii.

20. Ajami, 13–14; Stanley Hoffman, "No Choice, No Illusions," *Foreign Policy* 25 (Winter 1976–77) quoted by Ajami, 14; see also Rupert Emerson's catalog of "Western sins and shortcomings," which includes spending large sums of money on the military while poverty abounds in the United States and throughout the world, imperialism in the third world, "the squandering of the world's limited resources and pollution of the environment," and, the coup de grace: "If the West has been the fountainhead of liberal constitutional democracy, it has also been the breeding ground of Fascism and Nazism." Rupert Emerson, "The Fate of Human Rights in the Third World," *World Politics*, xxvii (January, 1975), 201–26, quoted by Ajami, 14.

21. Cyrus Vance, "Law Day Speech on Human Rights and Foreign Policy," April 30, 1977, at the University of Georgia, in *The Human Rights Reader*, eds. Laqueur and Rubin, 301.

22. Carter quoted by Norman A. Graebner, "Human Rights and U.S. Foreign Policy: The Historic Connection," in *The Moral Imperatives of Human Rights: A World Survey*, ed. Kenneth W. Thompson (Washington: The University Press of America, 1980), 52.

23. Graebner, 55, 63, 64; J. Bryan Hehir, "Human Rights and U.S. Foreign Policy: A Perspective from Theological Ethics," in *The Moral Imperatives*, ed. Thompson, 2; George Keenan, *The Cloud of Danger* (Boston: Little, Brown, 1977), 43 as quoted in Arthur Schlesinger, Jr. "Human Rights and the American Tradition," *Foreign Affairs* 57:3, 1978: 517.

24. Graebner, 51, 52; Anthony Lewis, *New York Times* quoted by Graebner, 64.

25. Kenneth W. Thompson, "Introduction," in *The Moral Imperatives*, ed. Thompson, v; Abdul Aziz Said, "Human Rights in Islamic Perspectives," in *Human Rights*, eds. Pollis and Schwab, 86; Ajami, 9–10.

26. Hines, iii. The idea for the image of the self-righteous American came from a cartoon in which an American is portrayed looking through a telescope at "HUMAN RIGHTS VIOLATION ABROAD," and pointing condemningly while wearing blinders that prevent him from seeing those who suffer at his feet. The cartoon appeared on the cover of a World Council of Churches: Commission of the Churches on International Affairs publication, *Human Rights and Christian Responsibility*, dossiers 1 and 2, 1974.

27. John Salzberg, "The Carter Administration—An Appraisal: A Congressional Perspective," in *Global Human Rights*, eds. Nanda et al, 5–7, 14; Graebner, 55; Associated Press interview, 11 June 1977 in *Human Rights and American Diplomacy*, ed. Buncher, 253.

28. Hinds, 1. The growing isolation of the United States from international discussion of human rights—what Reinhold Niebuhr called America's "isolationist

imperialism"—is evidenced by the following report to the U.S. Congress: "The U.S. record on ratification of human rights treaties is not good. . . . The United States, through its failure to become a party to all but a few of the human rights treaties, has become increasingly isolated from the development of international human rights law" (United States House of Representatives, 93rd Cong., 2d Sess., Committee on Foreign Affairs, *Human Rights in the World Community*, Government Printing Office, Washington, D.C., in Ajami, 9).

29. "Human Rights Basic Program Paper: Human Rights and Christian Responsibility," in World Council of Churches, *Human Rights and Christian Responsibility*, bk I, 5; Lazreg, 41; Ajami, 10, 13.

30. Winthrop S. Hudson, *Religion in America*, 2d ed. (New York: Charles Scribner's Sons, 1973), 20–21.

31. See Martin E. Marty, *The Righteous Empire: The Protestant Experience in America* (New York: Dial, 1970). See also Robert Jewett, *The Captain America Complex: The Dilemma of Zealous Nationalism* (Philadelphia: Westminster Press, 1973).

32. Hudson, 20–21; Graebner, 41, 43.

33. Graebner, 41–44.

34. Ibid., 43.

35. Ibid., 44–45.

36. Lazreg, 34, 37, 40, 41; Eugene Kamenka and A.E.-S. Tay, "Human Rights in the Soviet Union," *World Review* 19:2 (1980): 51; *Human Rights*, ed. Pollis and Schwab, 3–5; Said, 86; Ajami, 9.

9

FROM CULTURAL HEGEMONY TO CULTURAL INTEGRITY

CULTURES SHOULD RESPECT OTHER CULTURES' MORAL VALUES

Max Stackhouse, James Sellers, Raimundo Panikkar and others have addressed the human rights issue from the perspective of contextualist theology and the discipline of comparative religious ethics. Despite the many areas in which these theologians disagree,[1] they achieve consensus on three important points. All recognize the unique worthiness of each culture, the need for reform "within" each culture, and the need for dialogue "between" cultures. These three affirmations form the essence of contextualist theology's response to the non-Western world's concern that the integrity of non-Western cultures be respected. Later on we shall see how these concerns are rooted in more basic questions of human identity.

The Unique Worthiness of Each Culture

Contextualist theology asserts that each culture is uniquely worthy of respect. The distinctives among cultures should not be blurred or mitigated. They should not, many would say, be compared favorably or unfavorably with one another. They should be respected. As one church document affirms, the movement for universal human rights should "according to the demands of flexible and pluralistic realism, respect the different conceptions and situations of all the peoples of the world." Another points out that although "the Bible is clearly critical of other cultures at many points," such as the baalism of the Canaanites and the emperor worship of the Romans, it is "highly respectful of the best in other traditions." The first eleven chapters of Genesis clearly draw on non-

Hebrew sources. The Pauline epistles show respect for many Greek and Roman ideals.[2]

Each culture has its own distinctive ways of viewing and doing things. In the West, literacy is defined as the ability to read and write in one's native language. In many parts of the East, a person is considered illiterate if he or she knows only one language. Even murder is defined differently from culture to culture. If a member of a lower caste starves to death in India, or if a schizophrenic prematurely released from an overcrowded state mental institution freezes to death on the streets of New York, Hindu and Western liberal cultures might consider these deaths to be results of natural causes. Marxist cultures would consider them murder. On the other hand, if a guerilla group kills certain influential politicians or wealthy businessmen, some Marxist cultures might view this as a righteous, revolutionary act. By Western liberal standards, this would be viewed as murder. Because of the wide range of values, "no culture, tradition, ideology or religion can today speak for the whole of humankind, let alone solve its problems."[3]

The Universal Declaration of Human Rights is far from being a culturally universal document. It makes a number of assumptions unacceptable to many non-Western cultures. Reading the declaration through Hindu eyes, Panikkar discovers that the declaration assumes that there is a universal human nature "essentially different from the rest of reality." This is at odds with the Hindu view that sentient beings, not human beings, comprise a distinctive ontological category. The declaration assumes that the individual human being is endowed with dignity. This implies the separation of the individual and society, the "autonomy of humankind vis-à-vis and often versus the Cosmos," and the abstraction of rights from duties. Each of these is inimical to Hindu values. The declaration assumes a democratic rather than a hierarchical social order and a negative view of society. "Society here is not seen as a family or a protection," Panikkar comments, "but as something . . . which can easily abuse the power conferred on it." This implies that each individual has the right to stand up for his or her convictions even against the common good of society. The lengthy delineation of individual rights implies that "the individualization does not stop at the individual, but divides this segregated entity even further into separated freedoms."[4]

Considering the Universal Declaration to be "universal" could imply that all contradictory concepts be eliminated and that "the culture which has given birth to the concept of Human Rights should also be called upon to become a universal culture." Thus, non-Westerners have responded to the promulgation of universal human rights by expressing "fear for the identity of their own cultures." Considering the Universal Declaration to be "universal" would imply that most non-Western cultures are today where Western cultures were two to three centuries ago (when Western concepts of human rights were developed)—in transition from feudal structures to a "rationally" and "contractually" organized society. There are some parallels, but there are also some differences that should not be minimized.[5]

The diversity of cultures and the failure of the Universal Declaration to be a truly universal document suggest the difficulty of one culture dictating morality to another. This can be insidious even if in the name of such a noble ideal as human rights. Noble ideals can be twisted to serve ignoble purposes. Throughout Western history a number of injustices have been couched in human rights jargon. I have already mentioned the colonial enterprise. Within Western nations, human rights have been around for some time but were once only extened to whites, or males, or adults, or property owners, or heterosexuals, or Christians (or Anglicans, or Puritans, or Catholics, as the case may be). Deductive reasoning suggests that groups denied equal human rights must not be fully human. Even though the noble intention of early human rights efforts was to bestow a more dignified status on human beings, the ignoble consequence was the insinuation that nonwhites, women, and so forth were not fully human because they did not deserve human rights. Even if human rights were extended to all people, Panikkar believes that they would be unacceptable to much of the Asian world because of the insinuation that nonhuman sentient beings are inferior to human ones and that their rights can be trampled on if to promote the rights of humans.[6]

Sellers strongly endorses domestic human rights initiatives but he too is skeptical about universal human rights. Each nation looks out for its own interests and each culture is unique. Even if nations and cultures agreed that human dignity must be respected, there would be "considerable variation, from culture to culture, and from nation to nation, about just how to honor these ideals." The protection of freedom and individuality is one way, and perhaps a very good one. "But simply to impose our list of rights, drawn from this ideology, upon others, would be morally doubtful even if it were possible." "Exporting the American version of rights," Sellers concludes, "is little more than cultural imperialism."[7]

Reform Within Cultures

The second claim of contextualist theology is that moral and political reform must be initiated from within each culture. There is no "glue" that holds all cultures and religions together, even those of the Western world. Reform must, therefore, be intracultural. "To call for worldwide observance of human rights is largely futile," Sellers writes. Secularism and pluralism have disintegrated the bonds (such as natural law and the authority of the Catholic Church) that once held Western culture together. If the West is fragmented to the point of there being no ideological or institutional bond capable of uniting it—except a negative one, fear of non-Western nations—then worldwide cooperation on human rights or any other issue is highly unlikely.[8]

Each culture must develop its own tradition of justice to its fullest potential, correcting its faults and maximizing its strengths. American concern for global human rights must begin at home. If we begin abroad, we run the risk of ignoring our own human rights problems at home. "Undue attention to the evil practices of others inevitably distracts us from the moral shortcomings of our own society," Sellers writes. "Obsession with rights violations elsewhere" is likely to "divert our attention from continuing injustice at home." The American tradition of justice, despite its many strengths, is in need of fine tuning, if not major repairs. Liberty and individualism must be "cut . . . down to size." Violence, high health-care costs, inequality, crime, unemployment, homelessness, and malnutrition are high prices to pay for our individual freedoms. Perhaps, Sellers suggests, liberty should be viewed as but one facet of justice, kept in check by other concerns such as the value of life and economic equality.[9]

Another reason that American concern for global human rights must begin at home is that this more modest, indirect approach is likely to be more effective in the long run. If we, as a powerful nation, promote global human rights too aggressively, Sellers believes that "we run the risk of moral chauvinism," not only because of the diversity of beliefs concerning human rights but also "because our own moral tradition contains limitations within itself that we ought not to seek deliberately to export." A "more modest and productive approach" would be "to reflect upon our own American tradition of justice and to ask first what it may offer for the reform of our own society." Only after doing this could we begin to consider how American justice might benefit the rest of the world. Such an approach is more effective because it takes into account the fact that justice "speaks for itself," because it does not offend or threaten other cultures, and because it operates from strength rather than weakness. Actions and positive examples speak louder than words of harangue. Reform and revival of justice in America would issue a silent invitation to other nations to imitate us—rather than a command to them to obey us. Such silent strength is more persuasive than haranguing, particularly when others perceive our own house not to be in order. "If our own values prove to have the promise and power to bolster the lot of the disadvantaged among us, they may have then some carryover value for the disadvantaged elsewhere." The extent of this "carryover value" is something that others must decide for themselves. We can only strive to make it as attractive as possible.[10]

Even for Stackhouse, who would like to convert the Marxists and Hindus to the liberal-Christian synthesis, the most important thing America can do is to get its own house in order. True conversion requires free choice. We cannot make that decision for others. "In the final analysis Christians will have to leave decisions on many of these matters to the Hindus and the Marxists. We cannot, must not, make their decisions." What we can do, Stackhouse says, is create the conditions that would make a decision for the liberal-Christian synthesis most likely. Non-Westerners will certainly reject the liberal-Christian synthesis if their exposure to it is largely negative. Any attempt to promote global human rights must, according to Stackhouse, be attended with "caution," "restraint," "willingness to listen," and "modesty about our capacities to surpass our own loyalties and bias." If the forms to which non-Westerners have been exposed "have been supportive of precisely that which stands opposed to universal ethics and human rights" (such as the obscurantism of evangelical Christianity, or the co-option of the church as an agent of repression) we should not expect them to appreciate Christianity or liberalism. Even for those who wish to evangelize and universalize the liberal-Christian synthesis, the best way to do this is for liberal-Christian culture to focus on reform and revival at home and use a "soft sell" approach abroad.[11]

Trying to become "a city on a hill" and respecting the self-determination of all people are ideas as old as the United States itself. In the previous section, I argued that the classical American identity is one of being a righteous example, not a global crusader. Here, I argue that the American ideal is not that we be such a good example that other nations would try to clone us but that we be such a good example that other nations would be inspired to develop their own traditions of justice to their fullest potential. If they discover anything new about themselves by admiring the American example, or if they discover anything useful from the American tradition that can be translated into their own cultural setting, then they may, of course, choose to borrow. What contextualist theology demands, "straight out of the American tradition, is *self-determination* for all peoples, and the development of a structure of justice appropriate to each nation or culture."[12]

Is this call, for America to begin at home, tantamount to a return to the isolationism of an earlier era? It is not, as long as reform at home is done with an eye toward how it might benefit the rest of the world. We begin at home not because we are unconcerned about other nations and cultures or because we have given up on them but because we believe this the most positive, effective way of influencing them. The third and final claim of contextual theology should allay the fears of those who worry that contextualism might be little more than a euphemism for isolationism.

Dialogue Between Cultures

The third claim of contextualist theology is that the universalization of human rights is contingent not only upon reform within each culture but also upon dialogue between the cultures. Even as each culture seeks to develop its own concept of justice, it should do so with an openness to the insights and criticisms of other points of view. "Even while we hope to let our tradition speak for itself," Sellers says, "we must also strive for a spirit of openness to what *other* traditions may have to commend them: perhaps these traditions can speak to us." In the same vein, Stackhouse believes that "if we are to embrace a *fundamental* understanding of humanity and thereby give a rooted content to human rights that is genuinely universal, we must work out our creeds fully aware of the strongest alternatives to our own positions."[13]

The best way to see your own culture is through the eyes of another, adds Panikkar, who has lived with one foot in Hindu culture and the other in Western Catholicism. It is difficult to distinguish the universal aspect of something from the cultural manifestation of it without comparing it to another culture and asking how the two cultures achieve similar objectives through differing means. Human rights are, for Panikkar, "one window through which one particular culture envisages a just human order." Those who live in that culture cannot see the window, only the landscape. Those of other cultures look at the same landscape through different windows. They cannot see their own window either but they can see others' windows. "Should we smash the windows and make of the many portals a single gaping aperture—with the consequent danger of structural collapse—or should we . . . make people aware that there are . . . a plurality of windows?" Panikkar prefers the latter option, a "healthy pluralism," not a global monoculture. In a healthy pluralism each culture learns about itself by seeing itself through the eyes of another. It does not preoccupy itself with hegemonic ambitions.[14]

Lucas and Will argue that, because of the East–West fighting over human rights, it is especially important that the church and other institutions foster "positive encounters." Their volume is an attempt to do just this. Amid the tension left in the wake of the Helsinki discussions and the Reagan administration's characterization of the Soviet Union as an "evil empire" and "the embodiment of evil," they attempted to promote dialogue so that each side could hear the other's perception. This was done not in an atmosphere of polemics and power plays but in a discussion among theologians and sociologists with no political stakes, whose only interest was in learning about their own culture through the insights of another.[15]

Cross-cultural dialogue is important not only to enable cultures to better understand themselves but also to enable each culture to benefit and

language, or even one set of moral values. Christianity is contextual. It can be adapted to and incarnated in the languages and customs of the various cultures of the world. The image of God can be reflected in Asian and African as well as European and American cultures. The Old Testament makes it clear the Yahweh's concern with the Hebrews was not to change their culture, nor to involve them in otherworldly interests, but to help them bear the image of God in this world and through the structures and limitations and potentialities of their culture.

What is needed is a dialectical view that incorporates both notions of humanity. I have tried to show that Christian anthropology offers the basis for such a dialectic. The Judeo-Christian tradition claims that humans are "a combination of both body and spirit who live in history"[23] and who, through their special relation to God, are able to transcend history. Hebrews emphasized the immanence of God; Greeks emphasized God's transcendence. God acted within history, yet transcended it. Because this is the God whose image we bear, we too are immanent-transcendent beings. Every aspect of human culture is significant—it has been graced with the presence of God. No aspect of human culture is absolute—God transcends it, judges it by a higher standard. Thus we try to develop the potentialities of our culture, all the while aware of its limitations. Thus we desire the development of all cultures, not the absolutizing of our own. Thus contextualist theology recognizes the integrity of each culture, the need for reform within cultures, the need for dialogue between cultures.

CONCLUSIONS TO CHAPTERS 8 AND 9

1. Non-Western cultures have accused the human rights movement of chauvinism, hypocrisy, and cultural and ethical imperialism.
2. This tendency is rooted to some extent in the American identity as a "redeemer" nation and culture. Originally this identity was expressed in terms of America striving to be an example of righteousness that others would be inspired to imitate. More recently it has been expressed in terms of America being an extroverted crusader for righteousnes. What is missing in both models is the humbler notion that America is a nation among nations and a culture among cultures. Having assumed the lonely role of a "a city on a hill" and a "lone ranger" crusader, America has refused to participate as a nation among nations and a culture among cultures in international dialogue and cooperation.
3. This tendency is also rooted in the liberal identity of humans as abstract beings that transcend history and culture. Liberalism defines humans in transhistorical, transcultural terms. Thus it conceives human rights in transhistorical, transcultural terms. From the perspective of many non-

Western philosophies of life, as Marxism and Hinduism, such a view fails to address the needs of persons as they exist in their historical-cultural milieu. It abstracts individuals from society and grants rights to the abstraction, not to any empirically extant being. From the standpoint of Western liberalism, viewing humans and human rights in abstract terms has the advantage of offering a transcendent reference point from which to judge injustice that is being condoned at the cultural level.

4. Christian anthropology insists on defining humanity and human rights in both historical-cultural and abstract-universal terms. Christian theology affirms that the historical-cultural realm is a legitimate area of divine activity and yet that God and humans made in God's image in some sense transcend history and culture.

5. Our thesis is held to be valid. At the root of the international conflict over human rights is a question addressed by theological anthropology. Christian theology suggests a dialectical relation between abstract and historical conceptions of humanity, which in turn makes possible a rapprochement between universal and cultural conceptions of human rights.

NOTES

1. Stackhouse focuses on three cultural-religious-political traditions: the American liberal-Puritan synthesis, the German Democratic Republic's Marxist way of life, and India's Hindu tradition. As he says, his is an exercise in comparative religious ethics and human rights is one among many themes he could have chosen as a basis for comparison. (Max L. Stackhouse, *Creeds, Society, and Human Rights: A Study in Three Cultures* (Grand Rapids: William B. Eerdmans Publishing Co. 1984).

   Stackhouse is convinced that all three traditions claim ultimacy, but that all cannot be ultimate. He believes the liberal-Puritan synthesis to be the "best" one, the "right" one. ("Because the ultimate presuppositions of a Christian, Marxist, or Hindu society are in principle accessible to all people . . . we have to discern which in fact more accurately grasps the fundamental structures of human life." "The issue, the decisive issue, is which fundamental vision is most true and most fully meets the widest range of basic human needs and thus *ought* to be adopted universally as creed and institutionalized in every society." "What view of human rights is right?" "Sooner or later we have to decide whether one or another of these is more or less true than the others. At such a point, confrontation occurs.") Stackhouse considers the liberal-Puritan synthesis superior because it provides "the truest description of the human condition." It describes humans as sinners vis-à-vis God. Such a view "preserves freedom and is rational; it is potentially universal and practically creates in particular settings the social space whereby the concrete social structures are opened up so that most basic human needs are likely to be met over time with a minimum of destructive violence." In Marxism "all heaven and earth depends on our human decisions and human actions," "humans are and ought to be masters of life," and "what we do, as humans, determine[s] everything." In Hinduism the other extreme prevails: "we shall be what we are, and cannot be other than what we are." In Marxism there is too much freedom and responsibility. In Hinduism there is not enough. The former is idolatrous. The latter is fatalistic. Christianity avoids these two extremes. Moreover, Christianity has Marxism's strength and Hinduism's weakness, a concern for equality. Christianity affirms that all are equally children of God, loved by God, and sinners in need of God's redemption. Christianity also offers its followers Hinduism's strength and Marxism's weakness—spirituality. Stackhouse believes that the church is a more effective institution than the political party (GDR) or the caste (India) in that it is voluntary. It is not in a position where it has to worry about maintaining the status quo, staying in power, and so on. (Stackhouse, *Creeds*, 20-21, 269-76.)

Stackhouse states on numerous occasions that all these virtues of Christianity refer more to Christian ideals than to empirical forms that he can identify. (See, for example, pages 276, 278, 280, and 281 of *Creeds*. See also page 206 of his article, "Theology, History, and Human Rights" in *The East-West Encounter over Human Rights: Its Religious and Sociological Context*, edited by Geroge R. Lucas, Jr. And James E. Will, *Soundings* 67:2 [Summer 1984, Special Issue]: 191–208.) This is one weakness of his work. He compares Marxist and Hindu ideals and realities, as he perceives them, with Christian ideals. He is quick to excuse the shortcomings of Christianity by saying that these reflect not "true" Christianity but only its historical expression.

If cultures must be compared, Sellers would rather let praxis, not ideals, serve as the basis. He would prefer that each culture concentrate on developing its own tradition of justice. Any determination of who is better could only be based on seeing who tries to imitate whom, not on a comparison of ideals. (James Sellers, "Human Rights and the American Tradition of Justice," *Soundings* 62:3 [Fall 1979]: 226–55).

Sellers and Stackhouse are concerned about two opposite problems: Sellers with the problem of Western cultural hegemony, Stackhouse with the problem of cultural relativism. Sellers identifies "cultural imperialism" and "moral chauvinism" as the main problem. Stackhouse identifies the "age of relativism" and "a great Kulturkampf" as the main problem. Sellers counsels Americans to take a humbler view of their role of the world. Stackhouse also counsels "modesty" and "restraint" and "willingness to listen" but, he says, "judgments do have to be made" and "human rights suffer as much by timidity as by dogmatic and arrogant ethnocentrism." The reason that Sellers and Stackhouse come to the problem from opposite directions is that Sellers writes during the Carter era, in which there was little timidity and plenty of dogmatism, arrogance, and ethnocentrism. Stackhouse writes during the Reagan era, a time in which, as he points out at the outset of the preface, Reagan withdrew from concern for universal human rights and simply promoted American interest, defining human rights as whatever he wanted it to be at the time. This explains Stackhouse's call for more forthright expressions of human rights and for a more stable, enduring, universal concept of human rights. In the Reagan era, he complains, "'Ethics' tends to become less a grasping and implementation of universal values than a convenient adjustment to the cultural drifts in the society in which one lives." (Sellers, 227, 248; Stackhouse, *Creeds*, x-xi, 3, and 271).

Panikkar, like Stackhouse, does comparative religious ethics on the human rights theme. (Raimundo Panikkar, "Is the Notion of Human Rights a Western Concept?" *Diogenes* 120 [Winter 1982]: 75–102). Panikkar is much more cautious than Stackhouse in trying to universalize Western understandings of human rights. He writes in defense of non-Western cultures. He explains that the reason they have no concept of human rights does not reflect a moral weakness on their part, but rather the failure of Western scholars to interpret non-Western cultures sympathetically and accurately. Panikkar suggests such a method, "diatopical hermeneutics," which attempts to determine the "homeomorphic equivalents" between cultures. For example, rather than looking for Western notions of human rights in non-Western cultures, diatopical hermeneutics requires that the scholar determine what function is served by human rights in Western culture and then try to ascertain what it is in Indian culture that serves the same function. He believes that "the function served by human rigths in the West is to help create a just order. "In order to have a dharmic order," Panikkar says "classical India stresses the notion of *svadharma*," the dharma which is inherent in every being. (See Panikkar, pages 95–97). This position is supported by Hindu scholar Kana Mitra. (See Mitra, "Human Rights in Hinduism," in *Human Rights in Religious Traditions*, ed. by Arlene Swidler [New York: The Pilgrim Press, 1982], 79.)

Evans and Evans and most of the contributors to the *Soundings* East–West dialogue would also disagree with Stackhouse's concern that the "best" view be determined. Writes Robert A. Evans:

(1) The "rights perspectives" of the three worlds could be complementary rather than competitive. Thus, we need to nurture a broader, more global perspective on human rights. This calls for greater understanding of the legitimate variety and diversity of claims for human rights.

(2) Human rights need to be understood as interdependent and as forming the basis for a positive vision of human cooperation . . . .

(3) In the midst of presently competing perspectives on human rights, issues of survival and liberation require that the global village to [sic] move toward some agreement on the priority of rights.

(See Robert A. Evans and Alice Frazer Evans, *Human Rights: A Dialogue Between the First and Third Worlds* [Maryknoll: Orbis, 1983], p 241.) Most contributors to *Soundings* also felt the need to develop a "public theology" that incorporated the strengths of both East and West.

2. Agnes Cunningham, Donald Miller, and James E. Will, "Toward an Ecumenical Theology for Grounding Human Rights," in *The East-West Encounter* eds. Lucas and Will, 219; "The Church and Human Rights," No. 92 cited by

Joachim Kondziela, "*Citoyen* Freedom and Bourgeois Freedom: Religion and the Dialectics of Human Rights," in *The East-West Encounter*, 179.
3. Panikkar 87, 75; Stackhouse, *Creeds*, 269.
4. Panikkar, 80-83. On abstraction and individualism, Panikkar (89-90):

> The individual is just an abstraction, i.e., a selection of a few aspects of the person for practical purposes. My *person*, on the other hand, is also in "my" parents, children, friends, foes, ancestors and successors. "My" person is also in "my" ideas and feelings and in "my" belongings. If you hurt "me," you are equally damaging my whole clan, and possibly yourself as well. Rights cannot be individualized in this way. Is it the right of the mother or of the child?—in the case of abortion. . . . Rights cannot be abstracted from duties; the two are correlated. To aggressively defend my individual rights . . . may have negative, i.e., unjust, repercussions on others and perhaps even on myself.

> There is certainly a *universal human nature* but, first of all, this nature does not need to be segregated and fundamentally distinct from the nature of all living beings and/or the entire reality. Thus exclusively *Human* Rights would be seen as a violation of "Cosmic Rights" and an example of selfdefeating anthropocentrism, a novel kind of apartheid. To retort that "Cosmic Rights" is a meaningless expression would only betray the underlying cosmology of the objection, for which the phrase makes no sense. But the existence of a different cosmology is precisely what is at stake here. We speak of the laws of nature; why not also of [her] rights?

On democracy, Panikkar says (91):

> "*Democracy* is also a great value and infinitely better than any dictatorship. But it amounts to tyranny to put the peoples of the world under the alternative of choosing either democracy or dictatorship. Human Rights are tied to democracy. Individuals need to be protected when the structure which is above them . . . is not qualitatively superior to them, i.e., when it does not belong to a higher order. Human rights is a legal device for the protection of smaller numbers of people . . . faced with the power of greater numbers . . . In a hierarchical conception of reality, the particular human being cannot defend his or her rights by demanding or exacting them independently of the whole. The wounded order has to be set straight again, or it has to change altogether.

5. Panikkar, 84.
6. Ibid., 86.
7. Sellers, 227-30, 247-48.
8. Ibid., 228-29, 248.
9. Ibid., 239, 243, 245, 248, 252.
10. Ibid., 227, 230, 248.

11. Stackhouse, *Creeds*, 271, 279–80

12. Sellers, 250, 252.

13. Sellers, 250; Stackhouse, *Creeds*, 3.

14. Pannikar, 78–79.

15. George R. Lucas, Jr. and James E. Will, "Editor's Introduction," in *The East-West Encounter*, 123.

16. Paul Peachey, "Person and Society: The Soviet-American Encounter," in *The East-West Encounter*, 151; Stanislaw Kowalczyk, "The Possibilities of Christian-Marxist Dialogue on Human Rights," in *The East-West Encounter*, 170.

17. Peachey, 141; Lucas and Will, 123–24.

18. It has been shown that dialogue between cultures is a valuable way of moving toward universal human rights. In what manner, then, is this dialogue to be carried out? The theologians under consideration offer widely divergent views on this, as indicated by the discussion in note 1.

19. Stackhouse, *Creeds*, 259; Karl Marx, *Theses on Feuerbach*, cited by Peachey, 140; Pannikar, 97–98.

20. Pannikar, 86; Kowalczyk, 170; Stackhouse, *Creeds*, 5.

21. Pannikar, 76–77.

22. Stackhouse, "Theology, History, and Human Rights," in *The East-West Encounter*, 196.

23. Stackhouse, *Creeds*, 3.

CONCLUSION

In the first chapter I proposed the thesis that failure to achieve universal human rights is due in large part to differing ways that nations and cultures conceptualize human being. I suggested that progress toward universal human rights could be achieved by utilizing the resources of Christian theological anthropology.

Dissimilar anthropologies evoke dissimilar notions of what constitutes a human right. After identifying four anthropological polarities that have emerged in the human rights debate between Western and non-Western nations—individual versus communal, pneumatic versus physical, benevolent versus sinful, and abstract versus cultural ways of defining human being—I then argued that the communal, physical, sinful, and cultural dimensions, often overlooked in Western liberalism, are affirmed by Christian theological anthropology. Since Christianity is like, liberalism, an integral part of the Western intellectual heritage, a reformulation of Western anthropology is possible, as is a rapprochement between Western and Communist, Moslem, and Third World notions of human rights.

In addition to making this point—that progress in international human rights is possible if we come to terms with differing understandings of what constitutes the human being—I believe this book has made a number of other contributions that should be noted at this time. First, it tries to rejuvenate interest in the United Nations at a time when U.S. support for the United Nations is waning. Much of that apathy and even hostility is being stirred within conservative Christian segments of our society. I have argued that, rather than promote isolationism or imperialist internationalism, the doctrines and motifs of the Christian tradition help lay the foundation for truly international human rights.

Second, the book offers insights into the whole range of conflicts between West and East, North and South, and the role of First World theologians in resolving those conflicts. The model of conflict resolution that I have proposed here, with regard to the human rights debate, could be utilized in a number of other areas of international concern: relations between rich and poor nations, territorial disputes, environmental disputes from acid rain to saving the whales, the right sharing of the world's resources, restrictions on international trade, the safety of nuclear power plants, and the nuclear arms race. I have tried to show that the Christian doctrine of humanity has relevance to such a seemingly distant field as international politics and, by implication, to a number of other areas as well.

Third, the book contributes to a better understanding of the relationship of politics and religion, an area of burgeoning interest around the world. Fourth, it helps clarify the meaning of human rights, both as an abstract concept and as an historical movement. Fifth, in showing the complementarity of Roman Catholic and Protestant contributions to human rights theory and practice, it contributes to the efforts of the ecumenical movement.

Sixth, the book should be useful to those interested in understanding the relation between recent human rights initiatives, such as the Carter foreign policy, the work of Amnesty International, and the divestment (from South Africa) movement, to earlier initiatives—namely, the founding of the United Nations. It shows points of contact between the earlier and later efforts. It suggests that the later efforts are, to a great extent, attempts to bring to fruition the ideals of the earlier efforts. The book argues that a major barrier to achieving universal human rights has been that the document that launched the movement, the Universal Declaration of Human Rights, is itself flawed—it contains a number of liberal biases that many non-Westerners find unacceptable and even offensive.

Seventh, although the subject of the book is American foreign policy, it contains a number of implications for missiology. The mistakes of American missionary organizations and of the U.S. State Department have in many ways paralleled one another during the cold-war period. Inasmuch as this book is an attempt to assess the mistakes of one, it should have some relevance to the foibles of the other.

Finally, our distinction between two modes of moral discourse, the polemical and the ethical, and our affirmation of the latter as the language most useful in conflict resolution will indicate (it is hoped) the practical importance of distanced reflection in bringing about social change and will silence those who caricature such reflection as "theological navel gazing" and "all talk and no action." Such detached reflection may, at least in the case of the current international human rights situation, be the stuff of which real progress is made.

BIBLIOGRAPHY

General Works

A. Theological

Abbott, Walter M., ed. *The Documents of Vatican II*. New York: Herder and Herder, 1966.

Allen, Joseph L. "A Theological Approach to Moral Rights." *Journal of Religious Ethics* 2:1 (Spring 1974): 119–41.

Aquinas, Thomas. *Introduction to St. Thomas Aquinas*. Edited by Anton C. Pegis. New York: Random House, 1948.

Barth, Karl. *Church Dogmatics*. Edited by G.W. Bromiley and T.F. Torrance. Translated by Harold Knight *et al.* Vol. 3: *The Doctrine of Creation*, Part 2. Edinburgh: T & T Clark, 1960.

Belkin, Samuel. *In His Image*. New York: Abelard-Schuman, 1960.

Bettenson, Henry. *Documents of the Christian Church*. Second Edition. New York: Oxford University Press, 1977.

———. *The Early Christian Fathers: A Selection from the Writings of the Fathers from St. Clement of Rome to St. Athanasius*. New York: Oxford University Press, 1977.

Cahill, Lisa Sowle. "Toward a Christian Theory of Human Rights." *Journal of Religious Ethics* 8:2 (Fall 1980): 277–301.

Calvin, John. *Institutes of the Christian Religion*. In *The Library of Christian Classics*. Edited by John T. McNeill. Translated by Ford Lewis Battles. London: S.C.M. Press, 1961.

Christian Legal Society. *Quarterly* ("Human Right") 5:3 (1984).

Cohn, Haim H. *Human Rights in Jewish Law*. Hoboken, New Jersey: Ktav, 1984.

Conde, H. Victor. "The Theological Basis for Human Rights." *Christian Legal Society Quarterly* 5:3 (1984): 10–12.

"Document: Report of a Limited Research Project on the Theological Basis of Human Rights." *Reformed World* 36:8 (1981): 370–75.

Falconer, Alan D., ed. *Understanding Human Rights: An Interdisciplinary and Interfaith Study. Proceedings of the International Consultation Held in Dublin, 1978.* Dublin: Irish School of Ecumenics, 1980.

Forell, George W. and Lazareth, William H., eds. *Human Rights: Rhetoric or Reality.* Philadelphia: Fortress Press, 1978.

Greidanus, Sidney. "Human Rights in Biblical Perspective." *Calvin Theological Journal* 19:1 (April 1984): 5–31.

Gremillion, Joseph B., ed. *The Gospel of Peace and Justice: Catholic Social Teaching since Pope John.* Maryknoll, NY: Orbis, 1976.

Hudson, Winthrop S., *Religion in America*, 2nd ed. (New York: Charles Scribner's Sons, 1973).

Husslein, Joseph Casper. *The Christian Social Manifesto: An Interpretive Study of the Encyclicals Rerum Novarum and Quadragesimo Anno of Pope Leo XIII and Pope Pius XI.* Milwaukee: Bruce Publishing Co., 1931.

Jenkins, David. "Human Rights in Christian Perspective." *Study Encounter* 10:2 (1974): 1–8.

Jewett, Robert. *Paul's Anthropoligical Terms: A Study of Their Use in Conflict Settings.* Leiden: E.J. Brill, 1971.

Krusche, G. "Human Rights in a Theological Perspective: A Contribution from the GDR." *Lutheran World* 24 (1977): 59–65.

Lazareth, William H., ed. *Theological Ethics.* 3 vols. Grand Rapids: William B. Eerdmans Publishing Co., 1979/1959. Vol. 2:*Politics*, by Helmut Thielicke.

Leo XIII. *The Church Speaks to the Modern World: The Social Teachings of Leo XIII.* Edited by Etienne Gilson. Garden City: Image Books, 1954.

Lissner, J., and Sovik, A., eds. "A Lutheran Reader on Human Rights." *Lutheran World Fellowship Report* Nos. 1 and 2 (1978).

Lochman, Jan Milicc. *Encountering Marx: Bonds and Barriers between Christians and Marxists.* Translated by Edwin H. Robertson. Philadelphia: Fortress Press, 1977.

Lorenz, Eckehart, ed. *How Christian Are Human Rights? An Interconfessional Study on the Theological Bases of Human Rights.*(Report on an Interconfessional Consultation, Geneva, April 30–May 3, 1980.) Geneva: Lutheran World Federation, 1981.

The Lutheran Church in America. "Human Rights: Doing Justice in God's World." *Social Statements.* New York: Lutheran Church in America, 1978.

Luther, Martin. *Martin Luther: Selections from His Writings.* Edited by John Dillenberger. Garden City: Anchor Books, 1961.

Manschreck, Clyde L. *A History of Christianity in the World: From Persecution to Uncertainty.* Englewood Cliffs: Prentice-Hall, 1974.

Marshall, Paul, and Vanderkloet, Ed, eds. *Foundations of Human Rights.* Toronto: Christian Labor Association of Canada, 1981.

McCormick, Richard A., S.J. "Notes on Moral Theology 1977: The Church in Dispute." *Theological Studies* 39:1 (March 1978): 76–138.

Miller, Allen O., ed. *A Christian Declaration on Human Rights: Theological Studies of the World Alliance of Reformed Churches.* Grand Rapids: William B. Eerdmans Publishing Co. 1977.

Müller, Alois, and Greinacher, Norbert, eds. *The Church and the Rights of Man.* New York: Seabury, 1979.

Nielsen, Niels C., Jr. *The Crisis of Human Rights: An American Christian Perspective.* Nashville: Nelson, 1978.

Pagels, Elaine. *The Gnostic Gospels.* New York: Vintage Books, 1981.

Presbyterian Church of the United States, General Assembly 1983. *Church and Society* 73:6 (July/August 1983).

———, General Assembly 1984. *Church and Society.*75:2 (November/December 1984).

Sanders, E.P. *Paul and Palestinian Judaism: A Comparison of Patterns of Religion.* Philadelphia: Fortress, 1977.

Schmithals, Walter. *Gnoticism in Corinth: An Investigation of the Letters to the Corinthians.* Nashville: Abingdon, 1971.

Sidorsky, David, ed. *Essays on Human Rights: Contemporary Issues and Jewish Perspectives.* Philadelphia: The Jewish Publication Society of America, 1979.

Todt, H. "Theological Reflections on the Foundations of Human Rights." *Lutheran World* 24 (1977): 45-58.

United Methodist Church. *The Book of Resolutions, 1984* Nashville: United Methodist Publishing House, 1984.

World Council of Churches. *The Ecumenical Review* ("Human Rights Issue") 27:2 (April 1975).

World Evangelical Fellowship. *Transformation* ("Focus on Human Rights") 1:3 (July/September 1984).

B. Other

Ajami, Fouad. *Human Rights and World Order Politics.* World Order Models Project Occasional Paper, No. 4. New York: Institute for World Order, 1978.

Amalrik, Andrei. *Will the Soviet Union Survive Until 1984?* New York: Harper & Row, 1970.

Andropov, Y.V. *Speeches and Writings.* Leaders of the World series. Edited by Robert Maxwell, M.C. Second Enlarged Edition. New York: Pergamon Press, 1983.

Bay, Christian. *Strategies of Political Emancipation.* Notre Dame: University of Notre Dame Press, 1981.

Bedau, Hugo Adam. "Human Rights and Foreign Assistance Programs." In *Human Rights and U.S. Foreign Policy.* Edited by Peter G. Brown and Douglas Maclean. Lexington: Lexington Books, 1979.

Bentham, Jeremy. *Anarchical Fallacies; Being an Examination of the Declarations of Rights Issued during the French Revolution.* In *The Works of Jeremy Bentham.* Part VIII, collector John Bowring. Edinburgh: William Tait, 1889.

Bolívar, Simon. *Selected Writings of Bolívar.* Compiled by Vicente Lecuna. Edited by Harold A. Bierck, Jr. Translated by Lewis Bertrand. Vol. 2: *1823–1830.* New York: Colonial Press, 1951.

Botwinick, Aryeh. *Rousseau's Critique of Liberal Democracy: Then and Now*. Notre Dame: Foundations Press of Notre Dame, 1983.

Brown, Peter G., and MacLean, Douglas, eds. *Human Rights and U.S. Foreign Policy*. Lexington: Lexington Books, 1979.

Brezhnev, Leonid I. *Pages from His Life*. New York: Pergamon Press, 1982.

Buncher, Judith F., ed. *Human Rights and American Diplomacy: 1975–1977*. New York: Facts on File, 1977.

"The Campaign for Universal Human Rights." *The Humanist* 26:6 (November/December 1966): 193–96.

Carter, Jimmy. *Keeping Faith: Memoirs of a President*. New York: Bantam Books, 1982.

Casey, Robert John. "The Difference Principle Versus the Priority of Liberty in Rawls' Theory of Justice." Ph.D. dissertation, Vanderbilt University, 1977.

Chernenko, Konstantin U. *Human Rights in Soviet Society*. New York: International Publishers, 1981.

_____. *Speeches and Writings*. Leaders of the World series. Edited by Robert Maxwell, M.C. Second Enlarged Edition. New York: Pergamon Press, 1984.

A Chronicle of Human Rights in the USSR. New York: Khronika Press, 1973–1984.

Congressional Quarterly, President Carter. Washington D.C.: Congressional Quarterly, c. 1977.

Cranston, Maurice. *What Are Human Rights?* New York: Basic Books, 1964 [1962].

_____. *What Are Human Rights?* New York: Taplinger Publishing Co., 1973.

_____. "What Are Human Rights?" In *The Human Rights Reader*. Edited by Walter Laqueur and Barry Rubin. New York: New American Library, Meridian Books 1979.

Dobrin, Arthur; Dobrin, Lyn: and Liotti, Thomas F. *Convictions: Political Prisoners-Their Stories*. Maryknoll, NY: Orbis, 1981.

Dominguez, Jorge I.; Rodley, Nigel S.; Wood, Bryce; and Falk, Richard, eds. *Enhancing Global Human Rights*. New York: McGraw-Hill Book Co., 1979.

Dowrick, F.E., ed. *Human Rights: Problems, Perspectives and Texts*. Westmead, Farnborough, Hants., England: Saxon House, 1979.

Encyclopedia Americana, International Edition, 1980. S.v. "French Revolution," by George V. Taylor.

Erikson, Erik H. *Identity, Youth and Crisis*. New York: W.W. Norton and Co., 1968.

Fagen, Richard A. "The Carter Administration and Latin America: Business as Usual?" *Foreign Affairs* 53:7 (1978): 652–59.

Forsythe, David P. *Human Rights and World Politics*. Lincoln: University of Nebraska Press, 1983.

Goodell, Charles. *Political Prisoners in America*. New York: Random House, 1973.

Green, James Frederick. *The United Nations and Human Rights*. Washington, D.C.: The Brookings Institution, 1956.

The Guide to American Law: Everyone's Legal Encyclopedia. 1984. S.v. "Human Rights," by Charles H. McLaughlin.

Hart, H.L.A. "Are There any Natural Rights?" *The Philosophical Review* 64:2 (April 1955): 175–191.

Hassan, Ibne. "Amnesty International as a Human Rights Organization." Ph.D. dissertation, New York University, 1977.

The Hastings Center Report 6:5 (October 1976): 33.

Henkin, Louis. *The Rights of Man Today.* Boulder: Westview Press, 1978.

Hinds, Lennox S. *Illusions of Justice: Human Rights Violations in the United States.* Iowa City: School of Social Work, University of Iowa, 1979.

Hobbes, Thomas. *Leviathan.* Glasgow: William Collins Sons, 1974 [1651].

Joint Committee on Foreign Affairs and Defence of the Parliament of the Commonwealth of Australia. *Human Rights in the Soviet Union.* Canberra: Australian Government Publishing Service, 1979.

Kadarkay, Arpad. *Human Rights in American and Russian Political Thought.* Washington, D.C.: University Press of America, 1982.

Kamenka, Eugene, and Tay, A. E.-S. "Human Rights in the Soviet Union." *World Review* 19:2 (1980): 47–60.

Kennedy, Sharon Ann. "Contemporary Doctrines of Human Rights: An Evaluation of the Contributions of C.B. Macpherson and Christian Bay." Ph.D. dissertation, University of Florida, 1978.

Lankevich, George J., ed. *James E. Carter: Chronology, Documents, Bibliographical Aids.* Dobbs Ferry: Oceana Publications, 1981.

Laqueur, Walter, and Rubin, Barry, eds. *The Human Rights Reader.* New York: New American Library, Meridian Books, 1979.

Lauterpacht, H. *An International Bill of the Rights of Man.* New York: Columbia University Press, 1945.

Lightfoot, Claude M. *Human Rights U.S. Style: From Colonial Times through the New Deal.* New York: International Publishers, 1977.

Locke, John. *Second Treatise of Government.* Edited by C.B. Macpherson. Indianapolis: Hackett, 1980.

Los Angeles Times, 13 December 1977.

Kant, Immanuel. *Groundwork of the Metaphysic of Morals.* Translated by H.J. Paton. New York: Harper & Row, 1964.

McDougal, Myres S.; Lasswell, Harold D.; and Chen, Lung-chu. "Human Rights and World Public Order: A Framework for Policy-Oriented Inquiry." *The American Journal of International Law* 63:2 (April 1969): 237–69.

Machan, Tibor Richard. "Human Rights: A Metaethical Inquiry." Ph.D. dissertation, University of California, Santa Barbara, 1971.

McKeon, Richard. *Introduction to Aristotle.* New York: Random House, 1947.

Macpherson, C.B. *Democratic Theory: Essays in Retrieval.* Oxford: Clarendon Press, 1973.

———. *The Life and Times of Liberal Democracy.* New York: Oxford University Press, 1977.

———. *The Political Theory of Possessive Individualism: Hobbes to Locke.* Oxford: Oxford University Press, 1962.

———. *The Real World of Democracy.* Oxford: Clarendon Press, 1966.

Martin, J. Paul, ed. *Human Rights: A Topical Bibliography.* Boulder: Westview Press, 1983.

Marx, Karl, and Engels, Friedrich. *Marx and Engels on Religion.* Introduction by Reinhold Niebuhr. New York: Schocken Books, 1964.

Mill, John Stuart. *Utilitarianism.* In *Utilitarianism, Liberty, & Representative Government.* Edited by Ernest Rhys. New York: E.P. Dutton, 1917.

Moskowitz, Moses. *International Concern with Human Rights.* Dobbs Ferry: Oceana Publications, 1974.

_____. *The Politics and Dynamics of Human Rights.* Dobbs Ferry: Oceana Publications, 1968.

Moulton, Eben S. "An Analysis of John Rawls' *A Theory of Justice.*" Ph.D. dissertation, Vanderbilt University, 1974.

Muravchik, Joshua. *The Uncertain Crusade: Jimmy Carter and the Dilemmas of Human Rights Policy.* New York: Hamilton Press, 1986.

Nanda, Ved P.; Scarritt, James R.; and Shepherd, George W., Jr., eds. *Global Human Rights: Public Policies, Comparative Measures, and NGO Strategies.* Boulder: Westview Press, 1981.

Nasr, Waddah Nassim. "John Rawls' Arguments for the Feasibility of His Theory of Justice: A Study of the Relationships between Normative and Empirical Considerations in Accounts of the Nature of Moral and Political Obligation." Ph.D. dissertation, University of Minnesota, 1975.

New York Times, 4 and 22 March, 4 November, 11 December 1977, 28 February, 20 March, 22 October 1981.

Newsweek, 4 March, 20 June 1977, 15 March 1982, 11 July 1983, 12 September 1983.

Nietzsche, Friedrich. *The Genealogy of Morals.* In *The Birth of Tragedy and the Genealogy of Morals.* Translated by Francis Golffing. Garden City: Doubleday, 1956.

Pence, Gregory E. "A Critical Examination of John Rawls' *A Theory of Justice.* Ph.D. dissertation, New York University, 1974.

Power, Jonathan. *Amnesty International: The Human Rights Story.* New York: McGraw Hill Book Co., 1981.

Rawls, John. *A Theory of Justice.* Cambridge, MA: Belknap Press of Harvard University: 1971.

Rees-Mog, William. "In Defense of the First Amendment." Speech at Rice University, September 24, 1982.

Rousseau, Jean Jacques. *The Social Contract or Principles of Political Right.* Translation and introduction by Henry J. Tozer. London: George Allen and Unwin Ltd., 1895/1948.

Sakharov, Andrei D. *My Country and the World.* Translated by Guy V. Daniels. New York: Alfred A. Knopf, 1976.

Schwelb, Egon. *Human Rights and the International Community: The Roots and Growth of the Universal Declaration of Human Rights, 1948-1963.* Chicago: Quadrangle Books, 1964.

Solzhenitsyn, Alexander. *Letter to the Soviet Leaders.* Translation by Hilary Sternberg. New York: Perennial Library, Harper and Row, 1974.

_____. *Warning to the West.* New York: Farrar, Straus and Giroux, 1981.

Stark, Werner. *The Social Bond: An Investigation into the Bases of Law-abidingness.* Vol. 2: *Antecedents of the Social Bond: The Ontogeny of Sociality.* New York: Fordham University Press, 1978.

Szymanski, Albert. *Human Rights in the Soviet Union.* London: Zed Books, 1984.

Thompson, Kenneth W., ed. *The Moral Imperatives of Human Rights: A World Survey.* Washington, D.C.: The University Press of America, 1980.

Timerman, Jacobo. *Prisoner Without a Name, Cell Without a Number.* Translated by Toby Talbot. New York: Random House, 1982.

Triska, Jan F., and Gati, Charles. *Blue Collar Workers in Eastern Europe.* London: George Allen and Unwin Ltd., 1981.

United Nations. *Never Again War! A Documented Account of the Visit to the United Nations of His Holiness Pope Paul VI.* New York: Office of Public Information, United Nations, 1965.

United Nations. *Yearbook of the United Nations 1948-49.* New York: Columbia University Press in cooperation with the United Nations, 1950.

United Nations Department of Public Information. *United Nations Bulletin.* Vols. 1-8 (1946-1950).

U.S. Department of State. "Proposals for the Establishment of a General International Organization." In *Dumbarton Oaks Documents on International Organization.* Revised edition, Conference Series 60, Publication 2257 (1945).

U.S. Congress. Senate. *Supplementary Detailed Staff Reports on Intelligence Activities and the Rights of Americans.* S. Rept. 94–755, 94th Cong., 2d sess., 1976. Final Report of the Select Committee to Study Governmental Operations with Respect to Intelligence Activities, bk. 3.

Walzer, Michael. *Radical Principles: Reflections of an Unreconstructed Democrat.* New York: Basic Books, 1980.

————. *The Revolution of the Saints: A Study in the Origins of Radical Politics.* Cambridge, MA: Harvard University Press, 1965.

————. *Spheres of Justice: A Defense of Pluralism and Equality.* New York: Basic Books, 1983.

Washington Post, 18 December 1977, 8 January and 8 March 1978, 1 February 1979, 31 December 1984.

Weinstein, Warren. "Africa's Approach to Human Rights at the United Nations." *Issue: A Quarterly Journal of Opinion* 6:4 (Winter 1976): 14-21.

Weisfelder, Richard F. "The Decline of Human Rights in Lesotho: An Evaluation of Domestic and External Determinants." *Issue: A Quarterly Journal of Opinon* 6:4 (Winter 1976): 22–33.

Wicker, Tom. "What Does 'Human Rights' Really Mean?" *The News and Observer* (Raleigh, NC), 12 October 1983, sec. A, 4.

II. PERSONALISM

A. Works by Jacques Maritain

"The Conquest of Freedom." In *Freedom, Its Meaning,* 637. Edited by Ruth N. Anshen. New York: Harcourt, Brace and Co., 1940.

Freedom in the Modern World. Translated by Richard O'Sullivan. New York: Charles Scribner's Sons, 1936.

Integral Humanism: Temporal and Spiritual Problems of a New Christendom. Translated by Joseph W. Evans. Notre Dame: University of Notre Dame Press, 1973.

"Introduction." In *Human Rights: Comments and Interpretations,* 9–17. UNESCO. New York: Allan Wingate, 1950.

Man and the State. Chicago: University of Chicago Press, 1951.

"The Meaning of Human Rights." In Brandeis Lawyers Society, Philadelphia, *Publications.* Philadelphia, 1942–51. 3 vols. Vol 2, 1949, 2–27.

"On the Philosophy of Human Rights." In *Human Rights: Comments and Interpretations* 72–77. UNESCO. New York: Allan Wingate, 1950.

The Person and the Common Good. Translated by John J. Fitzgerald. New York: Charles Scribner's Sons, 1947.

Reflections on America. New York: Charles Scribner's Sons, 1958.

"The Rights of Man: A Comment." *United Nations Weekly Bulletin* 3:21 (18 November 1947): 672.

The Rights of Man and Natural Law. Translated by Doris C. Anson. New York: Charles Scribner's Sons, 1949.

Scholasticism and Politics. 2d ed. Translation edited by Mortimer J. Adler. London: Geoffrey Bles: The Centenary Press, 1945.

"Ten Months Later." *The Commonweal,* 21 June 1940. In "Appendix," Sidney Hook, *Reason, Social Myths, and Democracy,* 102. New York: John Day, 1940.

B. Works about Maritain and Personalism

Doering, Bernard E. *Jacques Maritain and the French Catholic Intellectuals.* Notre Dame: University of Notre Dame Press, 1983.

Dunaway, John M. *Jacques Maritain.* Boston: Twayne Publishers, A Division of G.K. Hall, 1978.

Fecher, Charles A. *The Philosophy of Jacques Maritain.* Westminster, MD: Newman, 1953.

Gallagher, Donald, and Gallagher, Idella. *The Achievement of Jacques and Raissa Maritain: A Bibliography 1906–1961.* Garden City: Doubleday, 1962.

Graham, Aelred, O.S.B. "Reflections on a Critique of Jacques Maritain." *Blackfriers* 26 (November 1945): 426–31.

_____. "Mr. Gregory and Mr. Maritain: A Reply." *The Tablet* 186 (1 December 1945): 266.

Gregory, T.S. "Politics and Original Sin: A Criticism of M. Maritain's Recent Essay, 'The Rights of Man.'" *The Tablet* 184 (18 November 1944): 248–49.

_____. "M. Maritain's Politics." *The Tablet* 186 (18 August 1945): 78–80.

_____. "M. Maritain's Politics." *The Tablet* 186 (24 November 1945): 250, 252.

Hook, Sidney. *Reason, Social Myths, and Democracy.* New York: John Day, 1940.

Knight, Frank H. "Review of Jacques Maritain's *The Rights of Man and Natural Law.*" *Ethics* 54 (January 1944): 124–145.

_____. "Natural Law: Last Refuge of the Bigot." *Ethics* 59 (January 1949): 127–35.

Smith, Brooke Williams. *Jacques Maritain: Antimodern or Ultramodern? An Historical Analysis of His Critics, His Thought, and His Life.* New York: Elsevier, 1976. Includes extensive bibliography.

Yeager, F.S. "A Note on Knight's Criticism of Maritain." *Ethics* 58 (July 1948): 297–99.

III. BASIC HUMAN NEEDS

Crahan, Margaret E., ed. *Human Rights and Basic Needs in the Americas.* Washington, D.C.: Gerogetown University Press, 1982.

Colonnese, Louis M., ed. *Human Rights and the Liberation of Man in the Americas.* Notre Dame: University of Notre Dame, 1970.

Hennelly, Alfred, S.J., and Langan, John, S.J., eds. *Human Rights in the Americas: The Struggle for Consensus.* Washington, D.C.: Georgetown University Press, 1982.

Hollenbach, David, S.J. *Claims in Conflict: Retrieving and Renewing the Catholic Human Rights Tradition.* New York: Paulist Press, 1979.

Lederer, Katrin, and Galtung, Johan, eds. *Human Needs: A Contribution to the Current Debate.* Cambridge, MA: Oelgeschlager, Gunn and Hain, Publishers, 1980.

Sharkey, Philip J. "Human Rights: The Relationship among Civil, Socio-economic and Political Rights." Ph.D. dissertation, New York University, 1975.

Shue, Henry,. *Basic Rights: Subsistence, Affluence, and U.S. Foreign Policy.* Princeton: Princeton University Press, 1980.

IV. REALISM

A. Works by Reinhold Niebuhr

The Children of Light and the Children of Darkness: A Vindication of Democracy and a Critique of Its Traditional Defense. New York: Charles Scribner's Sons, 1944.

Christian Realism and Political Problems. New York: Charles Scribner's Sons, 1953 [1948].

Christianity and Crisis. Editorial comments and brief articles listed chronologically as follows:

'Common Counsel for United Nations." 2:16 (5 October 1942): 1–2.

"Plans for World Reorganization." 2:17 (19 October 1942): 3–6.

"The United Nations and World Organization." 2:24 (25 January 1943): 1–2.

"American Power and World Responsibility." 3:5 (5 April 1943): 2–4.

"Editorial Notes." 4:15 (18 September 1944): 2.

"Editorial Notes." 4:16 (2 October 1944): 2.

"Editorial Notes." 4:22 (25 December 1944): 2.

"Editorial Notes." 6:3 (4 March 1946): 2.

"World Community and World Government." 6:3 (4 March 1946): 5–6.

"Editorial Notes." 6:4 (18 March 1946): 2.

"Editorial Notes." 6:9 (27 May 1946): 2.

"The Conflict Between Nations and Nations and Between Nations and God." 6:14 (5 August 1945): 2–4.

"Editorial Notes." 6:15 (16 September 1946): 2–3.

"One World or None." 8:2 (16 February 1948): 9–10.

"Editorial Notes." 9:23 (9 January 1950): 178.

"Can We Organize the World?" 13.1 (2 February 1953): 1.

"Editorial Notes." 13:22 (28 December 1953): 170.

"The Changing United Nations." 20:16 (3 October 1960): 133–34.

Christianity and Power Politics. Hamden: Archon Books, 1969 [1940].

Christianity and Society. Editorial comments and brief articles listed chronologically as follows:

"Plans for World Organization." 7:3 (Summer 1942): 6–7.

"The World After the War." (Review of H.B. Parke's *The World After the War*) 8:1 (Winter 1942): 41.

"Nationalism and the Possibilities of Internationalism." 8:4 (Fall 1943): 5–7.

"Republican Internationalism." 8:4 (Fall 1943): 7.

"International Ideals and Realities." 9:3 (Summer 1944): 3–5.

"Realistic Internationalism." 9:4 (Fall 1944): 4–5.

"Dumbarton Oaks." 10:1 (Winter 1944): 3–4.

"Reason and Interest in Politics." 10:1 (Winter 1944): 8–9.

"The Outlines of Peace." 10:2 (Spring 1945): 3–4.

"The San Francisco Conference." 10:3 (Summer 1945): 3–5.

"World Order." Review of F.E. Johnson's *World Order*, along with MacIver's *Civilization and Group Relations.* 11:1 (Winter 1945): 43–44.

"The International Situation." 11:3 (Summer 1946): 3–4.

"The Ideological Factors in the World Situation." 11:3 (Summer 1946): 4–6.

"The World Situation." 11:4 (Fall 1946): 3.

"The United Nations." 12:1 (Winter 1946): 3–4.

"Scientific Man Versus Power Politics." (Review of Hans J. Morgenthau's *Scientific Man Versus Power Politics*) 12:2 (Spring 1947): 33–34.

" The Morality of Nations." 13:2 (Spring 1948): 7–8.

"Revision of the United Nations Charter." 13:3 (Summer 1948): 8.

"What Can We Do?" 15:1 (Winter 1951): 3–4.

"The Churches and the United Nations." 18:1 (Winter 1952–53): 3–4.

"The Growing Tension between Nationalists and Internationalists." 19:4 (Special Issue): 3–4.

"Conversation: On the International Affairs Report from the Evanston Assembly of the World Council of Churches." (Niebuhr and R.M. Fagley) 20:2 (Spring 1955): 7–8.

"Comment." *Public Opinion Quarterly* 17:4 (Winter 1954): 435–38. Comment on Elmo Roper's lead article, "American Attitudes on World Organization."

"Critical Analysis of Dumbarton Oaks Proposals." *Post War World* 2:1 (15 December 1944): 1, 3.

"Democratic Goals and World Order." *The New Leader* 27:39 (23 September 1944): 5.

Essays in Applied Christianity. Edited by D.B. Robertson. New York: Meridian, 1959.

"The Illusion of World Government." *Foreign Affairs: An American Quarterly Review* 27:3 (April 1949): 379–88.

An Interpretation of Christian Ethics. New York: Seabury, 1979.

Leaves from the Notebook of a Tamed Cynic. New York: Living Age Books, Meridian, 1957 [1929].

Love and Justice: Selections from the Shorter Writings of Reinhold Niebuhr. Edited by E.D. Robertson. Cleveland: World Publishing, 1967.

The Lutheran. Editorial comments and brief articles listed chronologically as follows:

"Creating a New World Order." 34:8 (21 November 1951): 10.

"The Future Can't Be Controlled." 34:17 (23 January 1952): 11.

The Messenger Editorial comments and brief articles listed chronologically as follows:

"Is World Government Possible?" 11:16 (6 August 1946): 6.

"Race and the United Nations." 12:3 (4 February 1947): 6.

"The Difficult Role of America." 12:9 (29 April 1947): 7.

"The Nation and the International Community." 14:19 (11 October 1949): 11.

"A Plea for Humility." 19:21 (16 November 1954), 7.

"A Plea for More Humility." 20:7 (5 April 1955): 6–7.

"The Moral Implications of Loyalty to the United Nations." *The Hazen Pamphlets,* no. 29. New Haven: Edward W. Hazen Foundation, July 1952; reprint ed., *Motive* 16:1 (October 1955): 17–20.

Moral Man and Immoral Society: A Study in Ethics and Politics. New York: Charles Scribner's Sons, 1932.

The Nation. Editorial comments and brief articles listed chronologically as follows:

ws12 "Thoughts on 'World War III?'" 155:2 (11 July 1942): 32.

"World War III Ahead?" 158:13 (25 March 1944): 356–58.

"Realist's Eye View." (A review of Leopold Schwarzschild's *Primer of the Coming World*) 159:4 (22 July 1944): 105–07.

"The Basis for World Order." 159:17 (21 October 1944): 489.

"Sovereignty and Peace." (Review of Hans Kelsen's *Peace Through Law*) 159:21 (18 November 1944): 623.

"Will America Back Out?" 160:2 (13 January 1945): 42–43.

"Is This 'Peace in Our Time?'" 160:14 (17 April 1945): 382–84.

"The Myth of World Government." 162:11 (16 March 1946): 312–14.

"Reinhold Niebuhr Insists." 162:16 (20 April 1946): 491–92.

"The World State: Illusions and Realities." (Review of Crane Brinton's *From Many One*) 166:21 (22 May 1948): 578.

"The National Interest and International Responsibility." *Social Action* 21:6 (February 1955): 25–29.

The Nature and Destiny of Man: A Christian Interpretation. 2 vols. New York; Charles Scribner's Sons, 1941/43.

The New Leader. Editorial comments and brief articles listed chronologically as follows:

"Democratic Goals and World Order." 27:29 (23 September 1944), 4–5.

"The U.N.: An End to Illusions." 44:9 (27 February 1961): 3-4.

Reinhold Niebuhr on Politics: His Political Philosophy and Its Application to Our Age as Expressed in His Writings. Edited by Harry R. Davis and Robert C. Good. New York: Charles Scribner's Sons, 1960.

The Structure of Nations and Empires: A Study of the Recurring Patterns and Problems of the Political Order in Relation to the Unique Problems of the Nuclear Age. New York: Charles Scribner's Sons, 1959.

"The Theory and Practice of UNESCO." *International Organization* 4:1 (February 1950): 3-11.

"The U.N. is Not a World Government." *The Reporter* 16:5 (7 March 1957): 30-32.

The World Crisis and American Responsibility: Nine Essays by Reinhold Niebuhr. Edited by Ernest W. Lefever. Westport: Greenwood Press 1958.

B. Works about Niebuhr and Realism

Bennett, John C. *Christian Realism.* New York: Charles Scribner's Sons, 1941.

————. *Foreign Policy in Christian Perspective.* New York: Charles Scribner's Sons, 1966.

Bingham, June. *Courage to Change: An Introduction to the Life and Thought of Reinhold Niebuhr.* New York: Charles Scribner's Sons, 1961.

Good, Robert C. "The National Interest and Political Realism: Niebuhr's 'Debate' with Morgenthau and Kennan." *The Journal of Politics* 22 (1960): 597-619.

Harlan, Gordon. *The Thought of Reinhold Niebuhr.* New York: Oxford University Press, 1960.

Kegley, C.W., and Bretall, R.W., eds. *Reinhold Niebuhr: His Religious, Social, and Political Thought.* New York: Macmillan Co. 1956.

Kennan, George F. *Memoirs: 1925-1950.* Boston: Atlantic Monthly/Little Brown, 1967.

LaFeber, Walter. *America, Russia, and the Cold War, 1945-66.* New York: John Wiley and Sons, 1967.

Lefever, Ernest. *Ethics and United States Foreign Policy.* New York: Meridian, 1957.

Merkley, Paul. *Reinhold Niebuhr: A Political Account.* Montreal: McGill, Queen's University Press, 1975.

Minnema, Theodore. *The Social Ethics of Reinhold Niebuhr.* Grand Rapids: William B. Eerdmans Publishing Co., 1960.

Morgenthau, Hans J. *Reinhold Niebuhr: A Prophetic Voice in Our Time.* Greenwich: Seabury Press, 1962.

Robertson, D.B. *Reinhold Niebuhr's Works: A Bibliography.* Boston: Twayne Publishing, A Division of G.K. Hall, 1979.

Schlesinger, A.M., Jr., and White, Morton, eds. *Paths of American Thought.* Boston: Houghton Mifflin, 1963.

Stone, Ronald H. *Reinhold Niebuhr: Prophet to Politicians.* Nashville: Abingdon, 1972.

Thelen, Mary Frances. *Man As Sinner in Contemporary American Realistic Theology*. Morningside Heights, NY: King's Crown, 1946.

Thompson, Kenneth W. "Beyond National Interest: A Critical Evaluation of Reinhold Niebuhr's Theory of International Politics." *The Review of Politics* 17:2 (April 1955): 168.

_____. *Christian Ethics and the Dilemmas of Foreign Policy*. Durham: Duke University Press, 1959.

_____. *Ethics, Functionalism and Power in International Politics: The Crisis in Values*. Baton Rouge: Louisiana State University Press, 1979.

_____. *The Moral Issue in Statecraft: Twentieth-Century Approaches and Problems*. Baton Rouge: Louisiana State University Press, 1966.

_____. *Morality and Foreign Policy*. Baton Rouge: Louisiana State University Press, 1980.

V. CONTEXTUALISM

Boston Theological Institute. *Human Rights and the Global Mission of the Church*. Annual Series, Vol. 1. Cambridge: Boston Theological Institute, 1985.

Claude, Richard P. *Comparative Human Rights*. Baltimore: The Johns Hopkins University Press, 1976.

Evans, Robert A., and Evans, Alice Frazer, eds. *Human Rights: A Dialogue Between the First and Third Worlds*. Maryknoll, NY: Orbis, 1983.

Jewett, Robert. *The Captain America Complex: The Dilemma of Zealous Nationalism*. Philadelphia: Westmister, 1973.

Lucas, George R., Jr., and Will, James E., eds. *The East-West Encounter over Human Rights: Its Religious and Sociological Context*. Soundings 67:2 (Summer 1984, Special Issue).

Marty, Martin E. *Righteous Empire: The Protestant Experience in America*. New York: Dial Press, 1970.

Panikkar, Raimundo. "Is the Notion of Human Rights a Western Concept?" *Diogenes* 120 (Winter 1982): 75–102.

Pollis, Adamantia, and Schwab, Peter, eds. *Human Rights: Cultural and Ideological Perspectives*. New York: Praeger Publishers, 1979.

Schlesinger, Arthur, Jr. "Human Rights and the American Tradition." *Foreign Affairs* 57:3 (1978): 503–26.

Sellers, James. "Human Rights and the American Tradition of Justice." *Soundings* 62:3 (Fall 1979): 226–55.

_____. "The *Polis* in America as *Imago Dei*: Neither Secular nor "Born Again," in *The Bible and American Law, Politics, and Political Rhetoric*, ed. James Turner Johnson (Philadelphia: Fortress, 1984).

_____. "Jonathan Edwards as an American Thinker," unpublished manuscript.

_____. *Public Ethics: American Morals and Manners*. New York: Harper & Row, 1970.

_____. *Theological Ethics*. New York: Macmillan Co. 1966.

Stackhouse, Max L. *Creeds, Society, and Human Rights: A Study in Three Cultures*. Grand Rapids: William B. Eerdmans Publishing Co., 1984.

————. *Ethics and the Urban Ethos: An Essay in Social Theory and Theological Reconstruction.* Boston: Beacon Press, 1972.

Swidler, Arlene, ed. *Human Rights in Religious Traditions.* New York: The Pilgrim Press, 1982.

World Council of Churches, Commission of the Churches on International Affairs. *Human Rights and Christian Responsibility.* 3 vols. 1974–75.

INDEX

Abortion, 4
Action Francaise, 45, 66-67
Africa, 24-26, 74, 134, 188-90, 192, 219. *See also:* Egypt; South Africa; Wai, Dunstan.
Ajami, Fouad, 73, 82-83, 142, 195-200, 204-05
Amnesty International, 8, 78, 83, 191-93, 226
Andropov, Yuri, 16, 188
Aquinas, Thomas, 40, 45, 51, 55, 56, 61, 67, 68, 117, 120
Aristotle, 51-52, 55, 61, 69, 120
Asia, 5, 22, 134, 211, 219. *See also:* China; Hinduism; Japan; Phillippines; South Korea.
Augustine, 20, 59-60, 117, 12

Bariloche Institute, 78-79
Basic human needs, 5, 6, 13, 26, 29, 35, 52, 65, 73-130, 187, 189, 212, 215
Bedau, Hugo Adam, 90-92, 101
Belgrade Review Conference, 135-36, 138
Bentham, Jeremy, 86-87

Bible and human rights, 34, 36-37, 61-62, 119-20, 123-24, 209-10, 219
Blacks, rights of, 1, 7, 11, 31, 187, 194-95, *See also:* Civil right movement; Racial discrimination.
Bolívar, Simone, 23
Brezhnev, Leonid, 16, 75, 79, 135, 139-40, 186-88

Calvin, John, 88-89
Capitalism, 16, 26, 27, 47-50, 73, 75-78, 105, 113, 121, 191
Carter, Jimmy, vii, 5, 8, 10, 11, 21-22, 74-78, 82, 97-98, 131-32, 135-43, 186-89, 193-96, 198, 221, 226
Carter, Rosalyn, 141
Castro, Fidel, 74, 79, 141, 189
Chernenko, Konstantin, 75-79, 136, 187-88
China, 2, 74-75, 157, 172
Christiansen, Drew, 119-20
Churchill, Winston, 1, 156

Civil and political rights, 4-5, 9, 14,
    23, 25, 26, 48-49, 57, 69,
    74-75, 78-84, 87-90, 93-94,
    97-108, 116, 117, 134, 191-95,
    215
Civil right movement, 1, 7, 191, 193,
    194, 198. *See also:* Blacks,
    rights of; Racial discrimination.
Cold War, 143, 187-88, 190, 198-200,
    226
Colonialism, 1, 21, 23-26, 75, 83,
    100, 112, 127, 133-34, 142,
    188-89, 190, 198, 199, 204,
    211, 217
Common good, 13, 14, 16, 21, 24, 27,
    36-40, 50, 53-56, 58-59, 68,
    114-15, 120, 179, 210
Communism, 5, 7, 46, 47, 62, 139,
    159, 190
Contextualist theology, 209-220
Cranston, Maurice, 90, 95, 101, 103,
    104, 127, 184
Cuba, 23, 73, 141, 189
Cultural pluralism, 22, 32, 57, 63-65,
    100-01, 131-32, 144, 149-50,
    163, 179, 190, 196-98, 209-220
Cynicism, 11, 86-87, 147, 155,
    164-69, 177-79, 197

Death penalty, 187, 193
Development, 23-25, 74, 114, 140
Dumbarton Oaks Proposals, 2, 151-52,
    162, 178, 181
Duties and rights, 14-15, 19, 28,
    37-39, 42-43, 49, 51, 56, 57,
    84-85, 91, 93, 108, 178-79, 210,
    223

Eastern Europe, 132, 136, 138, 145,
    215, 219. *See also:* Belgrade
    Review Conference, Helsinki
    Conference.
Eastern Orthodox Church, 37-38
Edwards, Jonathan, 201
Egypt, 19
Equality, 81, 84, 93, 169

Erikson, Erik, 11, 46
Eurocommunism, 139-40
Evans, Robert A., 205, 222
Evans, Alice Frazer, 205, 222

Fascism, 14, 15, 45-48, 50, 59, 62, 93,
    190. *See also:* Action Francaise,
    Nazi Party.
Federal Republic of Germany, 76, 193
France, 45, 127, 139, 170, 190, 202,
    203 Declaration of the Rights
    of Man and Citizen, 56, 84,
    86. *See also:* Action Francaise.
Freedom House, 78-79, 192

German Democratic Republic, 215,
    220-21
Germany, 49
Gnosticism, 122, 124, 130
Goodell, Charles, 193-94
Graham, Frank P., Conference on
    Human Rights, 5
Great Britain, 1, 2, 37, 100, 133-34,
    156-57, 172, 193, 203

Harakas, Stanley S., 37-38
Hart, H.L.A., 84-85, 101
Haughey, John, 119
Helsinki Conference, 10, 135-39,
    186, 214
Helwig, Monika, 119-20
Hennelly, Alfred, 119
Hinduism, 210, 213-16, 220-22
Hitler, Adolf, 47, 158
Hobbes, Thomas, 86
Hollenbach, David, 92-93, 120-22
Homosexuals, rights of, 1, 5, 48, 211
Hook, Sidney, 59-60, 62, 64, 70
Human dignity, 9-10, 27, 28, 39-40,
    49, 50, 52, 56, 58, 59, 62, 63,
    98, 100, 110-13, 115-16, 118,
    121, 122, 154, 174, 188, 204,
    210
Human nature, vii, 3, 30, 46-49,
    51-53, 83, 118, 216, 225

Abstract versus concrete notions of 3, 6, 10, 116, 176, 204-05, 216-19
Individual versus corporate notions of, 3, 6, 10, 27-40, 45-64
Pneumatic versus physical notions of, 65, 73, 79, 99, 108-09, 113-18, 122-23
Theological basis of, 56, 61-62, 108, 110. See also: Human dignity, *Imago Dei*, Sin

Idealism, viii, 11, 23, 146-50, 156-60, 168-69, 177-78
Ideals, human rights as, 60-61, 70, 85-87, 144, 146, 176
Ideology, human rights as, vii, 4, 7, 8, 14, 15, 24, 73, 75-76, 79, 82-83, 99-103, 187-88, 190, 199, 200, 204, 211-12, 216, 218, 226
Imago Dei, 61, 70, 111, 112, 121-23, 218-19
Imperialism, 8, 12, 16, 75, 133, 171-74, 190-204, 207, 208, 211, 215, 217
India, 157, 210, 213, 222
International law, 22, 29, 144, 149-50, 177
Islam, 19-21, 23, 81, 93-94, 188. *See also:* Egypt; Jullundhri, Rashid Ahmad; Said, Abdul Aziz

Japan, 5, 78
Jefferson, Thomas, 81, 84, 202
John XXIII, 40, 42-43, 110-11, 114-16
Judaism, 122, 182, 219
Jews, rights of, 15, 29, 34, 48, 93, 136
Jullundhri, Rashid Ahmad, 19, 93-94, 188

Kant, Immanuel, 20, 48, 150
Kissinger, Henry, vii, 11, 137, 186, 197
King, Martin Luther, Jr., 7, 194, 206-07
Knight, Frank H., 60-61, 70

Langan, John, 119-20
Latin America, 6, 7, 21-24, 74, 114, 119, 134, 141, 175, 189, 190. See also: Bariloche Institute; Bolívar, Simone; Castro, Fidel; Cuba; Theology of liberation; Nicaragua; Portales, Diego.
Lauterpacht, Hersh, 28, 150
League of Nations, 168, 171, 173
Legal positivism, 55, 146, 160-64
Leibniz, Gottfried, 51-52
Liberalism, 10, 18, 20-24, 27, 47-55, 61, 73, 83-109, 117-23, 147, 163, 176, 210, 213-18
Libertarianism, 36, 79, 81-82, 103, 131, 184
Locke, John, 31, 35, 55, 84
Love, 33-34, 37-38, 51-54, 61, 113, 148, 154
Lucas, George R., 205, 214-15
Luther, Martin, 20, 31, 35, 88-89
Lutheran social teachings, 35-36, 98. See also: Luther, Martin; Thielicke, Helmut

Machiavelli, Niccolò, 47, 56, 86, 165, 188
Maritain, Jacques, 13, 40, 45-66, 114, 147-50
Marx, Karl, 24, 36, 93
Marxism, 7, 18, 24, 34, 69, 89, 92-93, 119-21, 210, 213-16, 220-21
Medvedev, Roy, 186
Methodist social teachings, 22
Mill, John Stuart, 91
Moskowitz, Moses, 11

National security, 5, 13, 15-18, 26, 86, 165-66
National sovereignty, 65, 131-84
Native Americans, 18, 194, 195, 199
Natural law, 30, 47, 49, 55-57, 86-87, 142, 150-51, 160, 212
Natural rights, 83-87
Nazi Party, 2, 15, 29, 45-48, 59-62, 86, 169-70, 174, 218

Negative and positive rights, 14-15, 20-21, 87-92, 95, 104-09
Nelsen, J. Robert, 36-37
Nicaragua, 6, 7, 175
Niebuhr, Reinhold, 131, 146-50, 152, 155-84, 207
Nietzsche, Friedrich, 130
North Atlantic Treaty Organization, 141
Nuremberg Code, 2

Order and human rights, 15, 22-26, 35, 74, 155-56, 169-70, 174, 177-79

Panikkar, Raimundo, 205, 209-11, 214-17, 222, 223
Participation, right to, 26, 112, 133-35, 192, 217
Paul VI, 111, 113-14
Peace, 28, 159, 163-66, 170, 174, 203
Personalism, 39-40, 45, 47, 50-66
Plato, 120
Portales, Diego, 23-24
Positive law, 47, 55-57, 69, 85-88, 142, 144-45, 150, 160, 166-67, 183, 184
Poverty, 24, 34-35, 58, 74, 98-102, 105-07, 113, 117, 189, 195, 207
Power, 27, 30, 31, 64, 85-87, 157, 164, 166, 168, 170, 172, 174, 176-78
Property rights, 20, 22, 69, 86, 92, 116, 117, 211
Protestant social teachings, 36-37, 62, 119, 226. See also: Lutheran social teachings, Methodist social teachings, United Church of Christ social teachings; World Council of Churches.
Philippines, 204

Racial discrimination, 2, 15, 16, 22, 31, 46, 48, 50, 74, 75, 92, 103, 111, 187, 189, 194-96, 204, 211

See also: Blacks, rights of; Civil rights movement.
Rawls, John, 119
Reagan, Ronald, 5, 214, 215, 221-22
Religious liberty, 2, 6, 19, 38, 48-49, 57, 63, 64, 69, 111, 116, 136, 138
Rights. See: Basic human needs; Blacks, rights of; Civil and political rights; Duties and rights; Negative and positive rights; Participation, right to; Property rights; Racial discrimination; Religious liberty; Torture; Women, rights of; Workers, rights of.
Roman Catholic social teachings, 38-40, 62, 63, 66-67, 99, 110-22, 226. See also: Common good, Solidarity; Subsidiarity; Theological doctrines; Theology of liberation; Vatican II.
Roosevelt, Eleanor, 2, 144
Rousseau, Jean Jacques, 24, 48, 51

Said, Abdul Aziz, 19-21, 93-94
Sakharov, Andrei, 137-38, 187
San Francisco Conference, 2
Schwelb, Egon, 11, 28-29, 94
Sellers, James, 70, 205, 209-14, 221-22
Shue, Henry, 102-08, 120, 128
Sin, 3, 27-30, 65, 88, 146-49, 152-70, 175, 182, 198
Social contract, 85-87, 144
Socialism, 25, 73-78, 82, 117, 136, 138, 191
Solidarity, 35, 62, 114-15
Solzhenitsyn, Alexander, 7, 18, 38, 136-37
South Africa, 5, 86, 145-46, 199, 226
South Korea, 101, 142, 198
Soviet Union, 2, 14-18, 48, 73, 75-78, 82, 86, 92-93, 98, 113, 132-40, 143, 145-46, 152, 157, 159, 162, 165, 169, 172, 189, 190,

192, 193, 195, 200, 214-15
Criticisms of human rights
	initiatives, 132, 186-88
Constitution of, 16, 93, 186
Dissidents, 7, 15-18, 38, 135-39,
	186-88, 200. *See also:* Eastern
	Europe; Sakharov, Andrei;
	Solzhenitsyn, Alexander.
Stackhouse, Max, 119-20, 205, 209,
	213, 217, 220-22
Stalinism, 45, 50, 62, 92, 158
Subsidiarity, 117

Theological ethics, vii-viii, 3, 8-9, 30,
	35, 58-66, 108, 110, 118, 186,
	205, 216, 225, 226
Theological doctrines
	Body of Christ, 36-38, 62
	Creation, 112, 122-23
	Eschatology, 157
	God, 38
	Incarnation, 112-13, 123
	Kingdom of God, 89, 201
	Resurrection, 113, 124
	Trinity, 36, 38, 61, 70
Transcendence, viii, 6, 46-47, 121,
	132, 147, 218. *See also:* Bible
	and human rights; Human
	dignity; Human nature; *Imago
	Dei,* Sin; Subsidiarity; Theology
	of liberation.
Theology of liberation, 34, 119, 120
Thielicke, Helmut, 30-36, 42
Torture, 6, 103, 193

United Church of Christ social
	teachings, 194-95, 198
United Nations, 8, 24, 45, 131,
	155-56, 175, 189-91, 195, 225
	Charter, 2, 144, 162
	Covenants, 2, 9, 74, 81-82, 187, 199
	Formation of 2, 29, 143, 157-58,
		164-65, 181, 183
	UNESCO, 40, 77. *See also:*
		Dumbarton Oaks Proposals;

San Francisco Conference;
Universal Declaration of
Human Rights.
United States
	Congress, 194, 208
	Constitution, 161
	Declaration of Independence, 56, 86
	Foreign policy, vii, 10, 74-78, 91,
		98, 102, 104, 112, 118-22, 131,
		136, 137, 140, 141, 171-72,
		186-88, 195-99, 202-04, 226
	Human rights conditions, 16, 18,
		23, 74-78, 192-98
Universal Declaration of Human
	Rights, 2, 9, 14-15, 19-22,
	26-29, 36, 40, 48, 49, 56, 80-81,
	87, 93, 103, 127, 132-34,
	143-46, 156, 176, 178, 187,
	190, 204, 210-11, 226
Utilitarianism, 47, 51, 53, 59, 68,
	86-87, 128

Vance, Cyrus, 92, 97, 196
Vatican Council II, 38, 62, 67,
	110-10, 123

Wai, Dunstan, 24-26, 188-89
Welfare programs, 32-33, 35
Western Europe, 37, 92, 136, 139-40,
	170-73, 187, 192, 219
Wilson, Woodrow, 203
Will, James E., 205, 214-15
Women, rights of, 1, 2, 4, 5, 16, 19,
	22, 31, 75-77, 82, 92, 112, 211
Woodstock Theological Center,
	119-22
Workers, rights of, 4, 14, 16, 35, 61,
	76, 80-81, 89-90, 93, 111, 134
World Council of Churches, 30, 205,
	207
World War I, 173-74, 203
World War II, 1, 48, 50, 63, 152,
	156-58, 171, 174, 175, 181

Young, Andrew, 98, 195

ABOUT THE AUTHOR

Warren Lee Holleman is a Fellow in the Department of Family Medicine, Baylor College of Medicine, Houston, Texas. His current research focuses on ethical issues in the clinical, primary care setting. He was formerly Visiting Assistant Professor in the Honors Program of the University of Houston—University Park, and Instructor at the Houston Graduate School of Theology. He holds a Ph.D. from Rice University (1986) and an A.B. from Harvard (1977).